COPPOLA

A BIOGRAPHY

PETER COWIE

UPDATED EDITION

DA CAPO PRESS • NEW YORK

Library of Congress Cataloging-in-Publication Data

Cowie, Peter.
    Coppola: a biography/Peter Cowie. — 1st Da Capo Press ed.
        p.   cm.
    Includes bibliographical references and index.
    ISBN 0-306-80598-7
    1. Coppola, Francis Ford, 1939-   . 2. Motion picture producers and
    directors—United States—biography. I. Title.
    PN1998.3. C69C67 1994
    791. 43'0233'092—dc20
    [B]   94 -16270
                                                                   CIP

First Da Capo Press edition 1994

This Da Capo Press paperback edition of *Coppola* is an unabridged republication of the edition first published in New York in 1990, but here updated with new text, photos, and filmography. It is reprinted by arrangement with Charles Scribner's Sons, an imprint of Macmillan Publishing Company.

Published by Da Capo Press, Inc.
A Subsidiary of Plenum Publishing Corporation
233 Spring Street, New York, NY 10013

Manufactured in the United States of America

COPPOLA

Contents

Acknowledgments

I would like to thank Francis Coppola and his wife, Eleanor, for their time and amiable cooperation in the preparation of this book. My thanks also go to those friends, relatives, and colleagues of Francis Coppola who talked to me, often for many hours, about the subject: August Coppola, Carroll Ballard, Paul Bartel, Richard Beggs, Roger Corman, Frederic Forrest, Gray Frederickson, Barry Malkin, John Milius, Walter Murch, Michael Powell, Fred Roos, Mona Skager, and Dean Tavoularis. Valuable comments, anecdotes, and information stemmed from Lorenzo Codelli, Bill and Stella Pence, Gerald Pratley, and David Thomson. John H. Peters, chief executive officer at Zoetrope Studios, coped patiently and graciously with my queries at various stages of the project's long gestation. Anahid Nazarian, at Zoetrope in Napa, researched many elusive dates and names in the Filmography with her customary diligence and zest.

A majority of the photographs reproduced in this book come from the National Film Archive in London, the Ontario Film Institute in Toronto, and the personal collection of Francis and Eleanor Coppola. I am also in debt to Wim Wenders for the splendid picture he took of Francis Coppola and Akira Kurosawa.

The largest share of gratitude must go to Laura Morris, my editor at André Deutsch, who believed so passionately in this book from the start, and to Tom Luddy, whose gift for opening significant doors is matched only by his flair for discerning all that is bravest and most honest in contemporary filmmaking.

Introduction

As far as the eye can see, the grapevines march in soldierly rows out across the Napa Valley and along the flanks of the wooded hills that shield the home and property of Francis Ford Coppola. On this 1,700-acre estate, which was developed more than a century ago by a Finnish sea captain, Coppola presides over the cultivation and making of fine red wine. Yet to the world, Francis Ford Coppola's is a name that booms of modern Hollywood legend, a name synonymous with *The Godfather, Apocalypse Now*, and some of the most spectacular financial woes ever to rock the movie industry.

On a cloudless day in September the crushing of the grapes has already begun in a winery that fills the lower half of an elderly wooden building on the estate. A clutch of shabby automobiles and converted trucks deteriorates gently in the heat—among them the camper van in which Coppola and his friends traversed America while making *The Rain People* and the van in which Gene Hackman organized his clandestine taping sessions in *The Conversation*. Only "The Silver Fish" is missing, but this Airstream trailer has already departed for Rome where it will provide a portable headquarters for Coppola during the shooting of *The Godfather Part III*.

Above the winery stand two stories of books and equipment dear to the heart of the fifty-year-old director. His library comprises thousands of volumes on everything from botany to social history, from travel to the byways of criminal and aberrant behavior. Legions more lie hidden away in storage, waiting for the moment when the library can invade the rest of the building and resident wine-maker Steve Beresini can be consigned to a brand-new winery nearby. Upstairs is a private screening room where state-of-the-art sound consoles save Coppola's technicians the long commute into San Francisco.

Confidential screen-tests and rehearsals for *The Godfather Part III* are in progress. Al Pacino takes a phone call on the porch of the Coppolas'

1

elegant wood-frame house. Diane Keaton, his current girlfriend and co-star in the new movie, arrives in her own car and casts around uncertainly for the "stage" where Coppola is at work. Around the side of the house, near the chicken-run, veteran actor Eli Wallach strolls with a couple of colleagues. Coppola's wife, Eleanor, drives back from the stage with the director's father, Carmine. Asked why Francis should embark on a film he has always renounced, Ellie replies with a laugh, "Just say that they made him an offer he couldn't refuse!"

In the hushed dignity of the library, staffers deal with the incipient problems that accompany the preproduction of any major movie. Oscar-winning costume designer Milena Canonero phones for photographs of Talia Shire ("without the fringe"), while a harassed travel agent from L.A. switches reservations for Mario Puzo and Gordon Willis. Messages from Zoetrope Italia in Rome slither out of a fax machine. An accountant runs payroll calculations through a Macintosh computer. And always the chirp of half a dozen phones as Coppola's secretaries and assistants cope with the comings and goings of some of the most talented names in the business.

The trail to the stage sneaks back through a cleft in the hills and ends with an insulated barn that serves to accommodate the actors as well as more administrative offices. Relaxed in a director's chair in the sunshine, Dean Tavoularis marks up a third draft of the screenplay with his plans for the sets he'll be building in Rome's Cinecittà Studios. Tavoularis, who has worked with Coppola since the first *Godfather*, recalls that "Francis started mentioning *Part III* around September 1988." Tom Luddy, another loyal Zoetrope executive, arrives from San Francisco and notes how Coppola uses the same associates on film after film. "His attitude is that he didn't make *The Godfather* movies by himself, and so now he wants to reassemble as many of the original team as possible."

Soon, however, the mood at the stage grows tense. Several pages of script have been wrongly typed overnight, and Coppola finds he cannot start rehearsing for more than two hours. Even then, the scenes fail to jell. Coppola climbs into a station wagon and charges back down the trail to the bungalow he keeps as a writing den and slams the door behind him with significant emphasis. Dusk falls, and a light appears in the bungalow as Coppola and Mario Puzo labor on rewrites for the next day's rehearsals.

*

Flashback to a wet day in November 1987. With *Tucker, The Man and His Dream* already in the final editing process, Francis Coppola has a chance to pause between assignments for the first time in twenty years. One entire vineyard has been razed and the earth turned. Coppola looks across it to the mountains in the east, rising out of the valley floor. The field will be replanted, and named in memory of his son, Gian-Carlo, who died in a boating accident in 1986. After his death, Coppola says, "I began asking about priorities, how important is anything? What's important is to walk outside and see this field and see the cows and try to be as much a part of all that as you can be, rather than spinning your wheels to find $30 million and build a new studio and all that, trying to achieve something when in fact perhaps all you have to do to achieve is to be part of everything."

Born on the brink of World War II, Francis Coppola belongs to a generation that grew up to the sound of a crumbling Hollywood studio system, followed by the French New Wave breaking along the shores of European cinema. Both developments had a profound influence on him. Frustration in the face of studio methods and bureaucracy goaded him to establish his own independent operation in San Francisco. Admiration for the fresh breed of foreign director inspired him to experiment with movie form and language.

Perhaps it is not so strange that a man of such protean talents should have been treated with both adulation and hostility by the press. Many critics and journalists ignored the evidence of Coppola's gifts in *The Rain People*, damned even *The Godfather* with faint praise, and have spent the past ten years excoriating him for his lavish budgets and inordinate love of the Big Statement.

Of course Coppola remains the eternal outsider. He fascinates the movie industry as much by the flamboyance of failure as by the occasional magnitude of his success. Here is a man who has been beyond the edge of economic ruin and clawed his way back to some kind of solvency, and done so through sheer grind and application, not good fortune or a string of hits. When Francis was at graduate school, he lived on $22 a week, plus $65 per month for rent. During the 1980s, he became more accustomed to shelling out up to a million dollars in loan repayments each March. "I'm embarrassed by my duality of failure and success," he concedes disarmingly.

Through triumph and disaster, Coppola has remained an intrepid dreamer. He works hard at his fantasies, compelling some to see the light of day. When he and his brother August were growing up in the 1940s, "everything had to be remembered and told in stories, so that they became imbued with passion." It was, reflects the elder brother, "an emotional act rather than veracity." According to John Milius, originator of *Apocalypse Now*, "Francis has a wonderful, enthusiastic madness. He's the best filmmaker of our generation. I've often regarded myself as Marshal Ney to his Napoleon." During long, rainy nights on location in the Philippines on *Apocalypse*, Coppola would rap with designer Dean Tavoularis about their dreams of improving the world: "make a better telephone, develop a more efficient toaster, improve the style of baseball uniforms, build a beautiful little restaurant, run a revolutionary design school such as Germany's prewar Bauhaus." While mired in the turmoil of *The Cotton Club*, his thoughts turned to setting up an office at the top of the Chrysler Building in New York, and of buying a movie theater he had adored in boyhood.

Some of the minor conceits came true. Francis *did* launch a restaurant ("Wim's," after Wim Wenders) in San Francisco's North Beach. He piloted his own helicopter, as sound engineer Richard Beggs found to his horror immediately after landing in the Philippines, when Francis took him up for a spin over the jungle. He made a film (*One from the Heart*) using video technology from start to finish. He *did* establish an alternative studio in the heart of Los Angeles. He *did* run a magazine (*City*). He *did* buy and run his personal legitimate theater (The Little Fox in San Francisco).

Other dreams must wait. They range from the grandiose—endowing Belize with a communications industry so that the emerging nation can serve as a funnel between North and South America—to the fastidious —issuing Eisenstein's complete *œuvre* on video, transferred from original Soviet negatives.

Most of Coppola's fantasies, however, involve movies and are fired by the instinct of a gambler. Like the traditional Wild West, Hollywood beckons the gambler. But the movie business, again like gambling, measures success in monetary terms. There is ultimately no room for dreamers without profit. And Coppola has committed that most heinous of Hollywood sins: he has risked everything, even the smoke from his own chimney, on projects in which he believes. Michael Powell, the veteran British director engaged as an adviser to Coppola's Zoetrope Studios in 1980, likes George Lucas's story: "If we were stuck in a blazing building, I'd sneak down the back stairs and Francis would leap off the top at the front!"

The mythology enveloping Coppola makes it more and more difficult for him to do small things well. Ruined by the folly of *One from the Heart*, he recovered with *The Outsiders* and *Rumble Fish*, but all three films fell victim to a certain innate bombast, a kind of technological equivalent to the old Hollywood habit of cramming the 'Scope screen with extras—what Orson Welles once dubbed "the principle of the cast of thousands." Yet Coppola has never let himself be disheartened by financial calamity. "I always operate as if I'll be rich, because if I'm broke, that will take care of itself," he was quoted as saying during the 1970s. "I see everything in geometrical, spatial quantities, rather than numerical values," he says now. It is an approach that marks both his writing and his personal finances. For over a decade, he has been among the highest-paid film directors in the United States, his services regularly commanding in excess of $2 million.

Coppola is no Scrooge, however. His generosity covers a wide, if unostentatious spectrum, from sending friends and colleagues a case of Niebaum-Coppola wine at Christmas, to lending his support to directors in their time of need (the young George Lucas, the veteran Akira Kurosawa, the neophyte Godfrey Reggio). This helps to explain the loyalty of creative artists and technicians who have served with Coppola and his utopian vision of Zoetrope Studios through good and lean years alike.

European directors—Bergman, Fellini, and Godard, for example—have been accustomed to filming with the same team on one production after another. In America it is more difficult; technicians, too, have agents and understandably accept as many lucrative assignments as they can. But in his version of Orson Welles's Mercury Theater company, Coppola has retained the friendship and respect of a select band of collaborators: senior among them Barry Malkin, his editor; Dean Tavoularis, production designer; Walter Murch and Richard Beggs, maestros of sound; Fred Roos, the peripatetic producer.

Tavoularis sums up the feelings of many when he says,

> Francis is very likeable as a person. I always have a lot of fun with him, and it's great to collaborate together. From the moment a project is initiated, he wants ideas, and there's no jealousy involved. What's wonderful about Francis is that he never stops you, he's always pushing you. He never says your ideas are crazy, instead he'll want to know why you think that way. I like that, and it's this conversational aspect that builds and builds, and it starts becoming concrete, and you eliminate the chaff, and you focus in on things.

Coppola rewards this fealty with a degree of latitude and responsibility rarely found in Hollywood. Of course, Zoetrope has no board of directors, no stockholders. Francis is beholden to nobody. He has a knack of assembling groups of gifted individuals and then delegating creative functions to them. Not all welcome such independence. Some perceive it as a threat to themselves, as part of an instinctive bid by Coppola to forestall any risk of his being eclipsed by those in his circle.

He himself looks back to his youth to explain this situation.

> I think that it comes from a lot of things—one is my theatrical background. I always operated like a theater company, and I think theater companies traditionally stick together—"Let's get the show on the road" and all that. I also think that it's my Italian background and that I have always operated with people very affectionately, and people are starved of that. I feel they want that, they like the family attitude.

Most of the time, Coppola's fiscal and psychological authority has been exercised in a benevolent style. But deep within himself he must recognize the specter of Joseph Conrad's Kurtz, at the very heart of darkness, and the distortion of mind and principle that power can bring in its train. Steven Bach, a senior executive at United Artists at the time *Apocalypse Now* was being made, and the author of *Final Cut*, has written that "Coppola *is* the Godfather: to his own films, to George Lucas, Philip Kaufman, Carroll Ballard, the whole *Mill Valley Mafia* as it is called."

Harry Chotiner, a former reader for Zoetrope, has called Coppola "insufferable" in that "he totally believes in himself and his impulses and whims." Comparing him with Norman Mailer, and conceding his greatness, Chotiner sees both men as "giant gifted egos that are also awkward and infantile."

On larger productions Coppola will hire heads of departments, who are then responsible to him for those beneath him. In the words of a close colleague, Walter Murch, "Something that is destructive to his vision he will eliminate, but something that is *beyond* his vision, he may think of as wonderful and find ways of assimilating it." Bernard Gersten, former Vice-President for Creative Affairs at Zoetrope Studios, has said: "Francis is an individual. He's uncontrollable. He changes his mind. He makes decisions on an artistic basis and not on a financial one."

Gersten has identified a crucial trait in Coppola's character. The one trait, indeed, that mitigates the darker, more imperialist side of his nature as a mini-magnate and director of extravagant epics. The trait that fuels his courage when it comes to choosing new faces for his films. As Fred Roos has pointed out, the casting of Lee Strasberg as Hyman Roth in *The Godfather Part II* could have been disastrous. But it turned out that Strasberg was nominated for an Academy Award. With each passing year, some youngster selected by Coppola during the early 1980s makes his or her mark as a new star: Nicolas Cage, Tom Cruise, Matt Dillon, Raul Julia, Diane Lane, Ralph Macchio, Rebecca de Mornay, Mickey Rourke, Patrick Swayze . . .

*   *   *

Coppola's sexual politics breathe the conservatism of his Italian background, and if the occasional woman in his films escapes the customary ties of family, then like Natalie in *The Rain People* or Kay in *The Godfather Part II*, she must shoulder a terrible burden of guilt. Dishonor to the family is among the worst sins in Italian life. Like Hank and Frannie in *One from the Heart*, Coppola has returned to the side of his partner Ellie after even the worst crises in his professional and marital life. As he himself comments:

> When I was first married, I couldn't say I thought it would be forever. I didn't know. I could have thought of many other romantic eventualities if I had become an important director—I could have married Rita Hayworth! But I was crazy about that idea of having kids. I loved the little boys, taking them out, and it was just in my nature to like kids. My marriage has obviously gone through a few strains, but quite honestly I know that if I ever left my wife, and especially if I got involved with some other woman, then I might very well be in the same spot six years later except that I would have broken everything up. I'd just as soon keep my family together, and stay married, because I don't think that, unless you have a loser for a wife, or someone who's just a bad person, if you leave your partner and marry someone else you may very well leave the next person and go somewhere else, and you've disrupted one of the most important things you can have, which is a continuous family. It's hard to stay with one person. An old couple told me once that they had been married for sixty years and there never was a day when they didn't consider getting a divorce.
>
> I love my family—and I loved my previous family, my mother and father had great magnetic, magical charm. My mother's a bit of an immature kind of person, but with a lot of the magic that such people can have. My father was very dashing—I'd see him in a tuxedo, with his silver flute, and girls singing around him. He'd take me at 5 p.m. to Studio 8H at NBC and put

me in the glass box so I could watch Toscanini, and there'd be a knob in there that controlled the volume, and that just blew me away when I was a kid, when I realized that picture and sound were *not* connected! There was a tremendous amount of magical, emotional, mystical stuff connected to family, or women, or children. That part of life is very attractive to me.

Nothing has influenced Coppola's life and work so dramatically as his Italian blood. "In our family life," recalls his brother August, "there was great passion, creativity, belief in opera. The family was the literature incarnate." Francis has borne with him into his generation this unshakable faith in the sovereignty of the family. His wife and, when they were young, his children have accompanied him on location in the jungle and to festivals in places as far-flung as Moscow and Santa Fe. "We travel together like a circus family," says Eleanor, "with Francis on the tightrope and the rest of us holding the ropes." Two of those children, Gian-Carlo and Sofia Carmina, were christened with Italian names.

On a personal level, Coppola also relishes Italian tastes and habits. He installed superb espresso machines in his various homes and work sites —and even gave August a machine for the office of the Dean of Creative Arts at San Francisco State University. When outfitting his mini-restaurant in the Sentinel Building, he visited Biordi's, a nearby Italian store in San Francisco's North Beach, and purchased carefully selected pottery cups, as well as a pasta machine.

He loves big, Italianate parties. "What brings me the greatest joy," he said once, "is the company of nice people and to be able to go through all the rituals with them, to eat dinner with them, cook with them, talk with them. I'm very European in that respect." He denies any need to be the star attraction, however. "I'm always trying to have a party, and like everyone to have fun. I try *not* to be the center of attention, so that I can enjoy the party more. I'm embarrassed when I get that kind of attention. Even when someone says something complimentary to me, I become very embarrassed."

Film personalities visiting San Francisco's Bay Area have reveled in Coppola's hospitality at his home in the Napa Valley. The German directors Wim Wenders and Werner Herzog are more likely to be found at a Coppola bash than are the portable movie or agency executives one encounters on similar occasions in Hollywood. Carroll Ballard remembers "incredible scenes at [his] place, with people from all over the world, and Francis holding court." Ballard is not perhaps the most objective of commentators, since during one party in Napa he drank too much, called

Francis an asshole, and threw up all over the living room. But there is no doubt that the party as such manifests a yearning in Coppola to fulfill his role as a benevolent Godfather. Like many great hosts, he rarely shines at other people's parties. He is more relaxed when *chez lui*, enveloping his guests in a mood of largesse and civilized banter. Few outsiders would guess that Francis Coppola is by no means the brash, self-confident personality whom the press and public assume him to be. Francis will sit at the head of the long dining table, listening to courageous souls holding forth, whether it be his Uncle Anton giving a dazzling impromptu analysis of *Madame Butterfly*, or Russian poet Yevgeni Yevtushenko proclaiming the virtues of a script that he almost commands Coppola to endorse. His sensitivity may be detected in his leading screen characters, from Natalie in *The Rain People* to Peggy Sue Kelcher, and even includes Michael Corleone. They all carry within them a deep well of uncertainty, a tendency toward anguish in the face of commitment to family.

Except when wearing formal attire, Coppola looks rumpled and relaxed in his trousers, jacket, and a tie forever abandoning the struggle to stay in place. Often he will wear a casual brown corduroy suit, as though caught midway between Madison Avenue and Bohemia. Not tall, he carries his 250 pounds or so with distinctive flair, his ample midriff quelled by broad shoulders and a leonine head. Abstemious with alcohol, often reckless with food, he manages to appear at once unfit and bursting with energy. If, like most of his generation, he has smoked grass, he has bypassed the Hollywood standard diet of cocaine or more.

Few question Coppola's personal generosity or his quickness to foster those in need. The late Jean-Pierre Rassam, the French producer, was given sanctuary in Francis's home for several weeks so he could try to kick his addiction to heroin. Dennis Jakob, a kind of philosopher-in-residence at Coppola's side throughout the 1970s, lost his temper and vanished in San Francisco one day with a couple of reels of the final cut of *Apocalypse Now*. Once tracked down, Jakob refused to open the door until Francis promised to buy him a barbecue beef sandwich and root beer—a sentimental reference to the meal that Jakob had given Coppola at UCLA when the future emperor of Zoetrope was literally starving. Jakob turned down the offer, however, and sent Francis the reels in ashes, in envelopes. Fortunately the ashes were fake.

Coppola puts spontaneous trust in his friends, a feature exemplified in a modest way by his asking production coordinator Mona Skager to keep all his furniture when Seven Arts were transferring their Wilshire Boulevard offices to the lot at Burbank, and in a much larger way by his placing certain key assets in the names of close associates during his most turbulent financial crisis. "My worst fear," he says with a smile, "was that I'd lose my library—my books!"

Coppola has always been disposed to aid those talented figures who cannot cope with the pressures of selling their ideas to a Hollywood studio. He has lent his name to projects promptly and cheerfully. Should the end result prove disappointing, Coppola does not withdraw his imprimatur; he assimilates the failures of others as he must his own. When Walter Murch ran into difficulties on his first directing assignment—*Return to Oz*, being made in London—Francis flew the Atlantic just to be around his friend for a week, and to back up George Lucas's insistent plea that Walt Disney Productions should reinstate Murch after firing him from the set.

To some degree, such an attitude is bound up with Francis's own notion of the artist being the underdog. Deep down, his European mind may perceive success in the American context as damaging, even a sell-out. Like the Motorcycle Boy in *Rumble Fish*, he is a prince born in the wrong time. "I'm no tough cookie," he has said apropos his propensity to spend money, "I am extremely coddling of other artistic people. I always have a tough time saying no to someone who says it will be beautiful and we can afford it."

Coppola does not impose a specific style of delivery or demeanor on his actors. James Caan feels that "He lets you respond to a situation and urges you to throw in a few surprises of your own." This refusal to ordain the behavior of those around him accords with Coppola's dictum: "All talent consists of being comfortable with your instincts, and being able to act on them." It also explains the unusual measure of autonomy given to people like Vittorio Storaro, Tavoularis, Murch, and Richard Beggs whenever they work with Coppola. In Murch's words, "Francis's films invent themselves. You kind of organize the acts, but you can't control *all* the acts, and that makes it exciting in a certain way."

*   *   *

Francis *Coppola* (accent on the first syllable, as in "*tra*lala *co*pella"), or better still the now-banished triple assurance, Francis *Ford* Coppola, sounds so patrician, so different from even the most esoteric of Hollywood names. Francis eliminated the "Ford" in 1977, when he realized that others might share his distrust of a man with three names. Now, walking back to his house through the drizzle, he decides, tongue in cheek, to change his name again. "To just Francis. A letterhead with me and some birds on it, and it'll just say, 'Francis, Rutherford, California,' and people can write to me like that. That's when I become a saint!"

CHAPTER ONE

The Italian Connection

Francis Ford Coppola was born on April 7, 1939, in the Ford Hospital in Detroit, Michigan, the second son of Carmine Coppola and his wife, Italia. Both of Francis's grandfathers sailed from southern Italy about the turn of the century. The Italian immigrants of the period headed for two main areas—New York (especially Brooklyn), where they soon lived isolated in ghettos, and San Francisco, where they were assimilated more easily and could earn their livelihood from fishing. It was the New York families who kept the memory of home in the forefront of their daily lives.

Carmine had shown a pronounced musical talent as a small boy. His facility with the flute earned him a scholarship to New York's famous music college, the Juilliard School. Through a fellow student Carmine met, and soon fell in love with, Italia Pennino. Italia's father, Francesco, had brought a colorful personality to the New World when he landed in 1905. "He was a songwriter and a lyricist," says Francis, "and in those days the Neapolitan songs told stories, usually stories of the heart, of the nature of losing your mother, or the girl leaves you, etc."

Once settled in the States, Pennino championed the cause of the Italian silent movie, which with its melodramatic sparkle and eye for grandeur found a ready market in America. He ran a legitimate theater in Brooklyn and continued to create songs. According to Francis's mother, Pennino's firm was called the "Paramount Music-roll Company," and as he was a friend of one of the partners in the fledgling Paramount Pictures, he may even have contributed to the studio's name. Carmine would tease his wife

13

that her father Francesco enjoyed the company of Pearl White and that she often visited the Pennino house. Certainly he was fascinated by motion pictures and as late as 1949 presented Francis with a 16mm projector, when his grandson lay incapacitated by polio.

In 1931 Francesco Pennino, who by that time owned a number of movie theaters, returned to Italy to acquire some product to screen to the immigrant population. He visited various studios, and Francis maintains that "when one studio saw my mother, who was really quite a beautiful young woman—like Hedy Lamarr—they said, Well, maybe we could film her in front of the gate, saying, 'Through the courtesy of the Caesar Film Company, providers of the finest two-reel . . . ,' you know, whatever the hell it was . . . And they took a picture of her. But her father was shocked. 'No way is my daughter gonna be involved in this kind of thing!' "

Carmine's father, Augustino Coppola, on the other hand, could not boast such artistic qualities. The family stemmed from peasant stock in Apulia, on the Gulf of Taranto. Carmine's grandmother could neither read nor write. She was also handicapped by the loss of her nose. While crocheting, she habitually tickled her nostril with the needle. Infection set in, and doctors had to remove the nose. She was afraid to undergo plastic surgery, and remained disfigured to the end of her life. Carmine's mother, Maria Zaza, was pure Italian, but had been raised in Tunis. She spoke French and Arabic as well as Italian. She and her husband Augustino had seven sons, and an extraordinary life, according to Francis. The family lived in a small town called Bernalda. "There are wonderful stories of bandits," says Francis, "and murder for the honor of the sister, and the whole mythology of the family, leading to his father, who was a tool-and-die-maker and who built the first Vitaphone, producing sound on discs to accompany silent movies. He was the character we tried to portray in *The Godfather Part II* when the gunsmith, who was my grandfather, had the little boy play the flute (which was my father)." All the children of Augustino Coppola exhibited an early and abiding talent for music. Carmine would become a composer and arranger as well as a prominent soloist, and Anton opted for conducting operas and musicals. Both men are still active. Their brother, Michael Coppola, built an impressive model of the Corliss Steam Engine of 1876, and it stands today in the front room of the Coppolas' house in Rutherford.

In 1934 Carmine and Italia had their first child, August Floyd Coppola.

The five-year difference in age between August and Francis would prove crucial both to the brothers' relationship and to Francis's outlook on his life and career.

In Detroit, Carmine was first flautist with the Detroit Symphony Orchestra and official arranger for the *Ford Sunday Evening Hour* (hence Francis's middle name). Soon afterward, he moved back to New York, to occupy the most distinguished chair of his career, as first flute under Arturo Toscanini in the NBC Symphony Orchestra. He held the post for several years, and it was during this halcyon spell that his daughter Talia was born, in 1946. Talia remembers "half a dozen golden childhood years. [Mother] was loving and magical and so alive. She didn't need to put on a play—she *was* the play."

Francis remembers delighting in the showbiz world to which his father increasingly belonged. "We were brought around to the backstage of Radio City Music Hall every month. It was rices on the elevators behind the Music Hall, and we could see the chorus girls and the Rockettes, and watch my uncle conduct. There was a tremendous musical theater/opera influence on us. I think the first theater show I saw when a little kid was *The Desert Song*, on my brother's birthday."

"The family was a living presence," recalls August. "The relationship of brothers, aunts, etc., was like the declension of verbs." Although the Coppolas cherished their Italian origins, especially the heritage of music and painting, they reared their children in the mold of genuine Americans. From the age of three, August was told he would grow up to be a doctor. Francis, had Carmine had his way, would have become an engineer—curious because Carmine himself had been earmarked as a chemical engineer by *his* father. It was only through the efforts of his elder brother that Carmine had been allowed to indulge his passion for the flute.

Francis's childhood was anything but settled. His parents moved continually, in and around Queens. "Francis and I attended so many schools, it drove us crazy," says August. Carmine had endured poverty as a youth, and so when he began doing well himself he lavished toys on his children—with fireworks a favorite diversion. But in 1949 Francis was struck down by polio. "It was very dramatic," in August's words, "and our father was wiped out by it." Francis was attending New York City School, P.S. 109. He was not an outstanding pupil, and his teachers were constantly talking to Carmine and Italia about their son's failures in math and other subjects. His polio may have been contracted during an overnight Cub Scout campout. As Francis recalls:

It rained tremendously, and our tents all got soaked, and we were sleeping in the water. My mother believes that this soaking may have been connected with the whole business. I got up, and had a stiff neck. So I went to my father, who told me to go to school. But it kept bothering me, and I went to the school nurse. Before I knew it I was being whisked away in an ambulance, my mother was crying . . . But I was not very frightened; I was of good cheer, you know? The hospital was incredible. The epidemic was such that they had kids stashed in the bathrooms, three high on these racks, and in the hallways . . . The first night was pretty painful, and I kept calling out for my mother, but I was more frightened by the cries of the other kids.

Next day I was in a bed in some other part of the hospital, and I was in a very good mood. But I remember I tried to get out of the bed, and when I got out I went down; I couldn't lift myself up. That's how I discovered I had lost the use of my left arm. They kept me in the hospital for about a week and then, still paralyzed, I was taken home. My parents took me to a French doctor and he gave me one of those speeches about you're gonna be a soldier, and you're gonna have to understand you'll never walk again. I remember that after that interview we went to a Chinese restaurant, and we were all crying. Then began a long period at home, up in my bedroom. I had a television across from me, and puppets, and I had a 16mm projector, and a tape recorder. One of my problems was figuring out how to synchronize the sound between the film in the projector and the tape in the recorder. I'd invent all the "sound-track" myself, imitating Mickey Mouse and so on, and then I'd try to start the machines in sync. But I could never quite get it!

I stayed in bed almost a year, and with no other children for company because polio was such a contagious disease. So I just saw my brother (my sister occasionally) and people came in with gifts.

The Coppola household in Woodside was blessed with a TV set and although programming in those days was restricted to a mere two hours a day, Francis watched with avid interest, especially the Horn & Hardart's *Children's Hour* each Sunday morning. His ventriloquist's dummy replaced the children he could no longer mix with, and he managed to entertain his few visitors later with impromptu performances. Many years afterward, he said that the idea of Zoetrope surely grew from such shows, a studio "where we could work together like children, with music, puppets, scenery, lights, dramatic action, whatever we wanted to do."

The turning point came when Carmine Coppola rejected the instructions of the French doctor, who wanted to have Francis pinned into the bed, warning that he would damage the muscles if he tried to crawl around. Thanks to the March of Dimes, Carmine enrolled his son in a program in which a physiotherapist came to the house and helped Francis lift his arm a little more each day.

So after nine months of inactivity, he returned to school. There was a big assembly. "This is very significant," smiles Francis.

I always wanted to be a "Guard." A "Guard" had a badge like a monitor, and when the school welcomed me back at this assembly they made me a "Guard." After about a week my teacher, who hated me, said, "Why do you deserve to be a Guard, just because you've been sick?" And the next day the privilege was removed, and I was no longer a "Guard." That was the most dramatic part of the whole polio story!

Francis was left with a limp, not a pronounced one but, in his own words, "you can always tell a limp when you put your arm around a girl and you walk with her—that's when it's magnified!" The memory of that traumatic episode remained with him for years, however, and surfaces in the long monologue uttered by Harry Caul in *The Conversation*, about being paralyzed for months on end during childhood.

Once recovered, Francis joined August on forays into the famous New York City toy stores of A. C. Gilbert's and F. A. O. Schwarz. Creative toys of every kind, chemistry sets, and even a nuclear kit—for which Francis saved up some $50—held a particular fascination. August cut school with regularity and aplomb. He would take Francis with him to movie matinees at the Center Theater on Queens Boulevard around 45th Street and as Francis fondly remembers, "across from the White Castle hamburger stand." The inlaid floor of the lobby boasted the inscription "Center Theater, Home of Proven Hits." *Things to Come*, *The War of the Worlds*, and *The Man Who Could Work Miracles* were among his favorites. "We felt a bond between us," says August, "like the Corsican Brothers." They soon became so inured to the routine of moviegoing that they could enter a film in the middle and within seconds work out what was happening in the plot. Fantasy above all else impressed them—Walt Disney's work, and in particular Alexander Korda's production of Michael Powell's *The Thief of Bagdad*. Then there were all the Errol Flynn movies, and pirate and horror films (Bela Lugosi in *Dracula*), and even the staple comedy of Abbott and Costello.

"We were raised on Italian folk humor and Italian folktales," insists August. The Coppola family was spiritual to an extreme, but not religious; attending church was a means of finding girls. August proved the ideal elder brother in such circumstances. Tall, grave and handsome, he had no difficulty in attracting the opposite sex. Francis, by his own admission, "was funny-looking, not good in school, and didn't know any girls." The sibling relationship was intense and enduring, and throughout his most personal films Francis has focused on the need for a senior figure, part brother, part mentor, to be displaced. "As a younger man, the words I'd use of Augie are a purity, and a kindness," muses Francis. "A lot of brothers would dump a kid five years younger, but he would always take me everywhere. At one point we even lived in the same room, and you'd think he'd be dying to get rid of me even more. I was very charmed by him and very much wanted to imitate him." August could string words together, and won prizes at school for writing. Francis remembers handing in a long paper on Hemingway by August under his own name when he attended writing class in high school.

Technology obsessed Francis. He adored gadgets of every description, and at the age of ten was already experimenting with sound in his home movies. He edited pieces of film shot by his family, and liked to play the hero in them. He showed them "to other kids in the neighborhood. I had a little movie company there on 212th Street in Queens." In 1984, he confessed to being "the original video ranger. I read about the inventors of TV; in fact, I tried to build a mechanical television, but always had trouble trying to get the disc wheels to synchronize." He concocted his own color TV system, which he "dreamed of drawing on the blackboard" for his science teacher, in the tradition of whiz-kid Philo Farnsworth. Other kids gave him the nickname "Science."

In 1951, Francis's father quit the NBC Symphony Orchestra and moved full time to Radio City Music Hall on Sixth Avenue, where he arranged music routines for the Rockettes. But Carmine remained the eternally frustrated composer. Francis had admitted, to his chagrin, that when he was fourteen, and working during the summer vacation in a Western Union office, he sent a fake telegram to his father. The wire was signed by the head of music at Paramount Studios, and announced that Carmine had been chosen to score a new movie. "It's my break! It's my break!" exclaimed Carmine. But when Francis owned up, his father was shattered.

It was about this time that all the exposure to music began to bring results. Francis took not to the flute, but to the tuba. His playing was adequate, and in his early teens he enrolled in New York Military Academy at Cornwall-on-Hudson, which gave him a scholarship on the strength of his ability to play in the band. Francis disliked the place, and especially its emphasis on sports. He hated "the way the older cadets were always brutalizing the younger cadets." He made pocket money by producing love letters for his fellow cadets, at a dollar a page, inspired by photos of the girlfriends involved. While others played football at NYMA, Francis and his few studious friends would pass around a dog-eared copy of James Joyce's *Ulysses*.

After eighteen months he escaped, made his way to the center of New York, and wandered around the city for some days, "sleeping where I could and having certain crazy adventures, frightened that my parents were really going to be mad." Carmine and Italia were touring with *Kismet*, and did not know that Francis had run away. Some of his experiences during this taste of the big city would surface in Coppola's first studio film, *You're a Big Boy Now*, made in 1966.

August was at UCLA, and invited Francis to spend the following summer with him at his small house in Los Angeles. Augie was determined to become a writer, and proceeded to introduce Francis to the work of authors like André Gide and Aldous Huxley.

By now, Carmine and Italia were reconciled to the fact that their younger son would never become the engineer of their dreams. "My parents were concerned about my making a living," Francis reflects.

I can recall their talking in low voices about whether I should perhaps be a printer. A lot of people have an affinity for show business and things related to theater or music, but they don't ever allow that they would go into that as a *profession*, so at the same time they decide, well, I'll be an oculist, because my brother's going to be a doctor. So for many years I told my family that I intended to become an optometrist, just as my brother would be a doctor. And it wasn't until high school, and the first year of college, that what was my *hobby* emerged as my future profession.

To their credit, his parents encouraged his artistic leanings. Back in high school, Francis continued to play the tuba, but theater and movies remained his primary loves. He had been intrigued by the mechanics of the stage ever since, at the age of five, he went looking for Augie and discovered the huge lighting console behind the curtains of a large theater, the real "engine room" of the place. The concept of the movies as a show, a bravura performance, has colored much of his work on screen. According to Eleanor, the story goes that when Francis was about fourteen years old, "He was in the kitchen with his brother Augie and his wife. They were dancing around doing scenes from a romantic movie. Francis looked through his fingers like he was operating a camera, following their action." He liked acting out roles himself, and was eager to direct plays during his mid-teens.

And still Carmine Coppola sailed on with his own career. There were changes of job, and financial ups and downs throughout the 1950s. "I never knew where the family stood," said Francis in 1981. "One minute we had a little bit of money, the next, my father was saying he couldn't afford the mortgage." This did not quell Carmine's restless passion for his art, however. "My father was constantly at the piano," recalls August, "searching for the melody . . . If you sat at the family dinner table, you would understand why opera was born. When one of us was singing an aria, the rest had to stop and listen."

August had attended Hofstra University in Hempstead, Long Island. Praising the creative atmosphere of the school, he urged Francis to apply for a place. It was Francis's audition as Cyrano de Bergerac at Jamaica High School that prompted him to aim for a drama scholarship to Hofstra, which remains secure among the nation's top universities (its library alone boasts some 1,100,000 volumes). He entered the Theater Arts Department in 1956, and began immediately to assert his authority. In his own words, "the whole tone of my regime, and it was a regime, was to turn control of the Theater Arts Department into the hands of the students." Coppola recalls:

Hofstra was significant for me because after a career of going to many, many high schools, and not having many friends, and being the odd man out and the kind of boy scientist, my first year of college consisted of having a group of friends in the Theater Arts Department and actually going through four years at the same school. I got that partial scholarship to Hofstra by virtue of my playwriting—I'd already started writing at fifteen or sixteen years old, plays, short stories, etc. My brother was doing that and I wanted to do so too. I brought these fragments to the professor at Hofstra and as I could also act a little bit, I was given some 50 percent off my tuition fees.

It was a very good Theater Department. I was part of a pretty talented group at a very hot drama school in those years, and at first I worked for the shop and the scenery and the lighting and worked technical crews—they're always happy to have someone to do that—and helped run the light boards and stuff. While I was erecting the lights, I'd look down from the ladders and watch the rehearsals and see the professor direct the kids there. "Maybe I could do that," I said to myself. "I see what you do when you direct, you tell everyone where to stand and so on," and with my extraordinary technical ability I participated in a program of freshman student one-act plays. I did a Eugene O'Neill one-acter called *The Rope*. I staged it with music score and sets. But my technical ability made this production shine out; it was even better than the faculty production, and I became very fêted and kind of successful on the campus as this type of student.

By virtue of his popularity, Francis became elected as president of both the Hofstra drama organization ("The Green Wig"), and the musical organization ("The Kaleidoscopians"). As a result he was able to roll both societies into one new group, dubbed "The Spectrum Players," which presented a new production each week.

I discovered that the money for producing all the shows at the drama department did not come through the *college*, but through the extracurricular funding whereby every student paid a fee. In other words it was student activity money. So, being president of the student organization, I could take all that money away from the faculty and, instead of their producing the shows, *we* began to produce the shows. I made myself director of all of them! I have never achieved the success I had at Hofstra, in that political sense, out in the big world. Sure enough, the next year a rule was introduced stating that no student could direct more than two shows a year, and I had to remove myself from being a drama major to being an English major so they could not pin me down. It was a struggle with the faculty, even though they liked me.

Francis's greatest success at Hofstra was a musical play called *Inertia*, which drew its ideas from H. G. Wells's *The Man Who Could Work Miracles*, although Francis's most interesting recollection is of his staging of *A Streetcar Named Desire*. He had found a copy of Tennessee Williams's play lying around at home, when he was about fifteen. "It had a picture of a half-naked lady on the cover, so I thought I'd read it!" He fell captive to the magical, sensual, poetic world of Williams. Two of his future friends and colleagues were candidates to play Stanley Kowalski at Hofstra. One was Bob Spiotta, then a husky football player, later to become head of Zoetrope Studios in Los Angeles. "I didn't want the typical drama student to play Stanley who, after all, is supposed to be this young masculine guy. So I saw this football player who came to our auditions, and he wasn't at all bad, and we cast him, and he did quite well." Ron Colby, later to act in *Finian's Rainbow* and also to help produce Coppola's early movies, looked a natural choice for Stanley. He lost out to Spiotta in Francis's production at Hofstra, but played the lead in *Picnic*.

His striving for student independence at Hofstra was a foretaste of his efforts to break away from the authoritarian control of the Hollywood studios in subsequent years. He won three Dan H. Lawrence Awards for theatrical direction and production. He was also given the Beckerman Award in recognition of his outstanding services to Hofstra's Theater Arts Department. "I left Hofstra as really the top guy," he remembers with satisfaction. "When the faculty gave the last speech, they said, 'Well, we've seen a lot happen in these years. We've seen a new regime take over.' I think they were all proud of me. We got lots of things done, lots of imaginative, crazy things—and lots of stuff that failed."

In his final years, Francis sold his car and used the funds to acquire a 16mm movie camera (he had already made shorts, such as *The Lost Wallet*, on the 8mm gauge). He admired the genius of Soviet filmmaker Sergei Eisenstein. Francis had seen *Ten Days That Shook the World* when he was seventeen. "On Monday I was in the theater," he said, "and on Tuesday I wanted to be a filmmaker."

Now he was a visitor to screenings at the Museum of Modern Art, and immersed himself in books on the theory and technique of motion pictures. Francis's own first effort was a short about a woman who loses her children during a day's excursion to the countryside. Eisenstein and Pudovkin had placed great stress on the psychological power of "montage." They cited the example of Kuleshov's experiment intercutting the impassive face of a famous actor first with a bowl of steaming soup and then with the image of an open coffin. Viewers claimed to have seen a look of hunger and happiness on the man's face when confronted with the soup, and an expression of profound grief when matched with the corpse in the casket. In Francis's unfinished short, the idea was that the mother would regard the lush beauty of the countryside in a wholly different way once she had awoken from a nap in the orchard and found her children missing. Suddenly things that had seemed so attractive assumed a threatening quality, like some harbinger of the jungle in *Apocalypse Now*.

The following semester, in the autumn of 1960, Francis entered UCLA. At first he was despondent. "Once again I was like a cipher in a big group of guys—there were no girls at all when I arrived—and Colin Young made his usual speech about how only two of us would get through the course. . . ." Francis found the atmosphere so different from that of the theater, with its warmth and excitement, and the thrill of working together, all night if necessary, and then celebrating with the orchestra in the small hours. "My first impression of the Theater Department at UCLA was that it was dry, gray, and full of talk," he remembers. "I was a real production guy. I was ready to build the scenery. Little by little I began to see the lie of the land there, and I was not pleased with it. I looked at the UCLA Theater and that seemed rather more to my way of understanding. In those years there was always a pull for me, to forget this film thing and go back to theater, where I'd been so successful."

Although his professors may have found Coppola too theatrically in-
clined, there was no doubt that once again he was building a mini-empire.
Carroll Ballard and Dennis Jakob were fellow students who reacted to
Francis with a love-hate intensity. Another, Paul Bartel, would achieve a
pleasing notoriety with features like *Death Race 2000* and *Eating Raoul*.
"The image I had of Francis," he says, "was one of tremendous energy,
always friendly, always approachable. He also gave me the impression of
verging on the manic-depressive."

Their teachers at UCLA numbered the still-active French master, Jean
Renoir; one of Hollywood's few significant women directors, Dorothy
Arzner, who gave Francis much encouragement; and veteran screenwriter
Arthur Ripley, who died soon afterward. But a year or two later the
students across town at the University of Southern California (USC)
appeared just as impressive a bunch—George Lucas, Walter Murch, John
Milius, Caleb Deschanel . . .

Carroll Ballard, who went on to make his name with *The Black Stallion*,
offers a pungent account of life in the UCLA Film Department at the
time Coppola was holding court.

The whole department was housed out in the woods, behind the university.
The little sound stage was practically a closet. I'd wanted to be an industrial
designer, but dropped out disillusioned, joined the army, and had this dream
of getting into films. Loved Kurosawa and Dreyer. People at UCLA were
interested in film study and theory rather than the practical side. There were
only three moviolas in the entire department. There was an old Mitchell camera
locked in a closet, unlocked, shown and demonstrated, then wheeled back in
again. Don Shebib [*Goin' Down the Road*] was there. We'd go out to some
Mexican joint and drink beer and yell. A lot of interesting films were screened.
After about a year I found myself working as a grip on a picture that had been
put together by a guy who'd only been there a few weeks—Francis Coppola.
It was about a sculptor who only made statues of himself.

By all accounts, Ballard made the most talented student movie of the
time, a sharp and affectionate piece of observation called *Waiting for May*.

Francis's graduate work included making shorts like *Aymonn the Terrible*. More diverting were his forays into the burgeoning art of the nudie
picture. It was the era of *The Immoral Mr. Teas*, a 16mm release that
featured full nudity and managed to avoid prosecution. Some friends of
his brother's came to Francis and suggested that they produce a short
nudie film. Big money rewards beckoned, now that screen nudity seemed
legal. "I just wanted to make a film," pleads Francis,

so we shot *The Peeper*, about a little man who has reason to believe that pin-up sessions are being photographed near his house. The whole movie is the equivalent of a Tom and Jerry cartoon, with this guy trying to see what's happening. He peeks through a telescope but sees only a belly-button, or he hoists himself up with a block-and-tackle, and then falls down . . . Some people saw it, and offered to buy, but they themselves already had shot a vast amount of footage of a Western nudie, about a drunken cowboy who hits his head and sees naked girls instead of cows. They wanted me to intercut my film with theirs to leaven it and thus make the package sellable. So they gave me money, and we devised a plot gimmick whereby both characters meet and tell their stories, and that's how we'd unveil the two films, under the title *Tonight for Sure*. Sixty to 70 percent of it was not my work, but I was so eager for recognition that I shot the credit sequence and printed "Directed by Francis Ford Coppola" up on the screen!

Coppola also received another naughty commission. This involved shooting about twelve minutes of 3-D sequences with the buxom June Wilkinson and inserting them into an already existing German black-and-white movie.

In the final analysis, the quality that set Francis Coppola apart from his fellows at UCLA was his screenwriting. During his mid-teens he had already started writing, but now as he returned to the craft after years of stage directing, he found he had more facility than he thought and, in his own words, "*much* more facility than anyone at UCLA. I could sit down and write a script!"

A characteristic story involves the military draft. Francis was eligible, despite his polio attack and the fact that he was a minor epileptic.

I wanted to flunk my physical, so the night beforehand I started to drink a hundred mugs of black coffee, and I just started to write this story, high on all this caffeine, and I thought if I didn't go to sleep that night, and if I couldn't keep my eyes open during the physical, I wouldn't get taken into the army. So I wrote an entire script [*Pilma Pilma*] in a single night, on the level, about seventy to eighty pages, typed it right out. I went to my physical, passed it with flying colors, and fainted eight hours later when it was too late!

Francis did manage to avoid the draft, but at a later stage of proceedings.

Francis's incipient flair for screenwriting received another boost when he won the Samuel Goldwyn Award. It was an important competition, although usually novels were preferred to screenplays by the selectors. Francis wanted to enter *The Old Gray Station Wagon*, which was an early draft of what would become *The Rain People*, but as it was unfinished he submitted his original screenplay, *Pilma Pilma* ("It was pure Tennessee Williams," he admits nowadays). Carroll Ballard took the runner-up prize.

Not every student attending film school contrives to enter the industry. Francis seized the first opportunity that came his way. Roger Corman, uncrowned king of schlock movies, had bought the rights to two Soviet films boasting big special effects. "I needed someone to edit and dub them," says Corman, "so I contacted the Film Department at UCLA and asked them to send some students along. I talked with several, and chose Francis. He shot a couple of special effects scenes for *Battle Beyond the Sun.*"

Francis recalls the tension surrounding his "appointment."

I heard in school that Corman was looking for some kind of assistant. I remember my phone was ready to be cut off, because I hadn't paid it, and I called the lady who was handling affairs at Corman's office and told her I'd got the message late and wanted to be considered. "I'll call you back and tell you what I think," she said. "Send over some of your writing." So, I'm sitting by the phone saying, "Please, please don't cut off!" And sure enough it rang (although it *was* cut off a couple of hours later).

Not knowing Russian, Francis had to study *Battle Beyond the Sun* and concoct the entire story, with the dialogue to accompany it. He laughingly recalls:

There was one scene where the astronaut is confronted by a kind of golden astronaut of peace. Roger wanted to replace this vision with not just one, but *two* monsters, a male and a female. He wanted them to fight, and eventually the female would devour the male. So I went off with some of my theater friends and we set to work in the bathtub and with lots of latex, trying to make these monsters out of rubber, and film them—and we did!

Roger was the perfect guy for me because I lived my life a little faster than everyone else, and if we were to say, "Now let's go, we're gonna do something," I'm already thinking, "Let's get the trucks," so the real world is a little slow for me.

Being involved in production struck Francis as infinitely more stimulating than endless sedentary discussions at UCLA.

When word came through that Coppola had won the Samuel Goldwyn Award, Corman had announcements placed in the trade papers. The commercial savvy of Corman's enterprise remained underestimated for many years. "Roger's training was that of an engineer," reflects Francis, "so he looked at a product, said we're gonna spend $50,000, and we're gonna have a poster and that, and we're gonna make $5 million—and he did. He became very wealthy doing that."

The fee for converting *Battle Beyond the Sun* into an American Z-movie amounted to just $250, but as Ingmar Bergman at a similar stage of his life had declared a willingness to film the phone directory if someone had asked him to, so Coppola did anything to keep his foot in the industry.

Within a short space of time, Francis had become Corman's Man Friday, serving as script doctor, production assistant, second-unit director, and even sound recordist. He was dialogue director on *The Tower of London*, starring Vincent Price, for example. For *The Terror*, a typical Corman quickie featuring Boris Karloff and Jack Nicholson, Coppola went up to Big Sur and shot a week or so of scenes involving Nicholson.

In early 1962, Corman shipped his tiny unit to Europe for a movie about car racing, *The Young Racers*. "On race days there would be just three cameras," recalls Corman. "I handled one, Francis another, and somebody else a third. We bought a Volkswagen minibus and rebuilt it inside, and put racks on the outside, so we could travel easily and compactly. Francis was very practical and logical in his ability to work this." In later years, Coppola would rely on a similar mobile set-up, eventually attaining the peak of sophistication with his "Silver Fish" vehicle on *One from the Heart*.

Francis also had responsibility for the sound, although he had no training. "I find it very amusing," he says, "when I read somewhere that Floyd Crosby [the cameraman] claims, 'The sound wasn't done well, because you could hear the camera and we had to redupe the whole picture'— which we did—with Bill Shatner replacing the voice of Mark Damon! We shot the picture with an Arri 2S without a blimp, and there's no way you can photograph a movie with that kind of a camera and *not* hear it, because it's not blimped."

Menahem Golan, former chairman of the Cannon Group, was another Corman apprentice of the period. He asked Corman to ship the bus to Israel so that he could use it to make a movie in his home country. But Corman demurred. "We had to go to Liverpool to cover a Grand Prix, and Francis had been urging me to let him do a movie. Because we couldn't stay much longer in England (on account of union regulations), I suggested he make the film in Ireland. We'd just take the ferry across the Irish Sea."

Coppola shrewdly exploited Corman's sensible policy of shooting two films on any foray, because the basic costs of getting equipment to the site had already been accounted for. He would turn a similar trick himself with *The Outsiders* and *Rumble Fish*, shot back to back in Tulsa in 1982. When Corman was about to return to the United States to make *The Raven*, Francis felt the time was ripe for a proposition. "So I went up to him and pitched him one idea for a film. As I described it, a man goes to a pond and takes off his clothes, picks up these dolls, ties them together, goes under the water, dives down . . . And Roger says, 'Change the man to a woman, and you can do it.' So I said sure, and I changed it!"

Such was the genesis of *Dementia 13*, Coppola's first feature film. It dealt with a theme that everyone now associates with Coppola—the turmoil within a family—but it celebrated the horror genre that had reaped such success for Corman.

Francis left for Ireland with no script and a couple of colleagues; he called some student friends in the States to come over and join him. Corman agreed to put up an initial $20,000 towards the budget, and injected a few thousand more toward the close of production. Francis met an English producer, Raymond Stross, at Dublin's Ardmore Studios, and Stross gave him a further $20,000 in exchange for British distribution rights (the film would be released there as *The Haunted and the Hunted*). The screenplay emerged from a few nights of hectic invention. As Francis himself has often declared, the seed from which everything for a film comes is the script.

During the shooting of *Dementia 13*, Francis became close friends with Eleanor Neil. Ellie, as she was known in her circle, came from a long-established Californian family in Los Angeles. She had graduated from UCLA in the Art Department, and was studying for a master's degree and teaching design classes. Her boyfriend was working with Coppola on the cinematography and Ellie asked if, during her vacation, she might accompany him to Ireland. "I was told that if I paid my expenses there and back," she recalls, "I could work for two weeks and get $100 or something like that. So I went over, and at that point my relationship with the cinematographer cooled, and when I arrived I began to assist the art director; since the crew was so tiny, I did a combination of everything." Francis also promised her 1 percent of the film's net receipts—something he offered to nearly everyone at the time in order to keep within his budget. Besides, he had noted Corman's dictum that 50 percent of the profits should go to the money people, and 50 percent to the talent.

"When I reached Ireland," says Eleanor,

I was conscious of going to work on a movie set, and assumed it would be very glamorous. I wore a new coat with a fur collar, and tried to look as chic as possible when I was taken to the house in the country where the film was shooting. They led me upstairs to the third floor, and Francis was sitting in his pyjama bottoms, no shirt, and about three days' growth of beard! He'd been up all night, and now he was typing the script on mimeograph masters. The production staff sat in his room, grinding out the pages. You had the feeling that he was a risktaker, and commanded a vision of what he wanted. You had a sense, too, of his focus and dedication and commitment to go forward—ready or not—into this production.

A crew of nine worked on the picture and the cast consisted of actors who had been playing in *The Young Racers*. It was intended, according to Coppola, "to be an exploitation film. *Psycho* was a big hit and William Castle had just made *Homicidal*, and Roger always makes pictures that are like other pictures. So it was meant to be a horror film with a lot of people getting killed with axes and so forth."

Dementia 13 survives as an impudent blend of suspense and half-baked psychology, a little shop of horrors that mirrors Corman's unique style of grade Z moviemaking. It also prefigures much of Coppola's obsession with the family as a source of strife and perverted loyalty. When the scheming Louise tries to capitalize on the sudden death of her husband, John Haloran, she finds herself embroiled in a struggle between brothers. As in later films like *The Godfather* and *Rumble Fish*, the elder brother assumes a powerful role in the drama, a consequence of Francis's own admiration for August.

In a plot brimming with incident, the long-dead Kathleen rises— literally—from the depths of a pond on the family estate, to haunt her relatives. In the end, the baby brother Billy Haloran is exposed as the murderer not only of Louise but also of Kathleen (in childhood).

Coppola uses his Irish location to create a convincing mood of mayhem, and Charles Hannawalt's photography traps us in a limbo of dreadful night. One remarkable shot, which certainly does not belong to the Corman idiom, shows Richard and Louise embracing passionately in the castle grounds before zooming out, back through a slender window, to focus on the disapproving gaze of the mother.

Many of the notable moments derive from other favorite films of Coppola's. There's a close-up of a medicine glass and spoon, slightly blurred at left of frame, as Louise lays the mother down on a bed after she has fainted; it virtually duplicates the shot of the glass beside Susan's bed in *Citizen Kane*. A painting of the drowned Kathleen dominates a salon in a way reminiscent of *Rebecca* or *Dragonwyck*. But *Psycho* seems to be the strongest influence. Coppola kills off Louise, whom we have just begun to accept as the main character, some forty minutes into the movie, just as Hitchcock disposes of Marion Crane in *Psycho*. Kathleen's locked room is a musty shrine, packed with gruesome toys, including a gremlin figure equipped with a hatchet. It all prompts thoughts of the Bates Motel.

Not every diverting aspect of *Dementia 13* appears derivative, however. Coppola uses the sinister, rasping voice of Patrick Magee (as the family doctor) to good effect, years before he became more widely known in Stanley Kubrick's *A Clockwork Orange* or *Barry Lyndon*—even if he had played the prison officer in Joseph Losey's *The Criminal* just a year or so earlier. Coppola also communicates the spookiness of recollected nightmares; he clearly enjoys directing the ritual ceremony enacted around Kathleen's grave.

Coppola's self-confidence was boosted by the favorable reviews for *Dementia 13* when it opened in September, as well as by the business it did at the box-office. He actually made money on the film. The *New York Post* put the entire operation in perspective: "The photography's better than the plot, the plot better than the dialogue, and the dialogue better than the recording. The latter is something very hard to distinguish, which may be a mercy." Francis remembers exulting prematurely over a notice in the *New York Times* that complimented the "solid direction." He called his brother August in high spirits. "No, dope, it says 'stolid,' not 'solid,' " responded Augie.

Coppola has always cherished his apprenticeship with Roger Corman. The sheer productivity of a man scorned by mainstream Hollywood appealed to him. "I tried to impress Roger. I'd deliberately work all night so when he'd arrive in the morning he'd see me slumped over the moviola." Martin Scorsese, Daniel Haller, Robert Towne, and Peter Bogdanovich served Corman in similar capacities over the years.

The Studio Grind

The romance between Eleanor Neil and Francis Coppola developed toward the close of shooting on *Dementia 13*, and when Corman asked him to supervise the dialogue on a movie being made in Yugoslavia, Francis enjoyed the excuse of traveling across Europe with Ellie. "I had to return to the States to complete my commitments at UCLA," she says, "and Francis came out to California a few months later. Then we worked on another Corman picture, *The Terror*; I remember dressing a kind of witch's cottage!"

They married on February 2, 1963, in Las Vegas. Eleanor ran a fledgling business, creating murals for restaurants and motels, and the marriage date coincided with a visit she made to Las Vegas to check the installation of a mural at the airport there. "I was twenty-six when I married, which in those days was considered old-maidish, and all my friends had already had their weddings," she remembers. "So it seemed like a nice idea to celebrate in Las Vegas, and you could do it without the California blood-test and all the waiting around, so we took the train with about ten or twelve members of family, and friends, which was a lot more festive."

The marriage has, despite the upheavals of Francis's career, endured for twenty-five years. Eleanor has been accused by some of Coppola's disgruntled associates of interfering in the management of his company. Her husband denied this in a notorious memorandum circulated to all his staff in the throes of producing *Apocalypse Now*: "My wife has no interest, no control, and no influence over my work." That was of course not strictly true. Ellie had traveled with Francis to the Philippines and in addition to making a documentary record of the shooting, she kept notes for a diary that was later published—to Francis's embarrassment. She is certainly no archetypal *mamma mia*, even if she has devoted her life to her children and to giving Francis a congenial space in which to work. She never requests anything for Christmas, and one year Francis rewarded her modesty by popping downstairs, making a cup of cappuccino, gift-boxing it, and then presenting it to her. "To this day she maintains it's the best present she ever got," he says, "because she really wanted that cup of coffee." Like her husband, she could never have stomached a Hollywood lifestyle. When the Coppolas purchased their big house over-looking the Bay in San Francisco, she confirmed that it was "mostly for Francis; these things aren't important to me."

A week after his marriage, Francis received a call from Seven Arts. They were looking for a contract writer, and had been impressed by his scripts at UCLA. He was offered $375 a week to write a screenplay based on Carson McCullers's novel, *Reflections in a Golden Eye*. "There was open resentment," he remembers. "I was making money . . . There was a sign on the [UCLA] bulletin board saying: *Sell out!*" The story was lurid. At a military camp in the deep South, a colonel (Marlon Brando in the eventual movie) writhes in the toils of his sexual perversion, as he watches his lusty wife capering by night with a handsome young soldier. George Byron Sage, one of Hollywood's most astute studio readers, was struck by the forceful slant of the script. "Morally this screenplay is shocking and revolting," he noted. "Dramatically, it is . . . completely absorbing and utterly fascinating . . . it is the most brilliant dramatization of this very challenging novel we are likely to see." Sage's final comment was prescient: "If he is a new writer for the screen—as our records indicate —his talent is something the entire industry will, eventually, recognize."

The studio liked Coppola's screenplay (even though it was never used), and raised his salary to $500 a week on a three-year contract. He accepted, quit film school, and by the end of the first year was making $1,000 a week, in the knowledge that his agent was refusing offers from, among others, Universal. He and Ellie lived frugally at first in a lovely house up on Laurel Canyon in Los Angeles. But soon they purchased a big A-frame home in Mandeville Canyon. "I had really wanted to be a married person, even years before I had a candidate for a wife," he maintains. "I missed a family. I was primed to have a home and a wife and kids. I like kids very much. I'd been a drama counselor in 1958 and I really liked it, doing plays with these little boys and so on."

Francis saved every spare dollar in the hope of financing a movie of his own. Soon, he and Eleanor had accumulated some $20,000. "I was really frustrated," he told Joseph Gelmis, "because I could buy a Ferrari or I could buy a sailboat but I couldn't make a film. So I decided I was going to risk it all on the stock market and either have $100,000 to make a film, or have nothing. I lost it, every penny of it. In one stock. Scopitone. The jukebox with the little films."

Not that he disliked the screenwriting chores—such as a script for *This Property Is Condemned*—which honed his facility for dialogue and plot development. "I feel that I'm basically a writer who directs," he said much later. "When people go to see a movie, eighty percent of the effect it has on them was preconceived and precalculated by the writer." He confesses to a deep-seated respect for the writer who may spend three years on a novel, by comparison with a screenwriter who takes his way through a script in three months or less.

Francis is reputed to have worked on more than fifteen screenplays for Warner–Seven Arts. The best of them, by all accounts, was *The Disenchanted*. But it never entered production. *The Fifth Coin*, *Arrivederci Baby*, and *My Last Duchess* experienced a similar fate.

He was one of ten writers on *Is Paris Burning?*, a ghastly imbroglio stemming from the bestseller by Larry Collins and Dominique LaPierre. The fact that Francis was awarded a final screen credit along with Gore Vidal did not mitigate the sense of failure he felt. "I quit and was fired at the same time." He was in debt to his bank, and in a mood of desperation he and Ellie flew to Europe, visiting Denmark for the first time.

He still had a project under wraps. He had read and liked a novel by the British author David Benedictus entitled *You're a Big Boy Now*. The book charted the rites of passage of a melancholy young clerk at work in a London shoe shop. Coppola bought an option on the rights for $1,000 down against $10,000, and wrote the screenplay during his spare time in France while at work on *Is Paris Burning?* He transposed the story to New York, trying to combine the feelings of an American boy with those already expressed in the novel. The character of Barbara Darling was much more developed by Benedictus, however, chronicling her early sexual hang-ups with ferocious glee.

Bypassing Seven Arts, Francis approached Roger Corman. His contract at Burbank would expire soon, and he assured Corman that he would do the film for his production company. But suddenly Seven Arts discovered that the screenplay had been written during Francis's time in their employ. Their decision was adamant. He must make the film for them, or forget about it. The anger felt by Francis was at least tempered by the knowledge that Seven Arts had encouraged other directors, like Tony Richardson and Ken Hughes, to embark on adventurous films of their own with the blessing of the company's funds. And, because Francis owned the rights to the book, he could engineer a pragmatic compromise with the studio whereby he both scripted *and* directed the movie.

So, with a budget of around $800,000, Francis Coppola began work on his first mainstream movie. His fee was a mere $8,000 for writing and directing, but he still found it preferable to writing scripts for other people's films at $75,000 a time. *You're a Big Boy Now* was shot in twenty-nine days, mostly on location in Manhattan. Coppola was desperate to use the hallowed New York Public Library, with its eighty miles of book stacks, as his main location. The library refused, in the face of scenes involving a pornography collection hidden in a steel vault. But Mayor Lindsay, eager to promote the city as a place for films to be made, prevailed on the library to change its mind. Coppola shot the scenes involving the porno books on a sound stage on 26th Street. Conversely, he found the owners of the dirty bookstores on 42nd Street quite welcoming, although permission had to be obtained from the nude models featured on magazine covers that appeared on camera.

"Sometimes we'd spend hours to get from one part of the city across to the other because of the traffic," said Coppola, who used a hand-held Arriflex to follow Peter Kastner through the streets. Kastner, a young Canadian actor who had impressed Coppola with his performance in Don Owen's *Nobody Waved Goodbye*, had the lead as Bernard Chanticleer, and Elizabeth Hartman, who had just scored a personal success in *The Group*, played his idol-cum-nemesis, Barbara Darling. Two distinguished stage actresses, Julie Harris and Geraldine Page, were signed for supporting roles, and Tony Bill and Karen Black, then quite fresh to the screen, also appeared in minor parts.

"I wanted it to be a farce. Because I think growing up when you are nineteen is very serious but when you are twenty-eight it's a farce, you know. So I wanted to have the antic craziness of that kind of world," declared Coppola after the film had opened. He also wanted "to make a *Catcher in the Rye* kind of film, because I had run away from military school and wandered around the city and a lot of funny, bittersweet things had happened to me".

The chief influence on *You're a Big Boy Now* was undeniably the free-wheeling work of Richard Lester. Coppola concedes that *A Hard Day's Night*, Lester's film with and about the Beatles, had inspired him, but he resisted those critics who accused him of copying *The Knack*, the wacky comedy that had won Lester the Palme d'Or at the Cannes festival in 1965. "I hadn't seen *The Knack* when we had done [*You're a Big Boy Now*]. I tried to use certain disciplines in the film that [Lester] chooses not to. I allowed only one filmic extravagance, which was the jump-cut, and there was no zoom or under-cranking or over-cranking, as he likes to use." But he did sympathize with the sheer energy of Lester's approach to filmmaking, and appreciated the principle of allying contemporary music (in this case, by the Lovin' Spoonful) "to a dramatic story rather than just a musical film."

You're a Big Boy Now remains, though, every bit as much a prisoner of its period as Lester's pixilated comedies, recalling Coppola's quip that "Andy Hardy gets hit by the New Wave." The technique looks more self-conscious than it did when the film was screened at Cannes in 1967, to the general satisfaction of audiences there. The humor has a sophomoric ring to it, even if Coppola's skill with timing and locations suffices to compensate for his relentless accent on whimsy.

Bernard is a Candide of a New Yorker who is finally released from domestic bondage by an overbearing mother (Geraldine Page) and installed in a rooming house in the city (actually, the lofty old Manhattan Club at 26th Street and Madison). His landlady is a cantankerous spinster, Miss Thing (Julie Harris), whose pet rooster is not the most predictable of pets. Bernard sallies forth to take a job in the New York Public Library, where his father is Curator of Incunabula but also addicted to golf. Bernard cares little for the girl assistant who flirts with him among the book stacks. Instead, he retreats whenever possible into a fantasy world, which consists almost entirely of sexual fulfillment. He gapes at sex magazines and frequents the peepshow parlors (one of the film's nicest moments describes Bernard's confusion when his tie gets caught in a peepshow mechanism and the girl from the library carefully snips him free). The roller skates that Bernard wears even in the sober corridors of the library suggest his "above the ground" sensibilities.

Bernard's dream-object is a statuesque go-go dancer. She gyrates in a cage at a Manhattan disco, her effortless rhythm contrasting with Bernard's frenetic pursuit of a box kite through Central Park. When, after an exchange of letters, Bernard *does* get into Ms. Darling's apartment, he's pinned to the floor by a collapsible bed. He also fails to perform as she would expect. "Your spirit was willing, I'm sure," she says drily as he leaves for work the next day. Bernard finds himself tackling more than a mere rooster in the form of Dolph Sweet's patrolman. Named Francis (after his director, no doubt), the cop sports some of the film's wittiest lines.

In the end, of course, Bernard settles for the clean-cut, uncomplicated girl from the library. The capricious and distinctly adult demands of Ms. Darling prove altogether too much for his immature, myopic personality. Besides, the saga of Ms. Darling is less amusing than Bernard's adventures in the bowels of the library, whence our hero flees in the final section of the movie, clutching a Gutenberg Bible and negotiating the crowds in a Fifth Avenue parade before hurtling into May's department store in an attempt to shake off his pursuers.

Amy, his admirer from the library, pays his bail, and the young lovers frolic through the city streets, devouring pretzels, that most pungent symbol of Manhattan life. Bernard has overcome his complexes at last; he has been accepted and molded by the world at large.

The zany incidents and the gallery of offbeat characters (an albino doctor with a limp, a dwarf actor, and a lecherous librarian, among others) have lasted better than the technical affectations applied in the lab— negative images of Elizabeth Hartman as she go-go dances, a brief clip from *Dementia 13* in the disco sequence, or typed words chattering across the screen as Michael Dunn writes down Ms. Darling's visions. John Sebastian's songs add a lot of fun to the film, with lyrics that match the mood and verge on the surrealistic. In one daydream, for example, Bernard imagines some blacks performing as bagpipers. "Niggers go home!" comes the cry. "Where's home? Where their hearts are. Where are their hearts? Hearts in the Highlands!" It's the kind of non sequitur Groucho Marx would have enjoyed.

Looking back at *You're a Big Boy Now*, one sees the latent strength of Coppola as a director. His willingness to take risks. His command of timing. The latitude he gives to his performers. The ebullience of his montage sequences. The knack of making locations appear more interesting than they are in reality.

Had the film flopped, Coppola might never have consolidated his place in the industry. Certainly he would never have been assigned to direct *Finian's Rainbow*. The selection of *You're a Big Boy Now* for the competition at Cannes introduced his talent to European critics, who have remained loyal to him (and none more so than the French) throughout the ups and downs of his career. The Oscar nomination for Geraldine Page also helped associate Coppola with quality moviemaking. From a practical standpoint, the film was acceptable as a thesis at UCLA, earning

Francis his coveted Master of Fine Arts degree. "It was a point of pride to me that it was my thesis. All the other guys at UCLA used to *talk* about making a feature, but I was always more of a *doer* than some of the intellectuals. For me to go to the Cannes festival, which I had read about, and to be received as well as we all were, meant that those were some of the great days of my life," he recalls.

When *You're a Big Boy Now* opened on March 20, 1967, the reviewers reacted with tolerance to the excessive zest of the movie. *Time* suggested that the faults and the freshness both stemmed from the same source, "the vast, undisciplined energy of its writer, producer, and director—all of whom happen to be Francis Coppola, 27." Judith Crist, in the *World Journal Tribune*, called it "a youthful film about young people—youthful in the best sense, in its imaginative irreverence, its compassionate ego, its earnest confusion and its offbeat inspiration. It's funny and it's sad and when it's good it's so very good that when it's bad we'll just call it imperfect." Andrew Sarris, in the *Village Voice*, noted the movie's reference to Jean-Luc Godard, Terry Southern, and even "Peanuts," while Howard Thompson in the *New York Times* referred to "Mr. Coppola's vibrantly visual comic strip" being "at its funniest and most appealing when the vultures aren't pecking away at a young soul. It isn't often."

Richard Schickel was more scathing in his notice for *Life*, condemning Coppola's "compendium of clichés partially disguised in fancy dress." Francis and the studio were probably quite content with *Variety*'s headline: "Nutty comedy about a young male virgin; okay for selected locations."

*   *   *

Just before the premiere of *You're a Big Boy Now*, Coppola finished his most important screenplay to date. It was a study of George S. Patton, the five-star general who had outraged everyone in the Allied High Command with his ruthless campaigning in North Africa and Europe during World War II.

Francis had been given six months to come up with a script. That was back in 1964. But Patton, although charismatic, proved a tough nut to crack. He had impressed his men, who dubbed him "Blood and Guts." He treated his peers and few superiors with a cavalier disdain. He had even struck a shell-shocked soldier in a fit of temper, for which he was stripped of the Seventh Army Command. His rhetoric suggested a yearning for conquest rather than the liberation of enemy-held territory. Patton relished war and was an expert on the great campaigns of history, from Hannibal to Napoleon.

Francis lapped up the available sources—Ladislas Farago's *Patton: Ordeal and Triumph*, General Omar Bradley's memoir (*A Soldier's Story*), and the diaries of Patton himself. He saw in Patton a quixotic individual "born in the wrong era, on the wrong side of the river," as the Motorcycle Boy is described in *Rumble Fish*. "God, how I hate the twentieth century!" exclaimed Patton on one recorded occasion. Coppola gives the general a mythic aura, tinged with megalomania and redeemed with a genius for bucking the system.

By the time *Patton* reached the screen in 1970, half a dozen rewrites by divers hands had blurred the outlines of the original screenplay. But George C. Scott had agreed to take the title role on condition that Fox use Coppola's version, and director Franklin Schaffner retained certain key passages verbatim. Coppola wrote the opening speech (based on three authentic Patton addresses), proclaimed by Scott in front of a huge American flag, and addressing an unseen audience. "You do not die for your country," he pontificates. "You make the other poor dumb bastard die for his." He also composed the majestic monologue among the ruins in Sicily, as Patton invokes the glories of the Carthaginians and dwells on the mystique of reincarnation. If Coppola can be accused of having an obsession with power, then *Patton* is the first real evidence of it. None of the other figures in the film is examined so profoundly as Patton himself. Like Kurtz in *Apocalypse Now* the General inhabits the unholy vacuum of war. Being "a damned good soldier" constitutes his be-all and end-all. Kurtz is actually a frustrated version of Patton. Both men hunger for domination; both love war per se rather than any particular crusade.

Francis found that the studio let his contract lapse after taking delivery of the *Patton* script. It was too bold for its time. But he would win an Academy Award for his share in the film, although he never met, let alone worked with, his "coscreenwriter" Edmund North, whose labor was in "restructuring" the script.

The high regard accorded *You're a Big Boy Now* did, however, sustain for some months Francis's status as "the fair-haired boy at Warners." He and Eleanor now had two children, Gian-Carlo ("Gio") and Roman (named after Roman Polanski and born in Paris), as well as that obligatory success symbol, a Porsche.

According to Walter Murch, Coppola was a legend in the film student community in LA because he was the one graduate who had gone out and made a feature film and used it to secure his degree, which was the secret dream of every film student. "Up to then there was no way a student could enter the industry unless he was part of the family and had been sent to school by his parents to brush up. Francis made film study into a door instead of a wall."

Francis recalls this key stage in his career.

> I made a promise to myself—the one I didn't keep—a vow that somehow what could make me exceptional was the fact that I could write original screen material—write the screenplay, and then execute it as a producer and director. Many people could write, and many could direct, but only a small group could do both. So I had promised I was going to write all my own stuff, and only direct what I had written. And I began work on *The Conversation*. But then came a call from a guy named Joe Landon, and he said, "Listen, we're looking for some director to do *Finian's Rainbow*, with Fred Astaire and Petula Clark. Do you have any ideas?" And I said I wanted to think about it. Then he offered the job to me.

Francis accepted the assignment, and pushed *The Conversation* screenplay to one side. One of his motives was to impress his father, who had spent his whole life in the musical comedy field. But Francis had been misled into thinking that *Finian's Rainbow* would be a full-scale Hollywood musical. After all, Warners had just completed *Camelot*, starring Richard Harris and Vanessa Redgrave; *Star!* and *Funny Girl* were being made at other studios in town. But these musicals belonged to a different ilk from *Finian's Rainbow*, which had startled the Broadway stage in the late 1940s, on the very threshold of the McCarthy period. By Hollywood standards the book by E. Y. Harburg and Fred Saidy was almost subversive in its sympathetic attitude toward underprivileged sharecroppers in Kentucky. Yip Harburg, who had written the lyrics for *The Wizard of Oz*, was known as a radical, and his ideals are reflected in the communal farming scheme in *Finian*. The racial bigotry of the southern senator in the show added a further twist to the social tensions on display.

But almost twenty years had gone by, and in the late 1960s the tone of *Finian's Rainbow* might well seem patronizing in its attitude to black liberation. As Coppola said, "A lot of liberal people were going to feel it was old pap, because of its dated civil-rights stance . . . and the conservatives were going to say it was a lot of liberal nonsense." Certainly it had been too liberal a vehicle for the major studios to handle in earlier years—although John and Faith Hubley had planned to make a full-length animated version in the 1950s.

Francis was a great fan of musicals. He can still sing many of the classic

Hollywood numbers from memory, and *Finian's Rainbow* offered him a chance to make a fresh contribution to the genre he loved so much. He phoned Carmine, who was out on the road with *Half a Sixpence*, and suggested he do some orchestration work on the picture. Both parents were delighted and came to California for what would turn out to be a permanent stay. But Francis did not know the book of *Finian's Rainbow*, only the score, and after studying the original play he urged Warners to let him make the musical on an altogether more radical scale.

The reality of the situation, he laughs, was that

> a couple of guys sitting around at Warners had the idea of hooking Fred Astaire into doing a very cheap re-do of *Finian's Rainbow* on the old *Camelot* sets. I, who liked studios, was the one to suggest that we take a company down to Kentucky and shoot the film outside. That's when I found out that they had very specific ideas about how they wanted to make it. At least I could do a three-week rehearsal, in this funny small building at Warner Brothers, and in the round, with an audience. My dad came with his flute, and we had a pianist and a drum, and we ran through the entire *Finian's Rainbow* with Fred Astaire, even if it did look like an Omaha high school production!

The budget for *Finian* was pinned at some $3,500,000 (as against $10,000,000 for really big musicals of the day). A twelve-week shoot began on June 26, 1967. During production, Francis met one of his future peers, George Lucas, then a film student. "I was like a fish out of water among all these old studio guys," he says, "so now I had a friend in George, who I'd noticed hanging around the set. We used to talk about the set-ups, and about movies, and I decided I'd had it, and wanted to make my own movie—*The Rain People*."

The lush title sequence of *Finian's Rainbow* (shot by Carroll Ballard) prepared audiences for exotic locations in the style of *The Sound of Music*, but in fact Coppola took his cameras outside the studios for a mere eight days, to Monterey, Carmel, Modesto, and San Francisco. Ironically, Tom Milne would write in *Sight and Sound* that Coppola's *Finian* was "a demonstration of the naturalness of the musical as a means of expression, with barely an interior visible throughout the entire film, with dancers pounding rough grass and muddy earth instead of carefully prepared surfaces, and with singers actually experiencing the emotions they celebrate."

Midway through the shoot, veteran choreographer Hermes Pan, who had worked on most of Astaire's classic movies, was fired, and Coppola took over the staging of the numbers, attempting to remain faithful to the 1940s original and yet give the film a relevance to the altogether more questioning contemporary audience.

Francis's loyalty to his own ethnic origins explains the pro-immigrant bearing of his *Finian's Rainbow*. Sharon and her eccentric pa, Finian McLonergan, bring from their native Ireland all the idealism and sense of wonder that have evaporated in the materialism of the New World. Not that Finian is scornful of money; his love of gold has led him to Kentucky clutching his stolen "crock," which he believes will multiply if buried in the gold-rich soil around Fort Knox. But Finian is quick to take the side of the underdog. When the sheriff of Rainbow Valley County arrives to auction off Woody Mahoney's land because of unpaid back taxes, Finian produces the dollar bills required to meet the interest due. He and Woody become partners in the "Rainbow Valley Tobacco Co-op" and revel in each other's Irish blarney and exuberance. Sharon falls in love with Woody, to the despair of an antic eprechaun, Og, who finally has to settle for the hand of Woody's sister, "Susan the Silent."

Sharon embodies the musical's social conscience. Finian is much more the dreamer, and much more selfish in his dreaming. When her father asks her what makes America different from Ireland, she retorts, "It has more Irishmen." Finian corrects her: "It has more money . . . Everyone in America is rich." Sharon bridles. "But father, are there no poor in America, no ill-housed and no ill-clad?" To which Finian's typically shrewd answer is, "Of course, but they're the *best* ill-housed and the *best* ill-clad in all the world!"

Finian, it transpires, has "borrowed" his crock of gold from Og, the leprechaun ("who else would have gold in Ireland?"), with the implication that its misuse "in the hands of a mortal can only bring doom and gloom." The villains of the piece, Senator Rawkins and his sidekick, Buzz Collins (played by Francis's friend and production associate Ron Colby), appear to be motivated by two things: money and racial bigotry. The senator wants to keep the black sharecroppers in their place, and is deeply suspicious of the Rainbow Valley Tobacco Co-op; and when he learns from some federal geologists that gold is lurking in the Valley he plots to oust Woody and Finian from the area. He embodies the cast-iron conservatism of the old South. "The festering tides of radicalism are upon us!" he proclaims, rehearsing a speech; "Forward to the sweet tranquility of the status quo. Forward—to yesterday!"

Buzz has tried to convert Howard, the black friend of Woody's, into a servant in the traditional mold. When Howard brings him a mint julep with insufficient servility, Buzz exclaims, "You educated or somethin'?"

But, in one of the film's funniest scenes, Howard plays up to the old image. The senator is lying in his rocking chair, desperate for an Alka-Seltzer. Howard emerges from the house, bearing the glass on a tray, and shuffling from left to right, drawling the while all the sycophantic hyperbole about the julep that Buzz has taught him. Rawkins screams at the top of his voice for the drink to be brought to him, but Howard's writhing convolutions keep him at a tantalizing distance until Coppola mercifully fades the scene out.

The senator gets his comeuppance, of course, when he tries to evict Finian on the basis of some cockeyed ordinance about Negroes and Caucasians not dwelling together on the same parcel of land. Sharon, her Irish temper roused, dashes along beside the senator's car and, in her exasperation, "wishes" him black. Comes a thunderclap, and Rawkins looks in the car mirror to find himself a distinct shade of brown. He flees into the forest, believing himself forever relegated in the eyes of society. But the leprechaun reassures him that his black complexion is "rather becoming." Og, though deprived of his magic crock, still summons up enough strength of will to reduce the senator's bigotry and pomposity. Rawkins is soon enjoying the black lifestyle, joining up with three singers to form a quartet to sing at Woody's wedding.

So *Finian's Rainbow* is by no means a paean to the virtues of the New World. Only the sharecroppers escape the lash of dialogue and lyrics. Even Finian is corrupted, adopting the local xenophobia as he accuses poor Og of being an immigrant without a passport and belonging to "an illegal, subversive group," taking his orders from Dublin. He redeems himself a short time later when, in a number that brings out Astaire's old twinkle-toed zest, he mocks the day "When the idle poor become the idle rich."

On Broadway, Finian had been created as a nonsinging role, but the choice of Fred Astaire for the movie version proved successful. Astaire might have lost his peerless, lissome grace on the dance floor, but his timing remains as sharp and precise as ever. His crooked smile suits the ambivalent personality of Finian, too, and his pork-pie hat and walking stick are the ideal accoutrements for this latterday Pied Piper, as he leads the denizens of Rainbow Valley on a jolly dance across fields and through streams. Petula Clark was cast as Sharon, the role almost immortalized on Broadway by Ella Logan. Then thirty-five years of age, Petula Clark had amassed a huge popularity in Europe first as a child singer during the war and then in the heyday of Radio Luxembourg. During the 1960s she had been featured in several specials on American TV. She was probably more familiar to U.S. movie audiences than Tommy Steele, another British import whose scintillating work in *Half a Sixpence* had brought him to the attention of the studio. "I felt the leprechaun should be more shy and timid and bewildered," said Coppola, who had hoped to sign Donal Donnelly (of *The Knack*) for the role. "I wanted it to be an introvert leprechaun, a guy who speaks in this quiet voice and then suddenly becomes a human being." Steele cannot be anything other than winsome and toothy, but this brings a refreshing quality to the film. Og is utterly free of guile, so that we side with him against Finian when he complains that the old man's theft of the gold has forced him to become *mortal*. Steele's best number is "Something Sort of Grandish" with Petula Clark.

Considering the leanness of the budget, Coppola performs minor miracles with some of the musical numbers. "If This Isn't Love," for example, is a sparkling montage of delight, with helicopter shots interspersed with scenes of Sharon catching a greased piglet, or riding on horseback with Woody. For once the locations look spacious and appealing. At other times the limitations of the studio are obvious. Voices in the "forest" suffer from that boxed-in timbre associated with radio plays. Barbara Hancock as Susan the Silent transcends this in her exhilarating "Rain Dance Ballet" in the moonlit glade.

Most of all, though, it is Coppola's inventive technique that saves the day. His skillful use of close-ups, which over the next few years would reach perfection, brings to *Finian's Rainbow* an intimacy of feeling that makes the background insignificant. A good instance is Petula Clark's first touching rendition of "How Are Things in Glocca Morra?" At the other extreme, he creates a feeling of space with his introduction of aerial shots in such numbers as "The Begat," belted out by the black singers as they drive along the country roads to the wedding in Rainbow Valley. Even "Woody's Here!" gains something from the intercut shots of the train hurtling along the track. Such exuberance catches the Irish spirit so vital to *Finian*. So too does the prevailing green of the production—the lush foliage, costumes, and so on.

Lack of location work proves a handicap in "Old Devil Moon," when Woody tells Sharon about the strange-looking sky and the full moon, and Coppola cannot cut away from Clark's eager face. Only as the number winds down is there a brief shot of the moon. But the potential wonder and romance of the number fail to ignite.

Francis would not return to the musical genre for another dozen years, with *One from the Heart*, but the experience gained on the journeyman assignment that *Finian's Rainbow* represented would help him to become a judge of rhythm and pace. Like any musical, the film can be dismissed as naïve and superficial, but Coppola's lightness of touch and sense of fairy-tale awe are undeniable. He is no longer an enthusiastic amateur. He had to wait more than a year before the film was released by Warner–Seven Arts. By then, much hinged on its reception. *The Rain People* was finished, and Coppola knew that if *Finian's Rainbow* flopped he would be forced to survive away from the major studios.

Warners had high hopes for the picture. As James Monaco has said, "They decided to make it a road show, blew it up to 70mm—and cut off Fred Astaire's feet in the process." The reviews stressed the quaint simplicity of the original 1947 stage *Finian*. Joseph Morgenstern wrote in *Newsweek*: "The terrible truth is that *Finian's* folklore was always fake, its sentiments always bogus, its social consciousness always a clumsy embarrassment, and we always knew it." Pauline Kael, in the *New Yorker*, declared that in seeking "freshness and speed and an ethereal *Midsummer Night's Dream* atmosphere," Coppola was making "a pastiche of visual styles and lyrical effects out of what was already a pastiche."

Independence and the Dream of Zoetrope

In a conversation with writer Gay Talese, Coppola referred to his own audacious, if not cavalier, attitude to money. "People are hampered by money. It does not free them. It does not encourage them to go on and try new things. It makes them more conservative."

When, in early 1968, he had the chance to make *The Rain People*, Coppola rejected the easy compromise at every turn. He felt frustrated when he saw *A Man and a Woman* and knew that directors like Claude Lelouch had the chance to make their personal kind of films. He abandoned (temporarily at least) his lucrative career as a screenwriter, and embarked on the project with a budget of just $750,000 from Warners. His total fee for writing, directing, and editing *The Rain People* was $50,000. "I lived on what I made from *Finian* . . . I supported that cast and crew of almost twenty for five months." He sank his own cash into various items of equipment, most of which formed a valuable inventory for Coppola's own ministudio, American Zoetrope, when it began operations at the end of 1969. "If you're not willing to risk some money when you're young," he announced at the time, 'you're certainly not ever going to risk anything in the years that follow."

His self-confidence and ingenuity enabled Francis to set up *The Rain People*. Sensing that *Finian's Rainbow* would not score well at the box-office, he spread the word around the Burbank studios of Warner–Seven Arts that he was at work on a hush-hush project. Then without warning he dropped out of sight, leaving a few shrewdly planted rumors to the effect that he was already shooting the new picture on location in New York. He *was* indeed shooting—but nothing more than a football game! The ploy worked. Afraid that another company might give Coppola the money he needed, Kenneth Hyman, the new head of Warners, signed a contract without seeing the script. Francis was free to do what he longed to do, filming away from the studios with a small group of trusted colleagues. He procured a salary for George Lucas to make a documentary about the production. In reality, Lucas was writing the screenplay for *THX 1138*, and Coppola had already committed himself to finding a way for George to shoot his dream picture. At the end of several months, Coppola brought *The Rain People* in for $740,000.

*   *   *

The source of *The Rain People* goes back to Francis's childhood, when his mother had disappeared for three days after domestic pressures threatened to overwhelm her. "After an argument with my father, my mother went to her sister's house for two days and wouldn't say where she had gone. She told me she'd stayed in a motel. It just clicked with me, you know, the idea of a woman leaving and just staying in a motel. I imagined her sitting in this motel, very frightened. A lot of time the ideas that make up something you write are just like a little snapshot, just like a mood."

Around 1959, while still at Hofstra, and under the influence of Tennessee Williams, Francis had developed a story about three wives, for his writing class, and called it *The Old Gray Station Wagon*. "Then several years later I got this very romantic idea in my head about Shirley Knight. I didn't know her, but I thought she was very good. She seemed like an American actress who had some substance." He met Shirley Knight at the Cannes festival of 1967, where Anthony Harvey's film, *Dutchman*, was being presented.

In *Dutchman*, Knight's performance as the purposeful, satanic woman on the New York subway was an alarming achievement, ominous in its neurotic progression toward murder, and repellent in its utter lack of guilt. After the screening, recalls Coppola, "She was crying, because someone had been rude to her or whatever. I went up to her and said, 'Don't cry, I'll write you a movie.' And she said, 'You will? That's sweet.' And I did. And I went back and I took out this old college draft and decided to make it just one character." It was the first of the screenplays that Coppola was able to write and make as he pleased. Today he regards it as an attempt to imitate the Antonioni–Monica Vitti creative symbiosis.

But the artistic relationship between Francis Coppola and Shirley Knight was not made in heaven. They had conflicting temperaments, hers introspective, his flamboyantly extrovert. Despite these clashes of personality, *The Rain People* is persuasive in its study of a woman fleeing her responsibilities and failing to adjust to new partnerships during an aimless journey across the country. The suspicion remains that the woman's character should have been warm and compassionate, whereas in Shirley Knight's interpretation she is cold and unsympathetic. Her most challenging encounter, with the handicapped football player "Killer" Kilgannon, fails to catch fire, even if Coppola views the relationship in more emotional terms: "It's the story of a human being becoming more and more responsible toward another human being It's like a woman sitting next to the kid she's going to have."

The film's shape is dictated as much by its trek into the past as by its movement forward to new horizons. Natalie (Shirley Knight) stirs awake in a dark dawn after what sounds to have been a quarrel with her husband. The very allusiveness of this introductory sequence suggests a new maturity in Coppola's approach to narrative. Nothing in the film is certain, just as Natalie herself remains a prey to uncertainty. Raindrops coalesce on the windows; rain cleanses the suburban Long Island street where Natalie lives. In *Finian,* Susan the Silent is exhilarated by rain, and in *The Outsiders* a downpour marks the victory of the Greasers over the Socs. Water purifies, washes away the dust and inertia of life. Natalie is making a fresh start.

She begins with her parents, dashing in like a drowned rat at 6 A.M., denying that she's "leaving" her husband. "I just want to be free," she complains, "even for five minutes." As her father and mother argue the issue, Natalie's mind flickers back to the happiness of her wedding day (the zesty dancing looks and sounds like something from *The Godfather,* with its tune scored by Francis's father).

More than any other film, *The Rain People* shows the influence of European cinema on Coppola's style and thinking. The mysterious opening, the short, abrupt flashbacks, and then a burn-out to glaring white to mark the passage of time—all this is reminiscent of Ingmar Bergman's *Persona* (released in the U.S. the previous year), while the brutal slivers of recollected action on the football field must be inspired by Lindsay Anderson's *This Sporting Life* (1963). Yet *The Rain People* is not derivative. It assimilates foreign influences and achieves a blank verse quality of its own.

Natalie's behavior verges on the schizophrenic. When she calls her husband from a booth on the Pennsylvania Turnpike, she drops into the third person, announcing that she is pregnant, and apologizing for her disappearance. She wonders if she was too set in her ways before marrying. It is not his fault, she assures him. "I just have a hunch I'm not ready to be a mother."

Coppola observes her in searching close-ups. Natalie's face, masklike, seems unrelated to the words being spoken. The camerawork is very subjective at this stage, reflecting Natalie's emotional turmoil. As she hangs up on her husband and leaves the phone booth, she glimpses pink wedding streamers fluttering on a nearby car. The images are fragmentary, inchoate, just enough to reinforce the mood of wistfulness.

Vinny, her husband, has sounded decent and appropriately concerned at the other end of the line. His presence, though unseen, is crucial to the film, serving as a kind of conscience reacting against Natalie's moments of self-pity. Coppola and his sound engineer, Walter Murch, treat this voice with care, reducing it to an incomprehensible mutter at some junctures and magnifying it at others so that it outweighs Natalie's.

So Natalie is by no means the usual browbeaten wife. She must earn the audience's sympathy and respect through her own conduct on screen—through her response to the people she meets along the way. Thus *The Rain People* is a road movie in the classic sense of the term. Its central character is affected by the individuals and incidents she encounters. As in *Apocalypse Now*, the journey matters more than the arrival.

After spending her first night in the grim anonymity of a motel alongside the freeway, Natalie speeds westward through a lush Pennsylvanian landscape. Coppola uses a helicopter to swoop over and ahead of her station wagon, and coats these freewheeling moments with surges of romantic music. So when Natalie pulls over for a hitchhiker on a lonely stretch of road, the audience guesses that she is ready for a small adventure. Even so, she almost drives off in panic when she sees the tall, good-looking guy running up to the car. Something in his manner makes her curious and she lets him get in.

For a long time neither speaks. The car radio grumbles away in the background. Finally Natalie asks his name.

"Jimmie," replies the man, "but you can call me Killer. People call me Killer 'cause my name's Kilgannon." In these few words, Coppola gives more than a clue to the man's naïve, forthcoming nature.

Names are identities, but also disguises. When they stop for a snack, Killer asks *her* name.

"Sara," she responds on a whim, and it stays that way until much later in the film. Like Harry Caul in *The Conversation*, Natalie is reluctant to divulge details about herself; it is a shyness close to paranoia. Killer, on the other hand, seizes eagerly on his new listener, recalling his days as a football star (although these stabs of memory make the players look like glory gladiators in the mud, and point to a shared inheritance of violence in the human personality).

Natalie sees Killer first as a plaything, a hulk of handsome muscle she can order around like a child. They stop for the night, and she titivates herself to a grotesque degree before inviting Killer into her room and indulging in some harmless power-play. Again she resorts to the third person, hiding her insecurity in the childhood game of "Simon says . . ."

"How obedient are you?" she asks with a barely suppressed thrill of pleasure. She makes him get down on his knees and bow to her. When she asks about the scar on his head, Killer suffers more flashes of memory, from the game in which he was critically injured. But then he recalls a kinder image, of his sweeping fallen leaves from the campus lawns. It is all he can do after the surgeons have finished with him, yet the gestures contain a liberating texture, as though the leaves were caged birds released into the air.

Natalie can only sense this past of Killer's. The audience is still way ahead of her perceptions. When Killer produces the envelope containing $1,000 in bills, and tells her that the college where he played football gave him the money as compensation, she realizes both the extent of his simplicity and also the burden she has assumed in picking him up.

There is an antic side to Natalie also. Next morning, as they drive through wet, verdant countryside, Killer engages her with his description of "the Rain People" who, when they cry, disappear altogether because "they cry themselves away." He claims to have seen them once. "They looked like ordinary people, only she is—very, very beautiful, and he's handsome and, uh, made of rain." Perhaps the parallel with Killer himself and Natalie is too obvious, but the metaphor lingers through the movie, matching the tremulous, evanescent nature of their relationship. In Coppola's words, the title refers to those "sad people who cry a lot over marriages that don't work."

As days slip by, Natalie and Killer begin to look more like an everyday couple. They buy ice cream. He has a haircut. They dash across crowded streets arm-in-arm.

Killer leads her to a drive-in movie theater, where the father of a former girlfriend runs the operation. The guy does not recognize Killer at first, but turns friendly when he does so, and sends him to the family home.

Ellen, the girlfriend, greets him with fear and hostility. Her mother is courteous to a fault, but Ellen has a tight mouth and a callous streak, and in front of her parents and Natalie, she condemns Killer for his handicap. "He got banged up, they put a plate in his head, and that's what came out."

Natalie is appalled, but psychologically she starts to drift away from Killer. As night falls, she tries to ditch him, urging him to go back to the mother of whom he has spoken so fondly. "I can't," he replies; "she died."

Natalie sees no alternative but to keep him, like an unwanted child. And just as a distraught mother abuses her cranky infant, so Natalie yells at Killer in her frustration. "Don't you see," she sobs, "I can hardly take care of myself." Nor, she dreads, of the baby growing in her womb.

She pursues the same lament when she calls her husband next. "I'm the one who's incompetent . . . I'm irresponsible, cruel, and aimless .... I lie to you all the time." But when she declares that she is going to have an abortion, Vinny loses his temper and harangues her for trying to purge her guilt by pouring it out over the phone. He hangs up. Natalie, stripped of pretension and vanity, finds Killer sitting patiently in the local bus depot, and blurts out her real name. Yet even at a moment like this, Shirley Knight fails to project any real warmth or vulnerability. So her attachment to James Caan's Killer gradually dwindles in conviction.

One motel may look like another across the whole width of the United States, but Coppola registers the subtle differences of region and attitude as Natalie's *voyage au bout de la nuit* progresses. The rich green fields of Pennsylvania and West Virginia give way to the small-town parade in Tennessee, and finally to the bare, unredeemed flatlands of Nebraska.

Natalie feels like an outsider, a foreigner, when she brings Killer to a "Reptile Ranch" off the highway where a job has been advertised. Alfred, the owner of the place, appraises them shrewdly and, once Killer has foolishly flashed his wad of bills, proceeds to inveigle him into a no-win situation. He takes Killer's $1,000 and promises to guard it in his safe. "You tryin' to palm off some cuckoo nut on me?" he snaps at Natalie. Alfred raises chicks and other creatures in appalling conditions. They are doomed, as Killer himself is doomed. Coppola's disenchanted vision of Middle America coincides with that of Dennis Hopper in *Easy Rider*, a film being shot at about the same time.

When she accelerates away from the ranch, Natalie is caught in a whirl of conflicting emotions. She is relieved to be rid of Killer at last, but shocked by her callousness in abandoning him to such gruesome circumstances.

She exceeds the speed limit, and is forced to the side by a patrolman, who writes out a citation. He starts asking insinuating questions about Natalie's husband and the reasons for her trip. She bridles, but finds the cop attractive (this was Robert Duvall's first role for Coppola). By this stage, Natalie has lost almost all her ties with the orthodox past.

An awkward gimmick in the screenplay, but one probably forced on Coppola by the pressures of time and budget, brings Natalie back to the Reptile Ranch to pay her speeding fine. The move introduces the cop to Killer, who is in the midst of liberating thousands of hapless chicks with the same benign care he gave to tossing the leaves in the grounds of his old college.

Topography, too, becomes strained in the film's gathering climax. Natalie agrees to spend the evening with Duvall's cop, but manages to call her husband from a nearby township while Killer watches with a pinched, hurt look. In the car they have admitted their love for each other, but Natalie—with neither justification nor real reason—has told him to go to hell. "At least I know you'll be taken care of there." So Killer manifests his pain by ripping out the cord from the phone booth, just as a reconciliation seems to be developing between Natalie and Vinny over the long-distance lines. Overcome with frustration, Natalie slaps and pinches Killer's face, thrusts him away, and jumps into her station wagon. Killer's last cry, "You hurt me!" pursues her as she drives away.

How and where she meets up again with Gordon, the cop, is unclear, but it may not matter, for Coppola is more interested in establishing a mood of despair and impenetrable darkness for the final sequence of *The Rain People*. Natalie will not see the light again. She enters Gordon's trailer that night. He turns on the lights and checks that his daughter Rosalie is asleep. She isn't, but Gordon and Natalie start necking anyway. A squabble breaks out between father and daughter which looks farcical in the cramped trailer but carries harsher overtones. Rosalie is chucked out into the night and Gordon and Natalie resume their petting.

When Rosalie in her pique snaps off the electric current to the trailer, Natalie welcomes the darkness. "Gordon?" she calls softly. When he replies, she says that it's like talking on the telephone. Coppola shows her face in profile, like a crescent moon surrounded by blackness. He recognises that in the sudden extinction of light lies a more profound and desperate truth. In his greatest films some of the most disturbing scenes unfold in shadow.

For the final time Natalie tries to learn about someone else. But Gordon is as uptight in his way as Killer, a captive to the traumatic memory of watching his wife perish in a fire. Natalie senses his lack of involvement with her, and draws back.

Killer and Gordon represent two entirely different kinds of man, the one apparently impotent, the other cocksure and aggressive. But Natalie can make it with neither, and holds both in some degree of contempt.

Killer finds his way to the trailer park, runs into Rosalie, and flings himself on Gordon when he sees the cop about to force Natalie into sexual submission. Remembering his battles on the football field, he hurls Gordon around like a rag doll. Rosalie's intervention saves her father; she shoots Killer with Gordon's police revolver.

Natalie weeps over the corpse of Killer, still talking to him in muted hysteria, sobbing that he can come back and live with her and her husband. But Coppola is unrelenting, and the darkness closes about her grief, and the film ends.

The Rain People, for all its improvised texture, is constructed with a discipline that even some of Coppola's later films lack. There is none of the self-indulgent milking of a scene that flaws an ostensibly similar picture like John Cassavetes's *Love Streams*. The dialogue is utilitarian and, save for the one exchange about "the rain people," unpretentious.

All three leading figures in the movie suffer defeat. Penetrating other people's lives to any significant degree is beyond each of them. "You've been stalling on me all night!" yells Gordon in his frustration, and the words and their anguish encapsulate the mood of the entire film. The only hope lies in Natalie's unborn child. Otherwise loneliness is, as so often in Coppola's world, inevitable.

Transcending this pessimism is Coppola's profound belief in the sovereignty of the family. "I wanted [the film] to be at once an understanding of those issues in a woman that would cause her to want her own freedom, and yet at the same time trying to collide them with a sense of family," he said some fifteen years later. "It was startling in those days to see a film where a woman gets up and leaves her husband. At San Sebastian, where it won [the top award], people were muttering, 'What kind of woman would do this?'"

In a career context, the adventure of making *The Rain People* proved to be much more significant than the film itself.

George Lucas, then "a skinny kid" who had met Francis on the set of *Finian's Rainbow*, wanted to work with *The Rain People*. Francis let him make a documentary about the shooting, and the result, entitled *Film-maker*, remains one of the most important analyses of Coppola's craft and incipient philosophy. It describes the romantic agony of living in trailers and converted buses, arguing with guilds, unions, and local authorities, and all the time fighting over the phone with the studio backing the production.

Bill Butler, lighting cameraman on *The Rain People*, recalls, "The theory was that we would travel from New York to as far west as we wanted to go. We had this little van; Coppola had a large camper van that we had an editing table in and there were several station wagons." Butler admired Coppola's willingness to gamble on a new idea, devoting himself to small-scale films with a modest supply of equipment, keeping the story simple, channeling his energy into working with the actors as closely as possible.

Although the shooting script was precise in terms of dialogue and plot development, there were no preset locations on *The Rain People*. The four-month trip through eighteen states began in early April 1968. From New Jersey, the convoy proceeded to Pennsylvania, West Virginia, Tennessee, Kentucky, and finally to Nebraska. Radio communication between the vans and cars was essential, as usually the next night's destination was not fixed. Eleanor trailed along in a Volkswagen van, with the children, staying with Francis in motels through the various states.

Beards (including Francis's) were shaved off in an attempt to enhance the respectability of the crew and to gain cooperation at the various locations.

In Kentucky, a ferry operator refused the crew permission to film on board, so Coppola went to the state authorities, then the state attorney, and in the end the police had to come down to the river to clear up matters. Such incidents tested Coppola's fast-growing reputation for persistence of vision when it came to production issues. In Lucas's documentary, Francis is seen arguing with some intransigent executive over the long-distance phone, condemning the hidebound studio system, and proclaiming his determination to finish the movie without further union hassles unless the state troopers stop him.

Improvisation was the keynote. Local people were co-opted in small parts, or as extras. In Chattanooga, Tennessee, Coppola learned that an Armed Forces Day parade was about to take place, so decided to use it as background.

The last eight weeks of production took place in Nebraska. An old shoe shop in Ogallala was converted into an office from which Coppola directed operations.

The Rain People is also notable for assembling for the first time actors and technicians who would remain loyal to Coppola throughout much of his career. Jimmie Caan, of course, as Killer. Robert Duvall as the cop. Sound engineer Walter Murch. Editor Barry Malkin, who had known Francis since they were both in their teens. Production associate Mona Skager. "He didn't know me," recalls Murch, "but we had one meeting lasting an hour, and three months later I came back with all of the sound mixed." This element of mutual trust contributes substantially to the professional quality of Coppola's films.

When *The Rain People* opened in August 1969, the critics unanimously admired Coppola's handling of the circumstances in which it had been made, but most felt dissatisfied, and regarded it as a flawed piece.

*   *   *

The exhilaration of making *The Rain People* with a tiny crew, against all the precepts and advice of Warners, provided the impetus for Coppola's dream to take shape.

The dream was called Zoetrope. Literally, its Greek root signifies "life movement." To film archivists, the zoetrope is familiar as one of the earliest precursors of the cinema—a drum circumscribed with images which when revolved rapidly gives the illusion of movement.

Francis yearned to go back to the basics, to create an environment where young, independent filmmakers could work with state-of-the-art equipment without the disagreeable pressures of the big studio environment.

When we made *Rain People* we had this unusual format, a very small caravan that could strike anywhere. We began to feel like Robin Hood and his band, we really had the filmmaking machine in our hands and it didn't need to be in Hollywood, it could be anywhere. So then we thought, well, if we can do it successfully on the road out of a few cars and things, imagine if we went to a beautiful city like San Francisco and implanted ourselves as a filmmaking community. We would have independence, and we'd still be close enough to LA to be able to draw on talent from there.

Associates of Coppola recall the ideal behind Zoetrope. "It was intended as an alternative place," says Fred Roos, producer of so many

Above left: *Francis as a baby.* Above right: *His mother, Italia.*
Below: *His father, Carmine Coppola.*

Above left: *Carmine Coppola* (at left) *with his parents.* Above right: *Francis's paternal grandfather, the machinist who built the prototype for the Vitaphone sound system.*
Below: *Francis with his elder brother August and sister Talia.*

Above left: *Francis in the uniform of New York Military Academy (with his mother).* Above right: *Francis with his wife Eleanor at a screening of* The Godfather.
Below: *Francis and Eleanor in the Philippines, with Vittorio Storaro during a break in the shooting of* Apocalypse Now.

Roman, Eleanor, Francis, and Gio in San Francisco in 1969.

Above: Dementia 13: *'It was meant to be a horror film with a lot of people getting killed with axes and so forth'' (Coppola).*
Below: *Elizabeth Hartman as Barbara Darling in* You're a Big Boy Now.
(Seven Arts)

Francis and Eleanor on location for Apocalypse Now.

You're a Big Boy Now: *Bernard (Peter Kastner) roller-skating in the New York Library. (Seven Arts)*

Above: *Francis with Elizabeth Hartman and Phil Feldman on*
You're a Big Boy Now.
Below: *Shirley Knight and James Caan in the final shots of* The Rain People.

The Rain People: *"Actors and technicians who would remain loyal to Coppola throughout much of his career": Francis "in uniform" third from right against skyline; George Lucas standing atop van, with Shirley Knight and James Caan just below him, and Robert Duvall (in white shirt, hand in pocket).*

The Rain People: *Francis on location with Shirley Knight (above) and Shirley Knight behind the wheel (below).*

Finian's Rainbow: *Petula Clerk and Fred Astaire arrive in Rainbow Valley County* (above). *Barbara Hancock as Susan the Silent* (below).

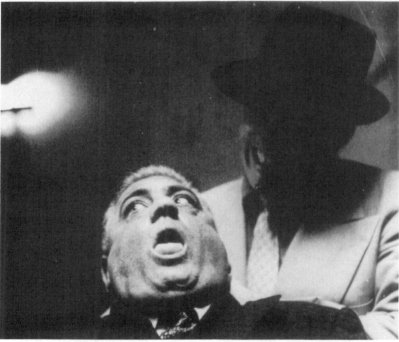

The Godfather: *"The alfresco exuberance of a Sicilian wedding, resurgent in the Long Island estate of the Corleones"* (above). *"A vicious portrayal of violence"*: the end of Luca Brasi (Lenny Montana) (below).

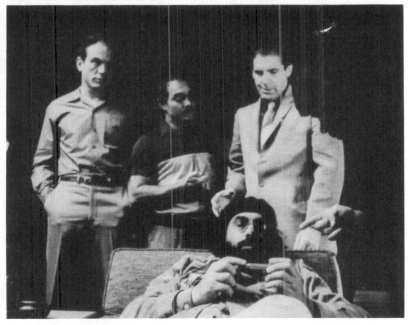

The Godfather: *"The Family is Coppola's dominant preoccupation."*
The Godfather Part II: *Francis slips into the role . . .*

The Godfather Part II: *Fredo (John Cazale) "is treated with thinly disguised condescension" by Michael (Al Pacino).*

The Godfather Part II: *The two faces of Robert De Niro as Vito Corleone: as the reasonable, quiet-spoken young immigrant* (above) *and as the ruthless killer* (below).

Francis with daughter Sofia during the shooting of The Godfather Part II.

Zoetrope movies, "where people could make their pictures with very little interference." Walter Murch emphasises the technical dimension of the facility. "The one big capital investment, the nonmovable investment, was the sound system, the idea being that if we could mix our films up in the Bay Area, we'd be free of a certain link to Los Angeles. Francis had had some frustrating circumstances mixing his earlier films in the big studios, and he intuitively knew that there was a lot more you could do with sound."

Two visits finally convinced Francis that Zoetrope was a feasibility. The first took place on Independence Day 1958, when along with George Lucas and Ron Colby, he drove up to John Korty's ministudio at Stinson Beach. They had come straight from the final days of shooting *The Rain People* and were exhausted. But the revelation that Korty's cottage industry actually functioned was exciting. Korty had already made an impact in the States and on the European festival circuit with independent, oddball movies like *The Crazy Quilt* and *Funnyman*. Indiana-born, he was genial, laid-back and persistent, a survivor beyond the system and above the underground. His equipment may not have been perfect, but it was at least all under the roof of his massive barn. Coppola and Lucas told him that the studio looked like a fulfillment of their fantasies. "He inspired us both," says Francis. "He was a real innovator. I produced his first TV film, *The People*. My father wrote the music for it."

Francis was sufficiently enthused to begin planning the move to San Francisco. "We were standing in the lobby of the Mark Hopkins in July," remembers Mona Skager, "when Francis suggested to Eleanor that she should move up here with the children." Soon afterwards, Francis followed up another introduction:

My wife had traveled in Europe as a young girl, and she had friends in Holland and Denmark and elsewhere, and when we were in Copenhagen, someone mentioned Mogens Skot-Hansen. I heard he ran a youthful film company. Part of the bohemian idea of people doing shows goes back to my Hofstra experience; socially it had been so much fun, and I always missed in film the sense of sitting around with your friends at the café and the pretty girls and that kind of theater life. Somehow Denmark had romantic connotations for me. I remember looking through the locked doors at Laterna Studios, and wishing I could make contact with Skot-Hansen. Later, I did find some people in Beverly Hills who knew him, so I got the Klampenborg address, down by the sea near Copenhagen, and visited Mogens Skot-Hansen and his family. Stayed there three weeks, in fact. I saw this mansion, and the pretty blond girls I'd always associated with Denmark, and the editing rooms and so on, and when I came back I told George Lucas that we too had to get a mansion somewhere.

We found a place in Ross that was known as the Dibble Estate, but after negotiating for it, and my selling all I had to raise the money, someone else purchased the property, which was very disappointing. Then we discovered that the person who'd bought the Dibble Estate had *another* property, another mansion, and we were ultimately prevented from acquiring that on zoning grounds. Now during my visit to the Cologne Photo-kina a few months earlier I'd ordered tons of new equipment. I didn't have the money to pay for it, but seeing all these editing machines and mixing studios was like being in a candy-store of technology. So when this equipment began arriving in the States, we had to put it somewhere. At the last minute I stored it in some extra space where there was a recording studio in San Francisco, on Folsom Street, and that's where American Zoetrope essentially started. You can still see the flagpole above the warehouse. The flag is gone, but the pole still stands!

As a permanent reminder of those days at the Laterna Studios, Francis cherishes a small collection of early cinematic toys and zoetropes. The patrician and idealistic Skot-Hansen, who had produced films for the United Nations, took pride in his collection of such devices.

Carroll Ballard recalls how Francis, fresh back from Scandinavia, took him out on a sailboat. "We exchanged ideas about what was wrong with the system. I expressed the view that there was no way one could work within it. The best chance was to get out of LA and find alternative financing. I'm sure Francis had similar conversations with lots of people."

In the dying weeks of the decade, American Zoetrope was established in San Francisco. Francis was owner, George Lucas was vice-president and Mona Skager acted as treasurer and secretary. The actual facility was at 827 Folsom Street, a warehouse found by Korty and converted by Coppola with some money advanced by Warner–Seven Arts.

The Hollywood studio, headed at that time by Ted Ashley, had succumbed to Coppola's glib assurances that George Lucas's feature, *THX 1138*, was ready to roll, and so agreed to fund the development of five projects. Warners later claimed that the deal called for Coppola to "buy back" the money spent on such Zoetrope productions should the screenplay fail to satisfy the studio, and Paramount eventually paid up to enable Francis to proceed with *The Godfather Part II*.

Not much cash was available either. "Warners were paying $2,500 a week seed money," says Mona Skager, "but I had to rent out all the equipment just to keep things going."

There was, however, a mood of optimism at the official opening of the

Folsom Street headquarters on December 13, 1969. Only Coppola and Lucas were aware that Warners might try to force Francis to buy all the projects and equipment should Zoetrope founder.

Anybody entering the three-story loft building on Folsom was immediately aware of the offbeat, anti-Hollywood flavor of Zoetrope. There was a silver espresso machine in the hall, Marimekko fabrics from Finland hung from the walls, their bold primary colors echoed in the purple, yellow, and orange paint of the freight elevator. The facility comprised seven editing rooms, and in one stood the pride of Zoetrope, a Keller three-screen table, the only such machine in California. Closed-circuit TV enabled the big screen to be used for other purposes. There were rooms for wardrobes, props, design, transfer, and coating, as well as optical work, film loading and unloading, and refrigerated film storage. Coppola did not hesitate to order a $40,000 Mitchell BNCR camera. "Francis likes to buck the system," says Skager. "He has the power of his convictions." Inspired by his visits to Photo-kina in Cologne, he resolved to match and even surpass the orthodox studios where technology was concerned. Soon, lightweight Arriflexes appeared at Zoetrope, along with portable sound recording equipment.

Coppola forgot one important factor—money. However complex the equipment at their disposal, filmmakers need, and unfortunately expect, to live well. Decades of lavish spending by the Hollywood majors have convinced anyone entering the industry that the fiscal rewards are high. Instead, in the words of his wife, Francis "dreamed of this group of poets, filmmakers, and writers who would drink espresso in North Beach and talk of their work, and it would be good. They would publish their writing in *City* magazine, do new plays at the Little Fox Theater, make experimental films at American Zoetrope." Cameras were lent to enthusiasts making shorts on everything from Buckminster Fuller in Mexico to tribal fishing rights in Seattle.

To Coppola's dismay, the studio suffered from theft and inefficiency. During the first year of operations, almost $40,000 worth of equipment vanished from the Folsom Street facility—simply borrowed or stolen by Bay Area filmmakers. According to Carrol Ballard,

> The fatal flaw was that it was never a cooperative venture. Everyone was off in his own little corner, competing. After Warners had lent Francis a lot of money, scripts were commissioned. I was working on a project, so were [John] Milius and [George] Lucas. The problem was that the conditions under which Francis wanted everyone to work were more than spartan—they were practically non-earning. My initial agreement with him called for me to make a

feature for a fee of $10,000—and I eventually made *The Black Stallion* for $35,000 and seven points of the net.

Roger Corman, godfather to Francis's son Gio, was visiting in San Francisco soon after Zoetrope had started operations. "I was an executor of his will, and Francis asked me what I'd do with all this equipment if he died. 'I'll put it in a truck and take it down to LA,' I said, 'because you're in the wrong city, Francis!' "

Even Francis conceded that his enthusiasm and imagination "far outpaced any kind of fiscal logic" at Zoetrope. The inevitable concomitant of his powerful personality was a need to be involved in every project, to sit on every committee. Some colleagues felt that Coppola drew his own ideas from this pool of talented people. Others noted his obsession with presentation—designing logos, envelopes, etc.—when he might have spent his time more fruitfully in the editing room. But the romance prevailed over the cynicism. The apprentice program they organized here led to Francis and his brother August later enrolling students from Bancroft Junior High School in Los Angeles to observe the various departments and technicians of Zoetrope Studios at work. And everyone loved the Thursday night screenings of new and classic films, with Chinese food on the side.

At no stage did Zoetrope seek to champion the contemporary antiwar fervor of the Bay Area, although Francis himself joined the huge demonstration there in 1969. During the 1970s he admitted that he had not understood the issues until he embarked on research for *Apocalypse Now*. His commitment to freedom of speech on the Vietnam controversy is confirmed by his lone public defense of Bert Schneider, the producer of *Hearts and Minds*, who read a telegram from the Viet Cong when receiving the Academy Award for Best Documentary.

Several projects competed for the green light at Zoetrope.

Coppola himself had already written the screenplay of *The Conversation*, which would not in fact be filmed until after the triumphant opening of *The Godfather*. At that stage of gestation it was, said Coppola, "a horror film—I hope!" George Lucas had shot *THX 1138* and was intent on proceeding with a script by John Milius entitled *Apocalypse Now*. Jess Ritter and Steve Wax were preparing a screenplay based on the People's Park Disaster at Santa Rita Prison Farm. Carroll Ballard, long before he won his spurs with *The Black Stallion*, was developing a project entitled *Vesuvia*.

None of these films was envisaged on an epic scale. At this point in his career, Coppola still felt that small was beautiful. He relished the idea of making inexpensive films, some even in 16mm. After all, Lucas had won prizes for his fifteen-minute student film at USC, which he called *THX 1138-4EB*. When Francis decided to give Lucas the go-ahead for a feature-length version of his SF movie, he wanted it to be at once innovative and low-priced.

The "exteriors" of *THX 1138* were photographed in the tunnels of San Francisco's BART subway system. There were no stars (although Robert Duvall once again pressed his claim to serious stardom with his performance in this movie). Walter Murch, whose calm, analytical skills influenced just about every Zoetrope venture, wrote the screenplay with Lucas. Sound therefore played a major role in the film—not so much human voices as the noise of the space-age: computer keyboards, high-velocity motorbikes, robotic commands. More science-fiction ballet than regular movie, *THX 1138* makes maximum use of the 'Scope screen to allow its characters to dart and writhe against a white, hallucinatory background.

The film's love story is fragile and frustratingly intangible. We never identify with Robert Duvall's haunted, hunted personality in a subterranean world of the future where computers and computer-programmed guards control a docile populace, their shaven heads and sheer-white uniforms sapping individual identity. Fritz Lang's *Metropolis* preached the same kind of message to much more powerful effect.

THX 1138 still appears like one long, exquisite commercial for Zoetrope's state-of-the-art technology. But its heartbeat is hard to hear. Like Alain Resnais's *Last Year at Marienbad*, its formal brilliance only spotlights the lack of human interest. The sterile surface of the film robs even the most intimate love scene between Duvall and Maggie McOmie of its potential fervor. Donald Pleasence's baleful, jokey attempts to chum up with—maybe even seduce—Duvall's THX lack conviction.

Without doubt, though, *THX 1138* lived up to the aspirations of American Zoetrope. Its technical alertness far outdistanced the experimental efforts of underground moviemakers of the late 1960s—many of whom worked in the Bay Area. It carried the imprimatur of a famous studio—Warners—as distributor. And it dared to suggest that an American film could be every bit as perplexing and imaginative as its European counterpart.

This terrifying, hermetic world suggested the dangers lurking in the wake of technological revolution. Ironically, the very concept of American Zoetrope encouraged this single-minded focus on technical excellence. Coppola proved later with *The Conversation* that he could reconcile human dilemmas with the mysteries of Newspeak. Lucas, in *American Graffiti* two years later, would direct as warm an evocation of the past as even the Beatles had accomplished in their songs.

If *THX 1138* is a significant harbinger of anything, then it must be *Star Wars*. In both its pretensions and its failings lay the clue to the break-up of Coppola and Lucas as a team during the 1970s. However much he, too, may have been attracted to the ideals of industrial light and magic, Francis Coppola continued to be more fascinated by the prospect of human beings at a crossroads of choice in their lives.

The Godfather

In late 1970, Coppola's career had reached a frustrating juncture. His dream of forging American Zoetrope into a viable alternative to the Hollywood studios was shattered. *The Rain People* had collapsed at the box-office and Warners had looked askance at *THX 1138*. The studio agreed to honor its commitment to distribute the movie, but the reaction to Lucas's ice-cold vision of an underground future patrolled by chrome-faced, leather-clad guards was frostier still. Warners' ties with Coppola's outfit were severed. All seven projects in development were rejected out of hand by Ted Ashley. They had included *Apocalypse Now* and *The Conversation*.

"Zoetrope was picked clean," said Coppola of those nerve-wracking months in 1970. "Everyone had used it, no one had contributed, and there was a time when I literally was staving off the sheriff from putting the chain across the door." He and George Lucas knew that vast sums —the figure ranged from $300,000 to $600,000—would have to be repaid to Warners under the terms of the original financing arrangement for Zoetrope.

Where should he turn now?

Francis was just thirty-one, and for whiz-kids that is a dangerous age. He had fought tenaciously for the chance to make *The Rain People* as he wished, and had been dejected by its failure. Privately, he was excited at the prospect of Eleanor's bearing their third child sometime in April 1971.

Of course his career as a screenwriter was still in excellent shape. *Patton* had won Coppola even more acclaim in Hollywood—and would earn him an Academy Award in the spring of the following year. Out of the blue, however, Robert Evans, vice-president in charge of production at Paramount, contacted him about directing a screen version of *The Godfather*.

This virile novel about the Mafia in the United States had appeared in 1969. Its author, Mario Puzo, had been hard pressed for money in the mid-1960s, and accepted a small advance from his editor, William Targ, at G. P. Putnam's Sons, New York, on the strength of a twenty-page outline. He had also found an enthusiastic response among Paramount executives, who were keen to option the eventual book for the movies. In 1968, Puzo had brought the completed manuscript to Putnam's. Even when the novel entered the bestseller lists the next year, Paramount was pessimistic about its potential on the big screen. The studio's previous Mafia movie, *The Brotherhood*, had flopped. Still, a low-budget production seemed like a reasonable risk.

Within its prodigious time span, *The Godfather* saga comprises the development of the Mafia from a crude secret society to a sleek, sophisticated brand of corporate government. In Sicily, the grip of the Black Hand over the local peasantry had tightened to a stranglehold throughout the nineteenth century. But by 1943, just two years before the movie opens, the Mafia's influence was implanted in the New World to such a degree that the American landings in Sicily were reputed to have been plotted through the good offices of U.S. crime bosses who had Sicilian roots and relatives. Italian soldiers may have an absurdist image, but the Mafia "soldiers" in New York have never been anything less than lethal.

Puzo's novel describes the ascendancy of the Corleone family in New York and Las Vegas. The young Vito Corleone comes to the United States at the turn of the century and builds a remarkable power-base in New York's Hell's Kitchen. He imports olive oil, but his stature grows by virtue of a benevolent despotism toward those immigrants weaker than himself. Pursuing a policy tinged with both ruthlessness and sweet reason, Vito Corleone supplants the old Mafia chieftains and eschews their ostentatious arrogance.

As the "Godfather" ages, so his sons, Santino ("Sonny"), Fredo, and Michael, come more into focus. The attempted murder of Don Vito precipitates a war among the five principal Mafia families. Michael kills his father's archenemy and then, after hiding out in Sicily for almost a year, returns to assume control of the Corleone domain. The corrupting effect of absolute power, and the transplantation of traditional Sicilian attitudes to the New World, underscore the novel.

Coppola was not the first director to be approached by Paramount. Al Ruddy, the producer, and his associate, Gray Frederickson, were finding the search for a director exasperating. Arthur Penn was busy; Peter Yates and Costa-Gavras, two hot names at the time, said no. Sidney J. Furie, the Canadian who had made *Big Fauss and Little Halsey* for Ruddy and Frederickson, divided the friends. "Ruddy really wanted him," said Frederickson, "but I fought him all the way."

Then Peter Bart, the Paramount executive who had optioned Puzo's original material, recommended Coppola. Bart was desperate for the project to succeed. He had worked on the screenplay with Puzo, and had brought Al Ruddy in as producer. It was becoming clear that the studio would clash with the Mafia and then with Italian-American lobbying groups as it progressed with *The Godfather*. Evans and Ruddy reasoned that Coppola, with his Italian name and ancestry, would keep the protests at bay. They also knew that, after the disaster of *The Rain People*, they could sign him cheaply. As Evans commented, "He knew the way these men in *The Godfather* ate their food, kissed each other, talked. He knew the grit" (even though, one might add, Francis was no relation to one of Vito Genovese's lieutenants, "Trigger Mike" Coppola).

At first, Francis demurred. He felt the book's sleazier aspects would mar any eventual film, and he thought the budget proposed by the studio was far too low. Evans had fixed a limit of $2 million. But the novel went on selling and selling, and selling. The film began to loom larger in the studio's plans for 1971, and the feeling was that it should be set in period, like the novel itself.

On behalf of the studio, Bart called Coppola at the home of George Lucas in Mill Valley. Lucas, anxious about the debts at Zoetrope, urged his young mentor to accept the assignment. So too did Coppola's father. Carmine met him by chance at Burbank airport. "I was at Paramount all day yesterday," said his son, "and they want me to direct this hunk of trash. I don't want to do it. I want to do art films." Carmine encouraged him to make some money from the project, and then use it to do the kind of movies he really relished.

Once he had changed his mind, Coppola aimed at the best deal he could hope for. After a late-night negotiating session at Paramount, he agreed to a fee of $125,000 and 6 percent of the gross rentals. He promptly called Mona Skager and announced with delight that they would all be sailing for Europe. Family and friends attended the Sorrento Festival in Italy, and enjoyed a glorious break from the strain of previous months, before Francis returned to start adapting Puzo's novel. A press release from Paramount implied that Francis Ford Coppola had been selected by virtue of his skills as a writer who could collaborate with Puzo and realize his vision on screen.

Puzo by that point was already laboring on the second draft of the screenplay. But the two men struck up a rapport based on mutual respect. Francis spent morning after morning at the Caffè Trieste in San Francisco, revising the script. "He rewrote one half and I rewrote the second half," recalled Puzo. "Then we traded and rewrote each other. I suggested we work together. Francis looked me right in the eye and said no. That's when I knew he was really a director." Puzo and Coppola retained this feeling of trust, enabling them to continue the collaboration on *The Godfather Part II* as well as "play baccarat and shoot dice" together.

Almost immediately, Bob Evans began to regret his choice of director. The studio was stunned by Coppola's insistence on signing Marlon Brando for the name-part. Brando's career was in the doldrums and he was notoriously difficult to work with. Although Mario Puzo had at first thought of Brando for the role, Paramount proved truculent. Stanley Jaffe, president of Paramount, proclaimed at an executive gathering that Brando would definitely not appear in the film. Bob Evans toyed with the idea of approaching Carlo Ponti, husband of Sophia Loren, for the role. According to Coppola, Frank Sinatra had put himself forward to play the Godfather—on condition he and Francis purchase the rights to the whole project from Paramount.

Jaffe's opposition failed to deflect Coppola, whose impassioned defense of Brando's skills swayed the board. Soon afterward, Jaffe resigned his post. Brando improvised brilliantly at a screen test taken on video by Coppola. This, and his agreement to work for expenses plus a percentage of the gross—which would net him $1,500,000—mollified the studio. It is interesting to note that Coppola had thought of Brando for the lead in *The Conversation*, before Gene Hackman had become a big name.

The casting of Al Pacino as Michael Corleone also caused ructions. Pacino had looked promising in his first major screen part, that of the junkie in *The Panic in Needle Park*, but did not carry the marquee clout of Warren Beatty, who declined the role.

Coppola's third key demand, that the novel's Sicilian scenes be shot on location in Italy, inflamed the mood and the budget still further. Returning from one preproduction trip to Europe, Francis was handed a wire at the airport from his agent, urging him, "Don't quit. Make them fire you!"

Undeterred, and beginning to show the flamboyant single-mindedness that would enrage bureaucratic executives and delight the media, Coppola perceived in *The Godfather* a journeyman assignment that might yet transcend the conventions of the gangster genre. With hindsight, *The Godfather* can be seen as the tide in Coppola's affairs which, taken at the flood, led on to fortune. "Dear Mommy," he had once written home, "I want to be rich and famous. I'm so discouraged. I don't think it will come true."

* * *

The love of family that runs like a filament through Coppola's life and work soon surfaced in the early days of production on *The Godfather*. Hiring the back room at Patsy's Restaurant, off Broadway, he assembled his cast and colleagues for an Italian dinner. Brando presided amicably at the head of the table, along with Jimmie Caan and Al Pacino, and Francis's sister, Talia Shire, served the spaghetti. "They'd never met before really," recalls Coppola, "and it was like playing at a family, a kind of sensual opportunity for them to relate to each other."

He was nervous about the casting of Talia as Connie, Don Corleone's daughter. He feared that she would appear too glamorous and inexperienced before the cameras. Their mother remembers one occasion when Francis started screaming, "Tally's too pretty for the part. I'm going to fire her! A guy who's going to marry into a Mafia family has to have a fat little dumpy Italian girl with an ugly face."

The director's parents were enlisted to make cameo appearances in the movie. They are among the diners at the Luna restaurant in the Bronx, where Michael guns down Sollozzo (who organized the assassination attempt on the Don) and the corrupt cop. Then Francis's mother, Italia, was cast as a switchboard operator in the Genco office scene, while father Carmine played the piano in a scene where the Corleone soldiers sit around in expectation of an attack by the other families. Francis himself lived in a two-bedroom apartment in New York, his two sons in one room and he, Eleanor, and their newborn daughter, Sofia, in the other.

The Italian-American community was at first opposed to the production. Paramount encountered intractable union problems in the New York area. In February 1971, the Italian-American League dispatched a mailing to virtually every elected official in national government, urging them to prevail upon Robert Evans not to allow *The Godfather* to defame Italian-Americans. Some days after this statement was released to the press, Al Ruddy asked to meet with representatives of the League. With Joseph

Colombo in the chair—the same Colombo who on June 28 that very year would be gravely wounded at an Italian-American Unity Day gathering in Columbus Circle—this meeting was held at the La Scala restaurant on West 54th Street.

On March 20, Ruddy declared to the *New York Times* that proceeds from the premiere of the film would go to the Italian-American Civil Rights League, and "In place of the words 'Mafia' and 'Cosa Nostra,' the crime syndicate will be referred to in the film as 'the five families' and other non-Italian phrases."

According to Mario Puzo, the word "Mafia" was never in the script in the first place, which enhances Ruddy's reputation as a negotiator. And while Vic Damone was at the time reported to have withdrawn from the role of Johnny Fontane because he felt that "it was not in the best image of Italian-Americans," it is more likely that Paramount's proposed fee was too modest.

Although the studio's union difficulties evaporated, not all prominent Italian-Americans endorsed the policy of appeasement. Senator John J. Marchi of Staten Island described the self-censorship as "a monstrous insult to millions upon millions of loyal Americans of Italian extraction." In the end, of course, *The Godfather* enjoyed enormous ethnic support at the box-office.

The central problem on the production turned out to be an escalating budget, which would climb finally to some $6 million. The additional expenditure was due in part to Coppola's meticulous attention to detail. By the end of the fifteenth day of shooting, production was lagging behind by up to two days a week. Francis was covering his scenes to a fastidious degree, ordering many more takes than usual. "I had told [the studio] it would take me eighty days to make the movie, and they gave me a schedule of fifty-three days," he explained later. Relations between the director and Gordon Willis, the cinematographer, were tense. Filming was disrupted on more than one occasion while the two men argued and then, overcoming their pride, rejoined forces to finish a complex scene.

Other snags conspired to push the budget up from its new ceiling of between $5.4 and $5.5 million: Al Pacino was injured, snow fell on a day when it should not have done, and so on. Ruddy had related how one sequence in particular cost $100,000. The slaughter of Sonny at the tollbooths was scheduled for filming on location near Jones Beach during a single day. But Paramount told Ruddy not to spare any expense at this stage, "So we went out to a deserted airstrip at Floyd Bennett Field which would be much easier to control than an actual location, and dressed it up to look like a highway." Dean Tavoularis designed the tollbooths, and filming took almost three days.

The Sicilian sequences were shot in the area of Taormina. "It's a little resort," says Coppola, "but within a radius of fifty to eighty miles we could find teeny, teeny towns . . . Taormina is not like Palermo; for a hundred years it's been a tourist place and the reactions of the Sicilians in Taormina and all around Etna are different; it's not a particular hotbed of Mafia activity. Of course Corleone *is* a little town in Sicily, near Palermo. Don't forget that Mario Puzo based *The Godfather* on genuine documents—he had access to all the Valachi Papers and so on . . ."

Paramount, aware of the need to create a box-office hit, were concerned about Coppola's refusal to emphasize the violence. At one point, a second-unit director was appointed because the studio, in Coppola's words, "felt I was great on character relationships and too timid with the violence." Elia Kazan was almost assigned to the production, in view of his track record in directing Brando in films like *Viva Zapata!* and *On the Waterfront.* "I kept dreaming," said Coppola, "that Kazan would arrive on the set, and would say to me, 'Uh, Francis, I've been asked to . . .' But Marlon, who knew about this, was very supportive, and said he would not continue to work on the film if I was fired."

Al Pacino also aroused Paramount's suspicions. "They looked at the dailies, and they wanted to recast the part," said the actor in a 1989 interview. "But Francis hung in there for me."

Brando, apart from exercising his superstar muscle by arriving late on set from time to time, approached *The Godfather* with professional devotion. He donned earplugs to make it more difficult for him to catch lines, strengthening the impression that the Don was hard of hearing. His voice assumed the hoarse texture of a faded tape recording. Special effects expert Dick Smith constructed a mouthpiece that caused Brando's jaw to sag and his cheeks to puff out. His eyes, according to one observer on set, drooped at the corners, and his skin was covered with a thin network of wrinkles fashioned from latex rubber. The star was also equipped with a padded false paunch beneath his suit, and weights were attached to both of his feet so as to give his walk a ponderous quality. Brando or Smith (or indeed Coppola) may have glanced at Orson Welles's old man Kane make-up before tackling the task, for those stuffed cheeks, straight-back hairstyle, and tucked-in jaw recall the Xanadu scenes of *Citizen Kane.*

August Coppola feels that Brando in *The Godfather* resembled Uncle Louis, Italia Coppola's elder brother, whose bulk had greatly impressed the boys in childhood. "If they had given *The Godfather* to a normal American director it would have taken on the stereotypes of Italian-Americans. Francis put it into everyday life, so that every aspect of the story is tied into our own family in some way—tone, coloration, rhythm. The irony is that you begin to respond to this Mafia story almost as a celebration." Francis insisted that Don Vito should look and sound like a New Yorker, rather than some comic-book image of the Italian mafioso.

August's reference to the story as a celebration touches on the most controversial aspect of *The Godfather*. Coppola invests a certain glamor in the hectic, unsavory lives of his characters, as much here as in *Apocalypse Now*. Yet the somber, profoundly critical study of Michael Corleone in *The Godfather Part II* must dispel any suspicion that Coppola was endorsing the Mafia's code of violence. Even this could not convince a fellow director like Nicolas Roeg, who found both films "a deeply unhappy experience. Here is this man [Michael] who has become a liar, murders his brother and others, slams the door in his wife's face and all in the interest of a little power. It was a doom-laden, black, nasty thing. He wouldn't even drink alcohol either, which was the last straw . . . I know it was very well made, but I lie awake because of its lack of decency."

Coppola concedes that the film projects a certain idealized image of the Mafia in the public consciousness. "People love to read about an organization that's really going to take care of us," he has said. "When the courts fail you and the whole American system fails you, you can go to Don Corleone and get justice." The entire opening section of Puzo's original novel underlines precisely this point. Where both book and film soften the Mafia image is in the Don's courtly behavior, which contrasts with the expletive-ridden argot of real-life Mafia chieftains, as recorded in court hearings and tapes produced in evidence. Robert Duvall's role as the *Consigliore* bears a distinct resemblance to Sidney Korshack, a celebrated lawyer for some prominent Families.

The notion of private justice takes forceful, verbal form in the very first scene of the film. Bonasera, the undertaker, beseeches Don Corleone for justice. His daughter has been brutally assaulted by two youths. "I believe in America," he declares like a credo in the opening line. This brilliant scene adumbrates the principal motifs of *The Godfather*. The camera's computer-timed lens retreats with scarcely perceptible stealth back past the head of Brando's Don as he listens to Bonasera's muttered lament. The scene stirs our awareness of the need of the simple-minded for a strong, protective authority. A quasi-religious mood is initiated by this ominous blend of fear and respect. The Don sits in monolithic silence, stroking a cat in a telling visual metaphor for the hooded claws of his domain. All this, and the conspiratorial shadows of Gordon Willis's photography, evokes the intimacy of some pagan confessional; Bonasera is a subject pleading not with God but with Mammon.

From the start, Coppola restrains us from classifying Don Corleone as a comic-book villain. Irritable because Bonasera does not accord him friendship, and appears only when he requires help, the Don growls to his adviser, Tom Hagen, "We're not murderers, in spite of what this undertaker says." Sniffing fastidiously at the rose in his buttonhole, he tells Hagen he wants the matter handled by "reliable people, people that aren't going to be carried away." The words, so mundane and unexceptional, mask the vicious street violence of the Mafia.

Beyond the shuttered study lies the alfresco exuberance of a Sicilian wedding, resurgent in the Long Island estate of the Corleones. The members of the family are introduced. Sonny, coarse, glittering, and priapic, smashing the cameras of those press photographers who try to penetrate the privacy of the occasion. Michael, sober and restrained in his army uniform (the film opens in 1945), enjoying the company of his WASP fiancée, Kay Adams, to whom he retails stories about the Corleones ("That's my family, Kay, it's not me"). Fredo, febrile and already drunk. Connie, the youngest, parading in her wedding finery. Mama Corleone, the most regal of all Italian mammas. Blood binds these individuals in more ways than one. Their indivisible loyalty—not to one another but to the concept of the family as such—has the strength not only of Sicilian tradition, but also of Masonic or Mormon custom.

The Family—this, more than anything else in either of the *Godfather* films, is Coppola's dominant preoccupation. When Brando declares that "a man who doesn't spend time with his family can never be a real man," the statement rings with hierarchical as well as sexual significance. Italian society is founded on the supremacy of the male; his "family" constitute his possessions, his very estate. This macho approach to life is both stated and implied throughout the *Godfather* saga. Luca Brasi solemnly voices his hope that Connie and Carlo's first child may "be a masculine child." Toward the end of *The Godfather Part II*, the sentiment is echoed in Michael's urgent demand after learning of Kay's "miscarriage": "Was it a boy?"

The origins of such a male-dominated society emerge during the Sicilian sequences of both films. Apollonia, Michael's demure young bride, is cherished by her family and village friends as a delicate, almost other-worldly icon, and not as a creature of flesh and blood who might have a will and desires of her own.

In Mafia parlance, the "Family" comprises not just the blood relatives, but a whole host of loyal soldiers and assistants. Clemenza and Tessio, the *caporegimes*, are regarded as just as integral members of the Family as Santino and Connie.

Coppola, discerning artist that he is, can afford to criticize the excesses of such a concept, even if he endorses the sovereign role of the family in his personal life, giving key roles in his filmmaking team to his father (as composer), his sister (as actress), his brother (consultant on script and creative issues), his late son Gio (as assistant director), and his nephew, Nicolas Cage (as actor), and retaining the loyalties of a host of other actors, technicians, and friends.

Even in the darkest days of Zoetrope, following the disastrous opening of *One from the Heart*, such people remained on call, certain that sooner or later Francis would emerge from the valley of the shadow.

Don Corleone himself stands tantalizingly beyond censure. In part, his ambivalent presence is due to the dignified, almost muffled performance of Marlon Brando. He is more of a congenial patriarch than his son Michael will ever be. He likes his wine, and he laughs a lot. At certain moments he seems ashamed of the Mafia's dependence upon violence. He refuses to be tempted by the quick profits likely to flow from narcotics. Respectability forms an essential virtue in the world of Don Corleone. Coppola has said in an interview that the character was a synthesis of two Mafia chieftains, Vito Genovese and Joseph Profaci. Genovese in particular ordered his soldiers not to deal in drugs, even if he himself did exactly that on the side.

Alone with Michael, in the serene aftermath of the attempt on his life, the Don refers wistfully to a career that might have been his—Senator Corleone (shades of the Kennedy clan), Governor Corleone—hoping that Michael would hold all the strings. "There just wasn't enough time," he concludes. "We'll get there, pop, we'll get there," replies a gentle Michael. In the midst of this scene—written by Coppola's friend, Robert Towne—the mantle passes almost imperceptibly to Michael. The son begins to draw on a dark reservoir of cunning and malevolence that lurks in the Mafia tradition.

Numberless crimes are committed in the name of the Family. Tom

Hagen is dispatched to Hollywood to deal with the intransigent producer who has dared spurn the Don's godson, Johnny Fontane, for a starring role. Later, in Las Vegas, Michael will chastise his older brother, Fredo, for speaking against the Family. Carlo Rizzi, the cocksure bridegroom of Connie, suffers more than most from this blood loyalty. When Sonny learns of his domestic cruelty, he administers a savage public beating to Carlo (and Sonny is no angel himself). Later when Michael detects the hand of Carlo behind the shooting of Sonny, he has no compunction in making his sister a widow.

The notion of family as a paradigm for American capitalism—survival of the fittest, the ruthless annihilation of critics, and the amassing of money which in turn purchases power—emerges more and more forcefully as this film and its sequel gather momentum. From the moment when Don Corleone and his sons, the *consigliori* and the *caporegimes* assemble like a corporate board to discuss drug trafficking with Sollozzo, to the electric moment in *Part II* when the ailing Hyman Roth confides to Michael that the pair of them are "bigger than U.S. Steel," there are frequent reminders that all the violence is a means to a single end—Big Business.

Michael's character steadily envelops both *The Godfather* and *The Godfather Part II*. He "has to *start out* ambivalent, almost unsure of himself and his place. He's caught between his old world family and the postwar American Dream," comments Pacino. In the first film he is contrasted with his aging father; in the sequel, with the young Don Vito. Like Cavaliers and Round-heads in seventeenth-century Britain, their attitude to power could hardly be more divergent: genial flamboyance set against ruthless calculation and efficiency. Michael arrives at the conclusion of *Part II* arguably, in Coppola's own words, "the most powerful man in the country," but he is somber and alone. Don Vito Corleone has enjoyed a serene finale, playing with his grandchild in the garden, stuffing his mouth with orange peel, and *pretending* to be a monster. And so even his death takes on a grace that surpasses the agony of his heart seizure. As the little grandson fusses over the stricken Don, Coppola cuts to a long shot of the tomato grove, with its white muslin billowing over the scene like a protective shroud.

Clearly, Coppola approves of the Don's grandiose manner more than he does of Michael's postwar idiom. Perhaps he sees in the father something of the spirit of pioneering America, an ample vision that has been displaced by a kind of colorless, industrial barony. Don Vito's humility is discarded by Michael and the new generation. Only the inner ruthlessness endures—diamond-hard and unforgiving, more devious, less personable—to rhyme with the real-life gangland of contemporary New York. Typical of this pragmatic approach is Sollozzo's comment to Hagen after the attempt on the Don's life: "I don't like violence, Tom. I'm a businessman. Blood is a big expense."

Michael's renunciation of religion and the Family, those two bastions of Sicilian life, symbolize his Luciferian fall. Both betrayals are illustrated in cinematic language that has become associated with Coppola's craft and vision. Michael continues to pay lip-service to the traditional ideals while others, like some ominous symphonic bass line, carry out his scheme of vengeance.

A prolonged coda to *The Godfather* describes the baptism of Connie's son (played by Coppola's infant daughter, Sofia), intercut with the Corleone "soldiers" gunning down the enemies of the Family. As the priest, catechizing Michael (now a Godfather in more than one sense) demands, "Do you renounce Satan?" so the slaughter begins. The editing takes up a heavy, inexorable rhythm, like the tolling of bells. The massacre both chimes with, and defiles, the lofty operations and minute details of the religious ceremonial. All his foes—Moe Greene, Barzini, Philip Tattaglia, Stracci, and Cuneo—are eliminated with clinical precision. Michael's adroitly engineered plot is the equivalent of blasphemy.

After the baptism, the *caporegime* Tessio and then Carlo are isolated and summarily executed for their treason. Michael's rejection of the Family concept begins at this juncture, when he orders the murder of Carlo without having the courage to admit his intention to the doomed man's face. In the very next scene, contractors start moving the Family possessions out of the Long Beach mall. Michael intends to establish a new organization in Las Vegas; the Corleone stronghold on the East Coast is being abandoned, along with the standards that Don Corleone had maintained (in his final conversation with Michael, the Don has remarked, "I worked my whole life, I don't apologize, to take care of my Family").

In the midst of this house-moving, Connie arrives in hysterics. She bursts into Michael's study and accuses him of ordering the murder of Carlo. Kay looks on transfixed, and when Connie has been ushered out of the room, she asks Michael softly and with great trepidation: "Is it true?"

"Don't ask me about my business!" snaps her husband with increasing harshness. Then, relenting, he permits her to put the question one more time. "Is it true?" she asks. "No," he replies quietly, staring at her with neither shame nor anger. In a brilliant touch, Coppola shows Michael embracing Kay in the wake of this monstrous denial. The intimacy of the moment, and the overtones of Family loyalty implied in other similar embraces throughout the film, only aggravates the appalling callousness of Michael's attitude.

Kay walks to the kitchen to make drinks. Turning, she sees the *caporegimes* surrounding Michael and offering their homage. Clemenza kisses Michael's hand and murmurs, "Don Corleone." The rites of passage are over, and Kay—Michael's last tie with the reasoned, sensitive world—is excluded from the inner sanctum. Slowly, inexorably, the door is closed like some dark curtain across her anxious face. *The Godfather* is at an end.

Coppola says that even before *The Godfather* he had always been interested in making a film about a father and a son at the same age—"in the father you'd see the potential of the son, and in the son the influence of the father." In the TV version (released in 1977), the similarities between Michael and his father as the young Don Vito are more pronounced. Both men, for example, win their spurs by destroying an arch foe of the Family. The manner of execution is almost identical: bold, unaided, and with a gun pointed unequivocally at the victim. On the mercantile side, both Michael and Don Vito look to the future for their prosperity—olive oil in the early years of the century, narcotics in the postwar era.

At every step Michael, like the young Don Vito, is forced to improvise in order to survive. Coppola places him in lonely, vulnerable situations, like the hospital where he visits his father, only to find the place deserted. The guards have mysteriously vanished. The Don lies helpless in an unprotected room, and there is only one nurse on duty. Michael's prompt assessment of the danger enables him to move the bed before any of Sollozzo's hoods can arrive to finish the job they failed to achieve on the streets of Manhattan a few hours earlier. Standing watch on the steps of the hospital with the shy young family baker as an unexpected ally, Michael has to feign strength and menace as the gunmen gaze up at him from the depths of a cruising sedan.

Soon afterwards, Michael decides to murder Sollozzo. The Family counsels against such a move. Besides, to gun down the police captain who will be with Sollozzo at the time seems certain to invoke the wrath not only of cops and politicians but also of the other New York Mafia families. So, just as his father's fearless attack on Don Fanucci a generation earlier had stunned his friends, so "little Mikey's" courage in going to the rendezvous with Sollozzo assures him of lifelong respect from Family and acolytes alike.

Coppola's sensitivity and inventiveness emerge from his filming of this assassination in the Bronx. Michael has been instructed to go to the john, find the gun that Clemenza's people will have taped to the toilet tank, and then "come out firing." Instead, he decides to delay for a moment. He returns to the table, and the camera closes in on his nervous face and roving eyes, while offscreen the blend of a subway train's rumbling and screeching below the restaurant, and Sollozzo's urgent patter of Sicilian, serves to fuel the charge of fury and resolve in Michael. So, when suddenly he does rise to his feet, shooting first Sollozzo and then McCluskey, we are as startled by the timing as he himself must be.

The Godfather acknowledges a debt to the classic gangster movies of the 1930s, with an elaborate montage of newspaper headlines rotating and gliding over images of the Corleone Family at war with its rivals (George Lucas helped Coppola make this sequence, which has an effect similar to a cadenza in a concerto). But in the action passages, Coppola opts for a vicious portrayal of violence that makes the original *Scarface* and *Public Enemy* look tame by comparison. Color, of course, and the dramatic improvement in special effects over the years, contribute to the visceral impact of scenes like the strangulation of Corleone strongman Luca Brasi, the slaughter of Sonny at the tollbooths, and Woltz's horrified discovery of his stallion's severed head in his bed. By creating a sense of impending doom, Coppola sucks his audience, as well as his screen victims, into a trap. If there is any manifestly obscene aspect of *The Godfather*, it is this feeling of complicity in the act of violence.

At a basic level, the appalling abundance of blood, combined with the impression of relentless physical power sustaining each outrage, undermines our defenses as viewers. While Luca Brasi struggles in vain against the silk noose flung around his neck, Coppola's camera gazes at his protruding eyes like some mesmerized onlooker. The absence of music, and the studied realism of the soundtrack (glasses crashing to the floor, Brasi's hoarse, animal groaning) reinforce the vicious shock of the murder. Coppola deals with the execution of Carlo Rizzi in similar fashion, much later in the film. From a set-up a few feet in front of the car windshield, we watch Carlo's feet thrashing against, and then smashing through, the glass, as he too is strangled.

Such moments register the fact behind the diverting phraseology employed by the Mafia—"I'll make him an offer he can't refuse," or "Mr. Corleone is a man who likes to hear bad news immediately." They also act as counterpoint to the cozy, family image of the New York mafiosi.

The violence in Sicily (the explosion that kills Apollonia, or the knifing of Don Ciccio in *Part II*) appears less repellent than its equivalent in New York, because it is tinged with a remote, operatic quality that diminishes the sense of physical violation. Yet one of Coppola's aims is surely to demonstrate how the Corleones' Sicilian origins still govern their American way of life. What in more sophisticated societies is identified as guilt, surfaces in the Mafia mind as vengeance. The cryptic, foreboding tone of such Sicilian messages as "Luca Brasi sleeps with the fishes," and Sonny's exasperated yearning for a Sicilian *consigliori*, point to a kind of folk reliance on the ancestral pattern of life—and death.

Behind the closely guarded gates of the Corleone mall in Long Beach, the ritual of Sicilian life is upheld to the last detail. The wedding of Connie and Carlo in the sunlit garden will have its counterpart in the Sicilian betrothal of Michael and Apollonia, and—in *Part II*—the alfresco celebration of Anthony's first communion at Lake Tahoe.

In one of the film's most engaging scenes, Clemenza instructs Michael in the niceties of cooking a stew for the entire Family, just as Coppola himself loves to prepare a meal in the kitchen. There is a sense of a recipe being handed down from generation to generation, and of the sublimation of self to some code of togetherness and Family. The stew becomes a potion, the mixing of which is every bit as important as the technique of wielding a gun or a knife. At the same time such passages in the film build a mood of ethnic identification, which explains to some extent the great public success of *The Godfather* in the United States. (In the original screenplay, this scene included the description: "Clemenza browns some sausage." Puzo made a sly note in the margin—"Clemenza *fries* some sausage—gangsters don't brown!")

The Godfather gives a romantic picture of gangster life. Francesco Rosi goes to the other extreme in *Salvatore Giuliano*, with its quasi-documentary unraveling of the Mafia's activities in Sicily. According to undercover agents, New York mobsters like to watch videocassettes of *The Godfather* films; one reputedly asked the waiter at his favorite restaurant to feed the jukebox with small change so he could listen to Rota's theme music.

Don Corleone's fear of drug traffic was justified. Art was vindicated by life in the spring of 1986, when Salvatore Catalano, Gaetano Badalamenti. and some twenty others were arraigned in New York and charged with importing $1.6 billion worth of heroin. The authorities had nailed their quarry thanks to evidence from Tommaso Buscetta, an informant worthy to rank alongside Pentangeli in *The Godfather Part II*. But the main families—Genovese, Gambino, Lucchese, Bonanno, and Colombo—continue to exert a powerful hold over the economic life of the city.

Betrayal, and the fear of betrayal, commands Mafia life in fact and fiction. The closer the bond between traitor and victim, the more cathartic the act of betrayal becomes. Tessio, about to be executed for fingering Michael to the rival family boss Don Barzini, gravely asks Tom Hagen if he can't get him "off the hook—for old times' sake."

"Can't do it, Solly," replies Hagen, his eyes averted in embarrassment. In such a moment Tessio, despite his treachery, appears human and sympathetic.

The most compelling revelation of disloyalty, though, concerns Fredo. Throughout *The Godfather*, Fredo is treated with thinly disguised condescension by Michael. In *Part II*, when Michael asks Fredo why he has betrayed him, the response comes in an explosion of impotent fury: "I was your older brother, Mikey, and I was stepped over!" Yet as Michele Pantaleone, author of *The Mafia and Politics*, has confirmed, "The recognized chief of the family is its most authoritative member, even if, as sometimes happens, he is the youngest."

Michael's decision to have Fredo killed for his act of weakness finally alienates him from the viewer in *Part II*. It bears the hateful stigma of fratricide, while Fredo's own lapse seems almost excusable, given the nature of Michael's evil empire.

Like all the best screen adaptations, *The Godfather* remains faithful to the spirit of the original novel. But Coppola and Puzo managed to agree on an audacious approach to the book. Many of what Coppola had dismissed as the "sleazy" elements in *The Godfather* were excised. "I can't do this as a Harold Robbins type of movie," Fred Roos reported him as protesting. The entire segment describing Johnny Fontane's predicament in Hollywood, for example, has gone as well as the disagreeable implication that Jack Woltz spends his free time screwing extremely young girls. Some changes, however grisly, are inspired. Take, for instance, the terrifying scene in Woltz's bedroom when he discovers that his beloved stallion has been slaughtered. In the book, he awakes to find the horse's head lying *on his bed*. Visually, Coppola's solution, with Woltz slowly and with mounting terror sweeping aside the bedclothes to reveal the head *in the depths of the bed itself*, is a masterstroke, prolonging the suspense and endowing the violation with a loathsome intimacy that utterly destroys the producer's self-confidence.

A sequence that required the script-doctor talents of Bob Towne showed Michael announcing that he will kill McCluskey. Coppola had put the declaration at the start, followed by the newspaper story and other ways of justifying the murder. Towne simply reversed the order, so that Michael's pronouncement has a more dramatic effect.

The pressures of producing a fast-moving film can, however, result in the blurring of certain nice details. Mario Puzo spends a paragraph on Clemenza's love of cleaning and polishing his Cadillac. But only the sharpest of viewers will notice the film's fleeting shot of the *caporegime* giving his car an affectionate wipe before driving off to gun down some of Michael's enemies during the brilliant cross-cutting between the baptism and the young Godfather's settling of accounts.

The most serious and intractable problem in the screenplay concerns Tom Hagen. In the novel, Puzo paints in his character in a series of beautifully modulated passages, pinning down the subtle inflections of his relationship, as a German-Irish orphan, with the close-knit Corleones. In the movie, though, his role as *consigliori* to the Family is uncertain from the very start. Michael tells Kay at the wedding that Tom will probably be given the post, yet in parallel sequences involving Hagen and the Don it is clear that Tom already enjoys a position of importance commensurate with that of *consigliori*. Until *Mario Puzo's The Godfather —The Complete Novel for Television* appeared, no mention was made of Tom's predecessor, Genco Abbandando, who in the novel lies dying of cancer and is regarded as the Don's childhood friend.

Later, when Michael returns from Sicily to take control of the Family's affairs, he dismisses Tom for no cogent reason, whereas in the novel we know that Michael is jealous of Hagen's closeness to Sonny, and this provides motivation for his downgrading of the *consigliori*. Next, Tom is seated beside Michael at the Don's funeral, and dares to damn both Tessio and Clemenza to his boss, suggesting him still to be every inch the relaxed confidant he was at the outset of the movie. No doubt Michael's rejection of his *consigliori* is intended to assert his new power and independence, but the act would carry more weight and resonance if Tom Hagen were to vanish from the film at that juncture. The pity is that Robert Duvall's portrayal of Hagen is second to none in its acute observation, economy of gesture, and communication of warmth and loyalty.

*   *   *

For all the rumors of tension and resentment on the set of *The Godfather*, the completed film is a tribute to Hollywood teamwork at its best. In each of the key departments, there is accomplishment of the highest order: the acting, with even the smallest speaking role presented convincingly; the cinematography of Gordon Willis, imbuing the images with a crisp, sunburned glow and richness of texture (dismissed by some naïve critics as poor lab work when Willis had striven for "an almost Kodachromey, 1942 kind of feel"); the production design of Dean Tavoularis, shaping the intimate interiors of the Family home; the costumes by Anna Hill Johnstone, which so dictate both mood and character (for example, the moment when Michael alights from his limousine to meet Kay outside her school, with his pitch-black coat and fedora giving off diabolical vibrations); and not least the music of Nino Rota, whose wistful lament for trumpet that heralds the film recalls his score for *Rocco and His Brothers* and reinforces the Italian atmosphere. Coppola had urged Rota to compose a central waltz, for he envisaged the film as a circular dance, generation meeting generation.

From its opening day, *The Godfather* was a triumph at the box-office. For the first few weeks it was attracting revenue at the rate of $1 million a day. There were the ritual accolades such as a cover story in *Time* ("an Italian-American *Gone with the Wind*") and—a year later—Academy Awards for Best Film, Best Actor (Brando), and Best Screenplay, even if *Cabaret* dominated Oscar night. The American critics were not quite unanimous in their praise, with Dwight Macdonald the most distinguished of the dissenters. Judith Crist thought the film essentially immoral. Typical of the excitement generated among reviewers, however, was Charles Champlin's judgment in the *Los Angeles Times* that *The Godfather* was "probably the fastest three-hour movie in history," while Vincent Canby, in the most influential of all papers, the *New York Times*, termed the film "one of the most brutal and moving chronicles of American life ever designed within the limits of popular entertainment."

The money generated by *The Godfather* was colossal. Before the end of 1972 it had become the all-time box-office champion, with estimated worldwide grosses of $150 million. Louis Malle "directed" a French-dubbed version that cost Paramount more than $150,000. On September 6, 1972, Paramount president Frank Yablans could announce that "Everyone owning a piece of *The Godfather* is a millionaire already." Al Ruddy, the producer, possessed 7.5 percent, Coppola 6 percent and Brando 1.5 percent (with a ceiling of $1.5 million).

The momentum continued through the 1970s. In July 1974, Paramount agreed to let NBC screen *The Godfather* on television, over two nights, for $10 million. A year later the same network paid $15 million for TV rights to the omnibus edition of both parts of *The Godfather* (see Chapter Six). Statisticians, analyzing the box-office allure of the film just thirty months after its premiere, estimated that 132 million spectators had paid some $330 million to see Coppola's masterpiece.

In the intervening years, other champions have come and gone, including *Jaws* and *Star Wars*. Never before, and never since, however, has the public flocked in such numbers to such a profound and richly layered film. Coppola makes no concessions to folksiness in *The Godfather*, and folksiness (often allied to an appeal to childhood fantasy) is the common denominator of such all-time money-winners as *Gone with the Wind*, *The Sound of Music*, and *E.T.*

Francis himself was stunned and delighted at the financial results of the film. "My dream of dreams was that *The Godfather* would net me one million dollars, and that, conservatively invested, could bring around fifty thousand dollars and with that coming in I could spend all my time writing my own stuff, without the interruption of having to deal with the studios."

During the final stages of editing the picture, he was despondent about its prospects. "I was sure people would feel I had taken this exciting, bestseller novel and transformed it into a dark, ponderous, boring movie with a lot of actors who were known to be my personal friends (excluding Brando)." He and Al Ruddy were willing to trim the 2 hours 55 minutes final cut to 2 hours 25 minutes in the face of studio pressure. But, to his eternal credit, Bob Evans admitted that the film played better, and faster, in its longer version.

Some months earlier, Evans had asked Coppola to write a screenplay from Scott Fitzgerald's novel, *The Great Gatsby*. Evans wanted Ali McGraw to play Daisy Buchanan on screen, and had grown frustrated at Truman Capote's failure to deliver a script. Then, anxious to escape the ballyhoo surrounding the premiere of *The Godfather*, Francis flew to Paris and holed up in the Oscar Wilde room at L'Hôtel, finishing the screenplay in three weeks. He stressed the visual aspects of the book and even borrowed lines from other stories by Fitzgerald. Inevitably, only certain elements in Jack Clayton's 1974 film of *Gatsby* corresponded to the Coppola screenplay.

Quite apart from this, Francis had been frantically busy, staging *The Visit of the Old Lady* at the San Francisco Opera as well as producing *Private Lives* for the American Conservatory Theater. He still could not believe that *The Godfather* would be such a smash hit. In fact, he never watched the movie once with a paying audience. "I can remember being in New York with him," says Eleanor. "He was looking out the window at the lines around the block for *The Godfather*, and then sitting in front of his typewriter, frustrated by the problems of converting *Gatsby* into a screenplay. So he by no means just basked in the glory."

Picking Up
The Conversation

Even as *The Godfather* opened, Coppola was dabbling again in his earlier hobby, the theater. His revival of Noël Coward's *Private Lives* opened on February 22, 1972, at the Geary in San Francisco, under the banner of the American Conservatory Theater (ACT). Paul Shrenar, who starred in the production, commented: "Francis turned the set upside down because he didn't want the usual clichéd production. I was very petulant about it until one day he reminded me who was director in a few choice words." Shrenar liked the "blood and guts" of Coppola's approach. "He directed us very specifically to be real and human. He hung up a sign at the pass door to the stage. It said: 'Look at each other, listen to each other.' "

Although the French director Jean-Luc Godard suggested that Coppola should donate some of his *Godfather* profits to "collective filmmaking on the class struggle," there was never any doubt that Zoetrope's main objective would be to support entertainment movies made in and around the Bay Area. As money flowed into Coppola's coffers, so space was rented at the Samuel Goldwyn Studios in Los Angeles, with Fred Roos at the helm of what was named "Cinema 7."

George Lucas had recovered from the failure of *THX 1138*, and had been trying all over Hollywood to place his original idea for a film about young people growing up in Modesto, an inland town in northern California where Lucas himself spent his formative years. Universal had agreed to take on the project, entitled *American Graffiti*, on a tight budget of $750,000 (really tight, because that included the purchase of rights to umpteen songs of the early 1960s to be used in the movie). A line producer was required, to give the project credibility at the studio, and Lucas turned to Coppola in early 1972, right after the opening of *The Godfather*. Universal, eager to secure an option on Francis's next picture, offered 10 percent of the profits to Zoetrope, in addition to the 40 percent already promised to Lucas. Francis agreed, if reluctantly. He did not realize that his share, even when reduced by agreed payouts to Gary Kurtz (the co-producer) and Haskell Wexler, who came aboard as "visual consultant" to Lucas during filming, would amount to around $3 million.

Some felt that Coppola's cut was too remunerative. Francis resents such an implication. "I had the job in Hollywood, I had the credits, I had the money, I had the houses. All of my young associates were broke, and I took them all with me and used everything I had to fund their, and my, projects."

George Lucas worked diligently, with a cast of unknowns. Many of them would achieve lasting status in the industry on the strength of this spirited launch—Richard Dreyfuss, Ron Howard (who turned to directing), Cindy Williams, Teri Garr, Harrison Ford, Candy Clark, and Charlie Martin Smith (an actor Coppola used to kid for resembling him when young). Ten years later Coppola himself would follow the same formula, on *The Outsiders*, and introduce stars of the future like Matt Dillon, Tom Cruise, and Ralph Macchio.

The studio, however, did not believe in *American Graffiti* at first. Following a preview at the Northpoint Theater in San Francisco on January 28, 1973, an altercation broke out between Coppola and Universal executive Ned Tanen. Audience reaction had been ecstatic, but Tanen wanted cuts in the film. "You should get down on your knees and thank this kid for what he's done for you!" protested Coppola. As usual, Lucas remained modestly in the background of this skirmish, but would later appreciate the fact that Francis had kept the trimmings down to a mere four and a half minutes or so.

American Graffiti opened on August 1, 1973, and struck an immediate chord with the crucial sixteen to twenty-four age group. It also appealed to those in their late twenties, who could fill in their own responses to the question, "Where were you in '62?" and found a kind of instant nostalgia in Lucas's evocation of the early 1960s and the small-town ritual of Saturday night cruising, local radio stations, impromptu auto races, and petting after dark.

At the box-office, *American Graffiti* showed remarkable stamina, outpacing even *Easy Rider*'s figures, and gave George Lucas the track record he needed to realize his dream of *Star Wars*.

*   *   *

The Conversation threads its surreptitious way through almost seven years of Francis Coppola's career. Even when it at last emerged, in March 1974, it seemed bent on sneaking away from the theaters as quickly as possible.

No more intense or impassioned film exists in the Coppola canon. Like a sinner hurrying home, head down, from the confessional, *The Conversation* radiates an abashed, self-effacing quality. Like Harry Caul, the central character, Coppola is a Catholic disturbed by the collision during the 1970s between a commitment to faith and an obsession with the new technology.

"It started" recalls Coppola, "with a conversation with [director] Irvin Kershner. We were talking about eavesdropping and bugging, and he told me about some long-distance microphones that could overhear what people were saying." Kershner then sent Coppola an article about a sound wizard called Hal Lipset who lived—and still lives—in San Francisco. Lipset was later summoned east to analyze the notorious eighteen-minute "blank" section of White House tape during the Watergate investigations.

So, in 1967, Coppola developed the idea of a film about a sound surveillance expert, based to some extent on Lipset (who is mentioned in the movie and also listed in the credits as a consultant), and inspired by Antonioni's *Blow-Up*. He had been impressed by the novels of Herman Hesse, and in homage to *Steppenwolf* named his main personality Harry. The last name, Caul, was a subtle reference conjured from a secretary's typing error—Caul for Call. Francis seized on the slip and retained the Caul spelling. In the finished film, Gene Hackman is seen wearing a plastic see-through raincoat, and frequently hides behind transparent or semi-transparent glass, suggesting the amniotic shroud that sometimes shields a child's head at birth.

The intention was for *The Conversation* to be made immediately after *The Rain People*. But although Gene Hackman agreed to take the lead, Francis was unable to begin photography on the film until he had behind him the insurance of a commercial hit—*The Godfather*. Meanwhile, Watergate had erupted and blessed *The Conversation* with a sinister relevance to its time.

Along with Peter Bogdanovich and William Friedkin, two other whiz-kids of the moment, Coppola formed "The Directors' Company." Each man, it was hoped, would direct two films for the company, and produce a third by one of the others. All would be released through Paramount. *The Conversation*, it transpired, was the only movie apart from *Paper Moon* to appear under the banner of the Directors' Company.

The production was structured on an intimate scale and limited to a modest budget (although its $2 million ceiling was far in excess of the $700,000 to $800,000 Coppola and Lucas had spent on *American Graffiti* earlier that year). Progress was never smooth. After only a week of shooting, in early December 1972, a sharp difference of opinion arose between Haskell Wexler, whose cinematographic brilliance had already won him an Academy Award, and Dean Tavoularis, Coppola's production designer. Wexler lost the argument; Coppola supported Tavoularis, and had to call on Bill Butler, who had served him loyally on *The Rain People*, to step in at short notice as cameraman. Tavoularis brought his customary vigilance to bear on every aspect of the production. One of the final scenes involved the dismantling of Harry Caul's apartment. "It was a real location," says Tavoularis, "and I remember the location people got into some trouble when Hackman started ripping up the floorboards. We had obtained two or three types of wallpaper, like from the 1920s and the 1940s, and placed one on top of the other, preparing layers of age, as it were, for him to peel away and make it look more authentic."

Editing took almost a year to complete. Walter Murch, who may fairly be regarded as cocreator of *The Conversation*, came into his own in 1973, when Francis told him, "Listen, I'm going to go straight from shooting *The Conversation* to preproduction on *Godfather II*. I won't be around, the way a normal director is around. You take the mix, do what you think right, and then show it to me when you think it's ready to be shown." In fact, Coppola contrived to spend some time over weekends on the editing process, but nothing can detract from the contribution of Murch, who marshals sound with the infinite subtlety of a major composer.

The Conversation looked like a winner prior to its opening. But although it won the supreme accolade of the movie intelligentsia—the Palme d'Or at Cannes—it failed to lure a sizeable audience to the theaters either in the United States or abroad, despite a promising $30,719 in its first week at the Coronet in New York City, in April 1974. The film's star was Gene Hackman, but no longer the crackerjack cop of *The French Connection*. Its director was Francis Ford Coppola, but not the man whose name was synonymous with gun-toting gangsterism in *The Godfather*. Its theme related to Watergate, but the public was offered the unsavory aspects of the bugging, not the glamorous political convulsions chronicled by Bernstein and Woodward.

Still, *The Conversation* was named Best Film of 1974 by the National Board of Review, and *Variety* waxed enthusiastic: "This is Coppola's most complete, most assured, and most rewarding film to date, and the years it took him to bring to the screen should be considered well worth the persistence." Epithets like "brilliantly original" (*Newsweek*), "enormous enterprise" (*Time*), and "fastidiously detailed" (*New York Times*) were invariably qualified by remarks about the slow tempo of the movie and comparisons with *Blow-Up*.

*   *   *

Coppola borrowed a mood as well as a name from *Steppenwolf*. There are several links with Herman Hesse's consuming study of a lonely man in search both of immortality and his long-lost youth. "For he was not a sociable man," says the narrator about Harry Haller in *Steppenwolf*, "indeed, he was unsociable to a degree I had never before experienced in anybody." The same description suits Harry Caul. The strategy of Hesse and Coppola is identical in its aim of extrapolating a commentary on contemporary society from the case history of one person. "Haller's sickness of the soul . . . is not the eccentricity of a single individual, but the sickness of the times themselves."

Both Haller and Caul suffer a tormented conscience on account of their religious persuasion—Protestant and Catholic respectively. Like his namesake, Harry in *The Conversation* despairs of finding what Hesse calls "the track of the divine" unless it be in the music that from time to time brings harmony to his existence. Like him, too, Harry Caul needs love and yet displays his disagreeable side to those whose affection he values most. Both men evince a world-weariness that in *The Conversation* stands in sharp contrast to the energy of modern American society. Harry's reaction to sex and violence is essentially passive, save for his one pathetic attempt to struggle with the guards at the Embarcadero Center.

The form of *The Conversation* corresponds to the slow, sly methods of professional surveillance experts. Coppola unravels the character of Harry Caul in sync with his unraveling of the mysterious conversation on Union Square, almost like two tapes running back-to-back on a cassette player. The dialogue during the last five reels of the picture amounts to no more than a few sentences and verbal expletives, until it shrivels away altogether, leaving the viewer free to concentrate on the soundtrack as much as the imagery.

The celebrated opening shot sets up the delicate equilibrium between sight (the camera's point of view, the audience's image) and sound (the wow and flutter of words picked up by Harry in the course of his work). We seem to descend at a barely perceptible speed *into* San Francisco's Union Square, with its bustle of lunchbreak activity on a sunlit winter's day. Like all great directors, Coppola is suspicious of the zoom lens in all but exceptional circumstances—the first shot in *The Godfather*, for instance. The motorized zoom serves him well again here, its slow, even, creeping pace pulling us into a shared conspiracy as surely as the eliding zooms that lead to the hotel room at the beginning of *Psycho*.

Even more than Hitchcock, Antonioni comes to mind as the film unwinds. Like the Italian director, Coppola lets his characters leave the frame before following them with the camera, shaping an awareness of psychological space—as well as tension—beyond the immediate image. The noise of the city is hushed; Harry travels by bus and subway without emerging from what Victorian novelists used to call "a brown study," at one remove from his surroundings. This fundamentally European pace may explain why *The Conversation* earned more admiration outside the United States (although it was nominated for Best Picture of 1974, and Coppola received a Best Original Screenplay nomination).

As the camera completes its descent and tracks Hackman's Harry Caul across Union Square, the changing focal lengths supply a visual equivalent to the tantalizing ebb and flow of sound on magnetic tape. High up on one of the buildings overlooking the quad, a technician maneuvers a three-stage directional mike, lining up the cross-hairs of his sight on the heads of a young couple strolling around the Square. It is a marvellous moment, communicating the concept of the mike as a weapon, threatening as well as recording its subjects.

Harry works from an innocuous-looking van parked on one of the streets bordering Union Square. When his assistant, Stan, starts clicking off snapshots of girls' faces through the van's two-way mirror windows, Harry is riled. There is a puritanical tinge to his character reminiscent of Michael in *The Godfather* when, for example, he dismisses the showgirls from his suite in Las Vegas (coincidentally, John Cazale plays the fallguy in both scenes).

Despite his sensitivity in this area, Harry appears to be so absorbed in the mechanics of his craft that he cannot hear the forest for the trees. "I don't care what they're talking about," he tells Stan, "all I want's a nice fat recording." Gene Hackman, when asked to characterize Harry Caul, replied: "Uptight, right-wing eccentric, secretive, but with no axes to grind."

Harry's vulnerable nature and spiritual hypochondria emerge from his reaction to situations and people around him. He comes home to his apartment and negotiates all three locks with the painstaking gravity of a native New Yorker rather than a Californian. Inside, he finds that the building's super has left a bottle of wine as a birthday treat. Harry is incensed, more at the realization that someone has penetrated his defenses than at the awareness of passing years—although that too irks him, and he tells his mistress later in the day that he is forty-two, not forty-four as stated on the super's greeting card.

The archetypal loner, Harry toils along to his workshop, where in the corner of a gaunt, echoing warehouse he can analyze the tapes on state-of-the-art equipment. First he synchronizes all three tapes of the Union Square conversation. He pins up some eight-by-ten glossies of the young couple, but the living images of their faces and movements dwell in his mind's eye. Stan watches and fiddles around.

Nothing is going right for Harry. The tapes at this stage yield little of value. When he calls in to fix a time to deliver the materials, Harry is informed that "the Director" cannot speak to him and that he should simply bring the tapes the next day. "Is that payment in full?" asks Harry, plaintively. "Whatever was arranged," comes the impassive reply. And when he takes the bus to see his mistress, Amy, he finds her boring and inquisitive.

Amy is the type who wears white socks in bed and nibbles cookies incessantly. Harry absorbs her inane banter for a while, then lets her head flop back against the bedboard. Even though he obviously likes her, he remains defensive, going so far as to deny the existence of a phone in his own apartment. Amy sings and hums to herself in a manner uncannily reminiscent of the woman whose conversation Harry's team has been taping. She and Harry pet for a time, until he breaks off without warning, accuses her of asking too many questions, and quits—for good.

In the blue ascetic decor of a BART subway train, Harry is haunted by a picture of the couple kissing in Union Square. A strain of jealousy infiltrates his professional curiosity, applied to a growing commitment to these characters he has never met.

Wrapped in his plastic raincoat, like a cocoon of loneliness and anonymity, Harry visits his employers in a huge office building in the Embarcadero Center. On an impulse, he rejects the $15,000 proffered him in exchange for the tapes. He wrests the package of spools from the Director's assistant and marches out of the offices. Coppola and Murch emphasize the suppressed roar of the elevator as Harry descends from the executive suite, having glimpsed first the man and then, as she enters the elevator, the woman from the Square: his "subjects." Combined with the intimidating noise is the plangent piano accompaniment of David Shire, which distills the melancholy in the style of Erik Satie. Shire's theme grows in volume and anxiety as the film proceeds.

Harry's dilemma, worthy of a Graham Greene loser, concerns the tapes. If he continues to meddle with them, he risks chastisement from his superiors. If he delivers them without further question, he may be turning a blind eye to murder. And the presence of the young couple in the Director's building disconcerts Harry even more.

Back in the workshop, he surrenders to the seductive hiss and burble, getting increasingly excited as he disentangles voices from the master tape. He brushes aside the protests of his assistant, Stan, and chides him for profanity and sloppy work. Stan leaves in a huff, and Harry applies himself again to the challenge of the tapes. The young couple's discussion includes a mysterious rendezvous—Sunday, 3 P.M., Jack Tar Hotel, Room 773. Gradually Harry isolates the most sinister line of dialogue: "He'd kill us if he got the chance." Shocked, he snaps off the switches, and goes to confession—for the first time in three months, so he tells the priest, and in need more of spiritual nourishment, one suspects, than forgiveness. Harry may be a slave to his technology, but he retains more than a vestige of human anxiety. This collision of interests, or duties, fascinates Coppola in his work as a storyteller on film, as well as being reflected in his private life.

Just as strong as the moral confusion that engulfs Harry is the craving to enter another world. The man and the woman in Union Square become Harry and Amy, at least to a foiled romantic like Caul, as he sits in the warehouse and dreams up images to match the voices on his tapes. The voyeur yearns to share the lives of those he observes. By the end of the movie, Harry Caul has identified with the young couple to such a vicarious degree that he regards himself as responsible for the murder at the hotel. And in sync with that, he finds that he has become the object of surveillance himself. Harry has passed through the invisible veil dividing nightmare from the everyday rituals of a prosaic world.

*

The film's central phase highlights the clash between Coppola's two cultures, Europe on the one hand, the brash New World on the other. They are personified in Harry and his rival wiretapper, Bernie Moran. When the two men are introduced to each other at a Bay Area convention, Moran comes on strong with the glitziness that stems from basic insecurity. He lavishes praise on Harry's legendary skills, and presents an item of his own equipment with all the glib naiveté of a detergent commercial. Harry, although embarrassed as "Europeans" often are by this aspect of American business life, does not yet recognize this dangerous streak in Moran. He is more alarmed by his loss of contact with Amy. Her phone is disconnected and, mysteriously, information has no listing for her. Harry also learns that the Director's assistant has been trailing him through the convention hall, passing him the message that he should deliver the tapes at 1 P.M. The following Sunday—to the Director in person. "Tell him I'll think about it," snarls Harry.

By now, for everyone involved, the film has become a search. Each character seems to be spying on another, observing and then betraying. This motif surfaces sometimes in visual ways (the TV monitor that shows Harry how the Director's assistant is watching him from a distance), and sometimes through verbal means (the recording of Harry's anxieties that Moran manages to make by planting a pen-mike in his coat pocket).

Harry's own quest for the gist of "the conversation" is so fixated that he allows Moran and his "part-time nun" of a secretary, Meredith, to join an impromptu party back in his warehouse. Moran's tone now becomes abrasive. He needles Harry, calling him "lonely and anonymous," toasting him as "the best bugger on the West Coast," and then opening old sores in Harry's past—a career in New York City that comes as news even to Stan, and a murder scandal involving the president and the attorney general's office in 1968. Like a ferret, Moran pursues Harry into the dark burrow of his subconscious. And Harry, with nowhere to hide, begins to unwind and think aloud, seeing in Meredith a surrogate confessor.

They drift away from the others, into the barren shadows of the warehouse. Inarticulate as always, Harry needs to be coaxed into voicing his concerns about Amy. His *sotto voce* tones are blurred and overlaid by the persistent piano variations on the soundtrack. He mumbles a hypothetical query to Meredith, asking if she would go back to a man who had "kept himself" from her, even if he had loved her. "How would I know if he loved me?" responds Meredith. Harry, according to Coppola, is "an anonymous person who observes and eavesdrops on the lives of other people, and he yearns to be personal with them, and tell them something of who he is, rather than just being the cipher."

When Harry discovers that Moran has been bugging these intimate moments, he loses his temper and tells him to leave. The party breaks up, but Meredith stays, intent on seduction. She manages to pry Harry away from his beloved recordings, but the tape continues running as the girl undresses and Harry lies back on his cot. In the most poignant passage in the entire movie, Coppola overlaps the two realities, as though dubbing them into a single new recording. We hear the young woman in Union Square referring to a bum on a park bench, "He was once somebody's baby boy . . . and he had a mother and a father who loved him," while the camera gazes horizontally at Harry as he lies defenseless on the bed, lulled into a vanished childhood.

And Coppola, rejecting the anticipated sex scene not from modesty so much as from an awareness that Harry's need for a mother figure is more significant, now conjures up a dream for his frail and inhibited protagonist. Harry is on a road in a park. He sees the woman from the tapes, and calls urgently to her. Smoke swirls around them obscuring faces and issues, as it does so often in *Apocalypse Now*. Harry, almost shouting, gives vent to a monologue about his youth, which even to the smallest detail must be a memory of Francis's own childhood illness.

> I was very sick when I was a boy. I was paralyzed in my left leg. I couldn't walk for six months. One doctor said I'd probably never walk again. My mother used to lower me into a hot bath; it was therapy. One time the doorbell rang, and she went down to answer it. I started sliding down. I could feel the water, it started coming to my chin, to my nose, and when I woke up my body was all greasy from the holy oil she'd put on my body. I remember being disappointed I survived. When I was five, my father introduced me to a friend of his, and for no reason at all I hit him right in the stomach with all my strength. He died a year later.

Harry breaks off, and remembers the reason for his signaling to the woman in his dream. "He'll kill you if he gets the chance," he yells, but without much conviction.

The next dream is a *visual* version of Harry's misinterpretation of the line. "He'd kill us if he gets the chance." Harry sees himself entering a hotel room at the precise moment that a man—the "Director"—dashes forward to attack the woman from Union Square. Only when this scene is "replayed" at the end of *The Conversation* does its true significance as the component of a different crime become clear.

And then he awakes, to find Meredith gone and the tapes with her. Like the Knight confessing to Death in *The Seventh Seal*, he has been cheated as a reward for being too careless with his sincerity. Like that medieval romantic, too, Harry refuses to abandon his self-appointed mission, to protect the woman he has begun to adore in a surreptitious, vicarious way. His paranoia increases when he comes home, calls the Director's office and finds that "they" know his unlisted number; the phone, secreted in his desk drawer, rings insistently until he answers it. "We have the tapes," he is told. If he reports right away, his money is ready for collection.

Harry wants his $15,000, but his conscience is fast gaining the upper hand. As he enters the Director's suite he hears his master tape blurting out at high volume. The brunet from Union Square is featured in a large photo on the wall. Then, as Harry counts his cash at a desk, he catches sight of another photo, showing the woman with the Director himself. The realization that they may be married unnerves him.

"What will you do to her?" he asks the Director. No reply comes to relieve him. Harry repeats his question to the Director's assistant as he enters the elevator. "We'll see," says the man in the noncommittal tones of a surgeon.

Coppola's Steppenwolf now becomes a symbol of caring humanity in a hostile environment. Harry walks outside the huge, menacing structure of the Embarcadero Center, refusing to give up the struggle. He checks in at the hotel where the young couple have set their rendezvous. His plastic raincoat, along with the mesh curtains and frosted glass in the hotel room, emphasises the spiritual myopia that obscures Harry from the crime about to be committed. And even when he has bugged the adjacent room, overheard a violent quarrel, and witnessed a bloodstained hand pawing at the glass balcony partition, Harry can only shrink in terror from the truth. He snaps on the TV, with its garbled references to Nixon, pulls the curtains together to shut out the light, and coils up in the bed with his hands covering his ears. His anguish springs from a deep well of shame; such violence could and should have been prevented by him, Harry Caul. The woman is *his* victim.

He surfaces from what seems like a deep, nightmarish sleep. He picks the lock of Room 773, and concentrates on the bathroom. Like Hitchcock in the similar scene in *Psycho*, when Sam and Lila examine the shower tub where Marion has been murdered, Coppola presents the gleaming white sterility of the fixtures as almost a manifestation of a hideous secret. Harry flushes the toilet. Blood writhes and wells from the inside. Harry retreats a step or two, and watches aghast as the crimson water spills over the rim of the bowl. A towel, perhaps something worse, surges to the surface.

Harry's instinct for bringing the murderer to justice urges him back to the Director's office, where he is manhandled by plainclothes guards. His explosion of fury on the stairs provides Gene Hackman with just about the only opportunity to reveal his natural, volcanic personality. Throughout the rest of *The Conversation* he must restrain his energy.

Coming out of the Center, Harry glimpses the woman he assumes to have been murdered, sitting in the rear of a massive limousine, its number plate a sinister C1. Almost immediately the final bits of the jigsaw start tumbling into position: the Director, not the young couple, has become the victim; the screams of the woman in the hotel disguised the fact that her lover had asphyxiated and stabbed the Director—*her* husband; and the allusive sentence on the tape becomes, "He'd kill *us* if he got the chance."

The tape may have conceded its mystery, but Harry cannot escape the consequences of his inquisitiveness. An anonymous voice warns him over his private phone that he should not get involved. "We'll be listening to you." Knowing for certain now that he must be bugged, Harry subjects his apartment to a systematic scrutiny.

He checks lamps, curtains, pictures, phone, and even his cherished statuette of the Madonna. Nothing. He dismembers the place, ripping up floorboards, stripping the wallpaper. Still nothing. Harry saves just one possession—his saxophone. Perhaps he guesses that it contains the mike. If so, he makes a conscious decision to cling to his dreams and his hopes, to the soul that the instrument indeed represents.

Coppola records this reduction, this quintessence of paranoia, in one of his most perfectly modulated sequences. While Harry loses himself in a long, melancholy session on the sax, the camera swings from one side of the apartment to the other and back again in a hypnotic arc, as though appalled by the spectacle of a life's debris. Shire's piano refrain dances and undulates off-screen, dominating and at last melding with Harry's saxophone lament.

The mood is one of tolerance and devotion. Harry is absolved. Free of the cage enclosing his workshop. Free of the drab encumbrances of his apartment. Free to seek some private peace at the heart of the music. Like Paul Muni in the final shot of *I Am a Fugitive from a Chain Gang*, who hisses, "I steal! I steal!" before retreating into the shadows, Hackman's Harry has come to terms with the sordid price of his profession.

Back to Corleone

In the euphoria that followed the release of *The Godfather* in early 1972, Coppola was soon persuaded to sign with Paramount to make a sequel. By now, he knew his street value. He insisted that he both direct and produce the film, and also that he should be allowed to devote his immediate energies to *The Conversation*. Charles Bluhdorn accepted his terms of $1 million plus 13 percent of the studio's gross rental profits. Shooting would be delayed until October 1973.

"What I wanted to do was part two, literally designing the second half so that some day they could be played as a six-hour movie," Coppola said. "It's really not a sequel; it's very novelistic in its construction." Paramount was startled by the classic simplicity of the eventual title: *Mario Puzo's The Godfather Part II*. The device was almost immediately copied by other studios, with *The French Connection II* being the first in a long line of sequels that owe their names to Coppola's decision.

Coppola realized that he could never match the financial bonanza of *The Godfather*. He prepared the ground, quite consciously, for an altogether more complex production. He wanted to scotch the notion that "sequels are usually cheap imitations of their parent. Usually made by different people, in an attempt to squeeze more money. I thought it would be exciting if I could reverse that: make a film that was more ambitious, more beautiful . . . more advanced than the first."

He had the freedom he yearned for, yet without risking his own money. Paramount had at first set a limit to the length of *The Godfather* of 1 hour 45 minutes. Now, with the clout that springs from box-office victory,

Coppola could dictate the shape and duration of *Part II*. At 200 minutes, it would outlast even its predecessor. Coppola was also concerned to reject the idea that somehow he *endorsed* Michael's behavior. This time, he said, he "didn't want Michael or the Corleone family to be destroyed by another gang, or by the attorney general . . . I wanted him to be destroyed by forces inside of himself; the very forces that had created him." At the close of the movie Michael Corleone is, in Coppola's words, "very possibly the most powerful man in America. But he is a corpse."

This time, Coppola took charge of the screenplay, including only one passage from the original novel and part of another script by Mario Puzo. Coppola had written scenes involving singer Enrico Caruso in Hell's Kitchen, Italian laborers putting up the mosaics in Times Square, and scenes of people sipping anisette in a horse-drawn carriage, on the Brooklyn Bridge. But time and expense denied them a place in the production.

Not until 1977 did Coppola manage to have the entire *Godfather* saga projected as one seven-hour-plus work—and then only on television (see page 113). Ironically, he was embroiled in the shooting of *Apocalypse Now*, and most of the reediting for that historic NBC presentation was undertaken by Barry Malkin. But there is no doubt that, from the moment he resolved to make *Part II*, he saw the film as a continuation rather than merely a sequel.

Assembling his team required persuasion and some mending of fences. After the friction with Gordon Willis on *The Godfather*, Vittorio Storaro was approached to join the production as cinematographer. Storaro had won many admirers in Hollywood for his work on *Last Tango in Paris*, but he declined this new offer. "The first *Godfather* movie was fantastic, and I didn't think the sequel could be as good." So Willis was contacted once more, and agreed to take the assignment. He would use the same camera and lenses with which he had photographed the first *Godfather*. "It was somewhat dated equipment, but I wanted the same thing to maintain that consistency."

Barry Malkin, who had edited *The Rain People*, returned to the cutting room on *Part II*, and would work regularly in the future for Coppola. Dean Tavoularis continued to create the production design, and Nino Rota was retained as composer—although Carmine Coppola conducted the score and added touches of his own at certain stages of the film.

A formidable responsibility lay with Walter Murch during this period. Not only did he have to ensure that *The Conversation* would emerge as planned, but also supervise the sound design of *The Godfather Part II*. Francis insisted that the cars in the film should make the authentic sounds of vehicles of the late 1950s. Murch located an automobile museum in San Francisco, and recorded the appropriate models in all manner of situations. "Francis gave me a cassette of music from the end of that decade," recalls Murch, "that a devotee had assembled in New York, and so for a number of weeks I just listened, and thought of ways of fitting it into the background of the film."

The casting allowed little room for maneuvering. Audiences would expect the familiar faces from *The Godfather*: Al Pacino as Michael, Robert Duvall as Tom Hagen, John Cazale as Fredo, Diane Keaton as Kay, Talia Shire as Connie. Brando would have been too old to play the young Don Vito, although Coppola intimated that there was a place for him in the movie if he wished to participate. But Brando demanded more money than Paramount was prepared to pay and besides, Gulf & Western boss Charlie Bluhdorn was still smarting at the actor's refusal to accept his Academy Award for *The Godfather*. The only occasion when his presence is truly missed is in the dying moments of the film, when right after Pearl Harbor the Corleone family gathers around the table to celebrate the Don's birthday. Coppola solves the problem of his star's absence by keeping the Don tantalizingly off-screen. Even had he participated in this tableau, however, Brando might have disturbed the audience's belief in Robert De Niro as the embodiment of the Don in youth.

De Niro had forced his way to the front in *Mean Streets*, Martin Scorsese's gritty, impressionistic film about Italian life in New York. He moved with the relaxed yet watchful grace of a closet assassin, and it was exactly this quality Coppola needed. He cast the American as Vito, the founder of the Corleone dynasty in the New World. *The Godfather Part II* describes his struggles for survival and gradual rise to power, in rhyme with the insidious regime of his son, Michael Corleone, in the late 1950s and early 1960s.

Among new names in the cast, B. Kirby Jr., was an inspired choice as the young Clemenza, and Michael V. Gazzo as Pentangeli projected the right image of sly, self-obsessed fallibility associated with minor Mafia figures. Gazzo was a playwright of some distinction, and author of *A Hatful of Rain* among other stage successes.

Francis's most courageous appointment was that of Lee Strasberg as the Miami-based mobster, Hyman Roth. Strasberg, lionized though he was as the influential apostle of Stanislavsky's "Method" in the United States, had never acted before the cameras. It was a considerable risk, but Coppola's skill at relaxing actors and letting them perform according to their own idiom proved an unqualified success.

The gamble almost backfired when Strasberg, in his seventy-fourth year, fell sick while the unit was shooting the Havana sequences on location in the Dominican Republic. Francis promptly adjusted the screenplay so that Hyman Roth himself would be portrayed as an ailing man. Al Pacino was also ill for three weeks in Santo Domingo. The role imposed an enormous strain on him. As Coppola concedes, "He's the same man from beginning to end . . . very rarely having a big climactic scene where an actor can unload, like blowing the spittle out of the tube of a trombone."

Location scouting for Coppola's productions usually falls on the shoulders of two key men, Dean Tavoularis and Gray Frederickson. "Francis is ready to delegate the search for locations, but if they're not right— well, you certainly hear about it," says Frederickson. Filming in the Dominican Republic made sense because Gulf & Western owned a lot of property on the island.

The Sicilian sequences were shot in and around Taormina, but the most unusual and most successful location was in Trieste, where the lofty old fish market served as an uncannily accurate replica of the Ellis Island building where immigrants from Europe were kept waiting for admission to the United States. Scouts had combed Milan, Turin, Rome, and other Italian cities without finding a suitable equivalent for this crucial scene. "We wanted the people in those scenes to look like immigrants," Frederickson recalls, "and extras in New York just do not look quite that way." Soon after these sequences had been photographed, shooting on the film concluded, in late April 1974.

The major set for the movie was built on the Henry Kaiser estate at Lake Tahoe, Nevada. This elaborate spread of houses and bungalows helped hoist the budget of *The Godfather Part II* to $13 million. The Coppolas were quartered for six months in a bungalow beside the lake.

*　　*　　*

In this sequel, Coppola abandons a linear narrative in favor of a tightly braided exposition. The film flits back and forth in time between the early years of the century and the end of the 1950s, from Manhattan's Hell's Kitchen to Cuba and Miami. Such a complex construction clouds the meaning of certain sequences—for example, the intrigue involving Frank Pentangeli in Brooklyn—and the demands that Coppola makes on his viewers may explain, as much as the absence of Marlon Brando, why *Part II* earned less than half of the original's revenue at the box-office.

But the rhyming pattern enables Coppola to develop a profound compound between Don Vito in his heyday and his son, Michael Corleone, during the most heinous years of the Mafia's influence in the United States. "The movie is meant to be like the *Oresteia*," Francis has remarked, "showing how evil reverberates over a period of generations."

The aim was to make each scene in such a way as to recall a shot or a moment from *The Godfather*. "It's something in the direction, or in the dialogue, or in the mood of each scene," explained Coppola. "It's like harmony where one note echoes another. As a whole, the first film ought to haunt the second like a specter." For example, in *The Godfather*, Michael assures Kay that in five years the Corleone family will be completely legitimate. In the sequel, a plaintive Kay reminds him of the promise. Metaphorically, too, the movie is bound to *The Godfather*. The murder of the rapacious Fanucci while a priest performs an alfresco service on Ninth Avenue echoes the rhythms of the murders that take place during the christening service at the end of the earlier film.

Coppola's meticulous attention to visual detail in *Part II* invokes painterly contrasts and expressions. Yet the noble sweep of the film, and especially that intricate weaving of past and present—the interweaving of themes in both time and geographical space—prompts a musical comparison: Italian *opera seria*, of course, rather than Wagner, for there are *buffo* moments that relieve the encroaching gloom. Although Luchino Visconti created an operatic tempo and weight in films like *Senso* and *The Damned*, he lacked the relaxed peasant humor of Coppola. The kinship with Bernado Bertolucci is much more profound; Francis could have made *The Spider's Stratagem* and been proud to do so.

The screenplay maps the rise of the Family during the 1910s and 1920s as much as its fragmentation and moral decay during the postwar era, under Michael's stewardship. Vito Corleone sails to the United States an orphan. His father has been assassinated for insulting the local Mafia chieftain in Sicily. His brother is gunned down in the movie's opening sequence; his mother is blown off her feet by a *lupara* shotgun as she screams for Vito to flee.

Vito in youth embodies the bright days of the family. Like countless other immigrants, he gazes in awe at the Statue of Liberty. The camera travels along these grave faces, seeing in them no guile or predisposition to violence, merely a candor and resolution to survive in a mysterious new land. After a bewildering series of examinations Vito, who can speak no English, is quarantined on Ellis Island. Coppola views him alone in his spartan room, as he stares out of a brightly lit window. *Vito Corleone, Ellis Island, 1901*, states a caption gently. There is a Pre-Raphaelite flavor of innocence about the composition and lighting. America is the crucible that generates the savagery depicted in *The Godfather* films. Yet for all his loyalty to his Italian blood, Francis rejects the romantic interpretation. An ugly filigree of violence courses through the Sicilian sequences, suggesting that when it surfaces in the New World it looks to its origins in these stony mountains and impoverished villages.

Brando's Don radiated an irresistible charm and nobility, and De Niro's Vito adroitly reflects these qualities, with the result that the audience allows itself to be duped, lulled into accepting the legitimacy of the young, budding Don's crimes. Clemenza initiates Vito into the glib, opportunistic life of the streets, asking him to hide some arms during a shakedown and then cajoling him into stealing a carpet for his apartment. Coppola presents these incidents with mischievous humor. Vito appears as the innocent bystander, startled by the revelation of such streetwise pranks.

Real life mimics the melodramatic gestures of the theater. When Clemenza holds his gun at the ready should an unwanted visitor disturb his theft of the carpet, Coppola almost freezes the moment and for a split-second the composition looks artificial. This cavalier attitude to existence is signaled too by the jaunty music that accompanies the shots for the streets crowded with immigrants, doing their shopping at open stalls.

Consequently, when Vito commits the murder that will propel him into a commanding position in Manhattan's Italian quarter, we accept it as, if not a heroic deed, at least as self-defensive. There is, however, no mistaking the ruthless premeditation that Vito brings to his assassination of Fanucci, the boss of the "Black Hand."

Vito catches his first glimpse of Fanucci at the theater, where Francesco Pennino's Italian melodrama distracts the spectators from the struggle for survival in the New World. Tavoularis's stage backcloth even includes a painting of the Statue of Liberty, shedding an ardent halo of comfort. While his friend draws back in fear at the sight of Fanucci's extorting money from the theater owner, Vito watches in fascination. He observes both the cruelty and the effectiveness of Fanucci's strong-arm tactics. When he is fired from the grocery to make way for a nephew of Fanucci, Vito remains calm, his voice already that hoarse, melancholy whisper associated with Brando's Don in *The Godfather*. This young Italian is perceived as a victim, a decent youth who minds his own business and then turns Robin Hood to free the neighborhood from the Mafia's grasp. Instinctively, he learns from Clemenza the time-honored Mafia habit of returning favors.

So the fundamental bass line of Coppola's entire *Godfather* suite traces the slow distortion of the Corleone character from altruism to unmitigated greed and self-interest. In *Part II*, the juxtaposition of these conflicting motives reinforces the mood of tragedy. Michael in the dying shot of the film is as pensive and alone as young Vito in the quarantine room on Ellis Island. Alfred Hitchcock, confirming in an interview the ambiguity of his movies, made the shrewd observation that "Our evil and good are getting closer together," and much of Michael's perplexity and insecurity can be explained in such terms.

Orson Welles once remarked that the greatest theme in Western literature concerned the loss of innocence. Vito Corleone, introduced to violence and malice while still a child in Sicily, is schooled by his experience, and resorts to similar methods. Protection of his burgeoning Family takes priority over everything; a "Family" that, as we have seen in *The Godfather*, comprises more than just relatives. Much later in time, during the Senate hearings into the affairs of the Corleones, the hierarchy of *caporegimes*, "buttons," "soldiers," and others is illustrated by a chart that looks at first glance like some august family tree. But the loss of his Family gnaws at Michael after the death of his father. Coming home to a snowbound Lake Tahoe, he ignores Kay as she sits at her sewing machine and trudges over to his mother's house instead.

"Tell me something, Ma," he says in Sicilian. "What did Papa think deep in his heart? He was being strong, strong for his Family. But by being strong for his Family, could he lose it?"

His mother replies that he's thinking of Kay's miscarriage. "You can always have another baby," she tells him, "but you can never lose your Family."

Michael, face half-obliterated by shadow, stares down into some private abyss and mutters, "Times are changing"—an utterance that provides simultaneously a bridge to the next flashback to Vito's youth and also a hint that Michael has lost faith in the concept of family. Fredo has betrayed him. Kay has suffered what he assumes is a miscarriage (and no more chauvinistic male than Michael Corleone exists). His father has passed from the scene. Santino, his elder brother, was cut down in an ambush while Michael was hiding in Sicily. Connie, his sister, has squandered her life to the detriment of her children and at the expense of the Corleone finances. Michael falls victim to an intolerable irony. He tries to "legitimize" and modernize the Corleone business, only to dismember (literally!) his beloved Family.

So Coppola's intermingling of past and present reminds his audience of the idea of loss and abandonment, even if at no point in the movie does Michael consciously reflect on the early years of his father's career. Each time we return to the modern strand of the story, Michael's movements seem to have grown more ponderous. He trudges rather than walks. He stares not at people, but past or through them. Coppola and his editors slow the cutting to a funereal cadence. As early as the scene in Miami when Michael visits Hyman Roth, his car and Johnny Ola's glide through the streets like a cortege. The music, too, sings of regret.

Father and son are joined, though, by an implacable, calculating streak. Vito may exude more physical courage than Michael, but the cold-blooded manner in which he thrusts his pistol into the mouth of the dying Fanucci, and pulls the trigger, springs from his Sicilian roots—*la vendetta*—as does his murder of the senile Mafia chieftain, Don Ciccio, with the dagger dragged in an ugly, emphatic swath across the victim's chest. As August Coppola has said, there is no such thing in Italian life as guilt, only revenge.

Like his son, Vito can switch from moments of cruelty to words of tenderness to his loved ones. The distinction here, of course, is that the men killed by Don Vito "deserve" to die. Michael's victims all possess a certain sympathetic quality—Fredo, Frankie, Hyman Roth . . .

Coppola is not appalled by Vito's point-blank shooting of Fanucci, but he recoils with loathing from even the most discreet of Michael's murders. Vito possesses the courage to carry out his own executions. Michael never soils his hands with blood. He issues orders, condemns his victims with a nod to his bodyguard, until even his brother Fredo must be killed in the remote expanse of Lake Tahoe, while Michael waits grimly in the boat house.

Both Corleones are withdrawn, watchful, and cautious with their words. Vito, however, could never be so harsh as Michael is in his Family relationships. The Michael who drinks only club soda and who strikes his wife with terrible force, as well as eliminating his older brother, remains light years away from Vito Corleone. Their methods may be similar, but their fundamental approach to life differs according to their circumstances and their epoch.

When Vito, like the hero of some Neapolitan melodrama, sallies forth to do battle with the penny-dreadful Fanucci on Ninth Avenue, he can utter the now-famous phrase, "I'll make him an offer he can't refuse," with a nonchalance and a brio that rob the words of their sinister ring. Michael, forced to assume responsibility for the Family at a time of crisis following the death of Sonny and the deterioration of his father's health, regards the world with profound suspicion. He fails to relax in the hot-seat—something that, even in the first days of the Genco Olive Oil Company, comes easily to Don Vito. Michael trusts none of his close associates. The few on whom he does rely are bodyguards, and no words pass among them. In comparison to the reptilian guile of Hyman Roth, Michael's conduct of his empire is forceful and unequivocal. But Michael could never be found watching American football in the middle of the afternoon, as Roth does when he receives him in his modest house in Miami.

Michael expects to possess everyone with whom he has intimate dealings. During the party at Lake Tahoe, he dances with Kay, clutching her in a bearlike embrace; an embrace moreover that is not so much passionate as proprietary. Later, ostensibly reconciled with Fredo, he fondles his brother's bowed head, caressing him like some domestic pet.

However much Michael struggles to assert his own brand of leadership he remains captive to the Corleone tradition. At every juncture he is reminded of his father, and of his role as successor. Both he and Vito share, as we have seen, a sinister ability to flick from cruelty to tenderness without the slightest compunction. Immediately after murdering Fanucci, Vito rejoins his family outside their tenement and takes the baby Michael into his arms, saying, "Michael, your father loves you very much." The need to protect his offspring seemingly justifies the crime. Michael in his turn speaks gently to his son, Anthony, revealing a side of his nature never available to adults.

When he kisses his son goodnight and tells him that he will be leaving in the morning, the boy asks if his father will take him with him too. "No, I can't," Michael replies; but there is great feeling in the exchange. Francis's son Gio resembled the Anthony of the film, and the drawing left on Michael's pillow by the boy was actually done by Gio himself for *his* father.

Even as he must condemn Michael, Coppola seeks to humanize him, for during the making of *The Godfather Part II* he became conscious of personal parallels. "To some extent I have become Michael," he admitted to Italian journalists while shooting the Ellis Island sequence in Trieste, "in that I'm a powerful man in charge of an entire production, and my wife . . . You see, there are personal things that emerge in this film more, perhaps, than I myself am aware of."

We notice that the monogram on the bed linen in Michael and Kay's room reads "MFC"—Michael *Francis* Corleone; and we recall the catechism in *The Godfather*: "Do you, Michael *Francis*?"

Coppola regards Michael as akin to George Minafer in *The Magnificent Ambersons*; alone at the last, rid of his enemies but with nothing to live for. That is his "comeuppance." The accumulated wisdom of Michael's career is contained in a remark he drops when discussing the assassination of Hyman Roth: "If anything in this life is certain, if history has taught us anything, it's that anyone can be killed."

In none of the truly great films directed by Francis Coppola are there any significant or mature female characters. In part this is explained by the subject matter—the Mafia, the Vietnam War—but Coppola's own Italian-American background accounts for the dominance of masculine roles. Women are either elderly, *mamma mia* matrons who cook the spaghetti and know how to withdraw from a room when the men start discussing "business," or, in youth, are essentially decorative, required to bow meekly to their husband's whims. In both parts of the *Godfather* saga, Kay seems fulfilled only by her children. Her "failure" to retain her third pregnancy wounds Michael to such a degree that he does not even speak to her when he returns from a trip after hearing the news.

Kay does not belong to the Italian-American world. Her maiden name, Adams, points to an entirely different tradition of American life. Her education allows her to acquiesce in some of the Corleone formalities, but at certain moments in both *The Godfather* and *Part II*, she articulates her resentment with a tendency that startles Michael. Like Emilia, who denounces Iago at the end of *Othello*, she pays dearly for this refusal to charm her tongue. And when Michael, in front of their children, shuts the door in her face, it is as terminal a gesture as the fall of an executioner's blade.

Kay tries to take her son and daughter away from Michael, and she suffers an abortion rather than bring another Corleone into the world. But in Coppola's eyes Kay remains no more than an irritant to Michael, Tom Hagen, and the staff surrounding the young Godfather. As an outsider by birth and breeding, she is useful in passing the judgment of "the world" on her adopted family. But she never transcends her intrinsic "weakness" as a female. Nor in all likelihood could Coppola develop her character if she were to do so. He is rarely at ease when writing major roles for women.

Even when their menfolk are less malign than Michael Corleone, Coppola's women stand in the shadow of their partners. Roth's wife dutifully prepares a tuna sandwich and retreats so as not to disturb her husband's conversation with Michael. The young Don Vito's wife serves supper from the kitchen, each plate carefully loaded, until she slips unnoticed into another room with her own meal while Vito reasons with Clemenza and Tessio.

Some women are simply ignored. Senator Geary takes pains to introduce his wife as "Mrs. Geary" before his fawning speech to the party at Lake Tahoe, but he is soon revealed as a man dependent on kinky sex with prostitutes, and in Cuba he eagerly requests a dancer as partner for the night.

In retaliation for such unrelenting machismo, women like Fredo's wife and Michael's sister Connie draw satisfaction from humiliating the men around them. Fredo's wife, drunk, has to be dragged off the dance floor by a Corleone bodyguard because Fredo himself cannot cope with her. Connie arrives at the party towing an insipid man named Merle, who absorbs a series of stinging insults from Michael without uttering a single word of protest.

What might be termed the passionate authenticity of *The Godfather Part II* is explained by Coppola's personality. Not just the witty asides, such as the discreet appearance of former mentors Roger Corman and Phil Feldman as senators in the movie, or Francis's screaming at Morgana King that if she could not bear to lie in an open casket on set, then he would summon his own mother to do Mama Corleone's death scene. But other, more poignant facets, like the tear-jerking musical attended by young Vito and his pal in 1917—excerpted from a melodrama about the immigrant experience written by Francesco Pennino, Coppola's maternal grandfather, and entitled *Senza Mama*. Or the lingering shot of little Vito shut up in Ellis Island, just like Francis's aunt Caroline at about the same period. Or the agonizing, almost embarrassing relationship between Michael and his brother Fredo which, like so many affinities in Coppola's work, reflects Francis's own complex attitude toward his elder brother August. In youth Francis was, in his own words, "the boob" and Augie the brilliant one whom he always looked up to. In *The Godfather* the roles are inverted, as it were. "I'm your older brother," cries Fredo in his despair, "and I was stepped over!" August, too brilliant in his own right ever to suffer such a fate, was nevertheless the Coppola whom everyone thought would make a big name.

Another kind of scene also reflects the Coppola lifestyle—the Family tableaux, from Vito and his meek Italian bride in their Manhattan apartment to a parlor gathering on the Don's birthday in 1942, which Michael recalls with such sadness in the final moments of the film. The strength of the Family is nourished by such gatherings. For Francis, the true Family meeting must be a private affair, away from the boisterous bonhomie of big occasions like Connie's wedding at Long Beach in *The Godfather*, and the celebration of Anthony's first communion at Lake Tahoe in *Part II*. The Family dinner that follows that latter reception in Nevada provides the first evidence that the Corleone Family may be about to disintegrate. "*Cent' anni!*" toasts someone at the table. "What's 'cent Anni'?" asks Fredo's dumb-blond wife. "It means a hundred years," says Fredo, and Connie adds, "It means we should all live happily for a hundred years— the Family. It'd be true if my father were alive." The exchange simply exposes the Corleone hostility toward outsiders, even in-laws, a point emphasized a few seconds later when Mamma Corleone grunts a Sicilian aside to Tom Hagen about Connie and her WASP boyfriend Merle: "Those two deserve each other." By comparison, Carlo Rizzi, Connie's first husband, is welcomed in relaxed style by the inner Family in 1942. He's okay, he's *paisan*. Already in *The Godfather*, Coppola has underscored the Sicilian heritage by showing the similarities of ritual between Connie's wedding at Long Beach and Michael's own betrothal to Apollonia in Corleone.

Comparison of the two *Godfather* films reveals that in the sequel Coppola has the courage to refer by name to the Mafia and the Cosa Nostra, an issue that caused severe teething problems for Al Ruddy and Paramount in the early days of producing *The Godfather*. But in *Part II* the stress falls much more squarely on the rise and decline of the Family as a metaphor for modern American history, with Michael Corleone as the personification of the United States. During the Senate hearings, as one of the Corleone killers refers to the "buffers" that stood between him and the upper echelons within the Family, associations with Watergate appear inescapable. When Roth, surrounded by lawmen at Miami airport, is shot by a stranger wearing a hat, the incident looks like a reconstruction of Jack Ruby's assassination of Lee Harvey Oswald.

But Coppola concerns himself with a larger vision. *The Godfather Part II* intones a lament for vanished ideals, for a time when people could walk the streets without fear, when men like Vito Corleone robbed the rich to help the poor, when America beckoned as the Land of Liberty (and of the Pursuit of Happiness).

Like the Corleone Family, the United States stands ostensibly for the rights of the individual and for the right to dissent. All too frequently, however, those who are not with America are deemed to be against her, and the CIA and even the State Department have practiced "dirty tricks" just as draconian and bizarre as those described in the *Godfather* movies. Paranoia and xenophobia tainted the Reagan era, supplanting—and perverting—the ideals of the 1960s. When Pentangeli says that the Corleone Family used to be like the Roman Empire, Tom Hagen responds wistfully, "It was—once," and the comparison with modern U.S. history is plain.

However pessimistic the mood of the film becomes, Coppola tries always to balance the darkness with scenes of light and festivity during the prime of Don Vito. By implication he and his coscreenwriter, Mario Puzo, blame various factors for the change in the quality of life: drugs, the unremitting drive for massive profits to a degree that mocks the original aims of capitalism, the growth of a covert system of government that enables everyone to shirk responsibility, and the acceptance of violence as a legitimate part of the pattern of daily life.

The episode in Cuba underlines the American predisposition to support dictators in the Third World. At the meeting with Batista, president of Cuba from 1940 and arbiter of power on the island from the mid-1930s, Coppola uses the boardroom table as a symbol of Big Business; round it are seated the CEOs of the top communications, mining, food, and sugar corporations, along with Hyman Roth and Michael Corleone (the latter welcomed with a nice touch of hyperbole as "representing our associates in tourism and leisure activities").

Michael can sense the imminent rebel victory on the island but Roth, who belongs to an earlier generation ("I was running molasses out of Havana when you were a baby") cannot adjust to the changing circumstances.

Roth may have been based on Meyer Lansky, the gambling king who fled Havana on the night of Batista's resignation. Coppola's blending of real history and fictional drama climaxes in the celebrations on New Year's Eve 1958. By dusk on the evening of December 31, barely half the city of Havana was held by Batista's forces, so Michael and his group could not have enjoyed drinks and a nightclub in quite the relaxed way they do in the movie. The president's hasty abdication speech is presented plausibly by Coppola, even though some sources contend that Batista was at Campamento Columbia with his chiefs of staff as the old year ran out.

Michael does not deliver the $2 million cash gift he has earmarked for Batista. He waits—and his doubts are justified by the events of New Year's Eve. "Fidel! Fidel!" is heard in the frenzied streets as Michael slips away to the airport. So Coppola gives his Manichaean antihero a measure of political savvy denied to his real-life counterparts in the U.S. government. Like his father, Michael survives by virtue of a streetwise pragmatism. Like America over the past twenty years, however, his fear of being unseated degenerates into paranoia and isolationism. His statement at the Senate hearings dwells on his patriotic role in the army in World War II, and on his never having been arrested or linked with crime in any way. And should the committee seek to challenge that statement by producing a witness, well, the Mafia has ways of dealing with that too. Sure enough, the following Monday morning Frank Pentangeli is smuggled into the hearings as the Senate's star turn, only to be confronted by the one presence that can assure his silence—his brother from Sicily, flanked and minded by Tom Hagen and Michael Corleone. In the long stares exchanged by the brothers across the crowded room lies the very essence of *omertà*, the Sicilian code of silence in the face of the authorities.

Despite its operatic tone, *The Godfather Part II* relies much more than its predecessor on references to contemporary pressures and prejudices. At the Senate hearings, Michael refers calmly to both the Mafia and the Cosa Nostra. Hyman Roth extols Cuba as a place where profits can be made beyond the reach of Kefauver—the zealous Democratic senator from Tennessee whose committee exposed a network of crime syndicates in 1950–1951 (and whose hearings were televised like those in *The Godfather Part II*). Frank Pentangeli speaks disdainfully of Roth as "that Jew in Miami." Fredo's wife, collapsing drunk on the dance floor at Lake Tahoe, screams, "Never marry a Wop!" And the most virulent abuse of all comes from Senator Geary of Nevada, who sits in Michael's study and declares, "I don't like your kind of people. I don't like to see you coming out to this clean country, with your oily hair, dressed up in those silk suits, trying to pass yourselves off as decent Americans. The fact is, I despise your masquerade, the dishonest way you pose yourself—yourself and your whole fuckin' family."

Much later, after Geary has been brought into line by the Corleones thanks to some sexual blackmail, he will deliver an impromptu paean of praise to the Italian-American community, while senators listen in astonishment and Michael sits impassive at the witness table.

The fundamental insecurity of immigrant families like the Corleones can be alleviated only by the exercise of power; and power in America stems from money. From olive oil to the most sophisticated of narcotics, the Mafia has tapped the primary sources of cash in modern American life. Nothing, then, can be more noxious to Michael Corleone than an insult that refers to the "alien" origins of his Family.

The secular strength and resilience of the Family transcend the sovereignty of the Catholic church. Both *Godfather* films (and *The Conversation*) contain elements of traditional Catholic ritual, but the priests are inconspicuous if seen at all. Don Vito and Don Michael deploy the gravity and ceremonial of the church to legitimize their actions. In the brief opening shot of *Part II*, members of the Family kiss Michael's hand in a gesture of fealty, something rendered usually to a bishop or a chalice.

This hypocrisy seeks to exalt even the most ghastly of murders—for example, the final massacre in *The Godfather*, which is timed to take place during the christening of Connie's baby; or the killing of Fanucci, which coincides with a *festa* in the streets below, and which is bound still more closely with the religious ardor of the neighborhood by means of a visual gimmick: the towel around Vito's gun ignites at the very moment the fireworks explode at the climax of the *festa*.

Nor can the church offer sanctuary from the profanity endemic to the Mafia. In the opening sequence of *Part II*, the funeral cortege of Vito's father is isolated by gunfire. In the final ten minutes of the film, Fredo is shot in the back of the head as he recites Hail Marys in the fishing boat on Lake Tahoe.

But homage to the church remains an important attribute of the big Mafia chieftains. Don Fanucci, swaggering along Ninth Avenue, ostentatiously pins a high-denomination bill to the cluster of notes dangling beside the shrine. The crowd applauds with respect. Michael Corleone celebrates his son's first communion in flamboyant style, with a vast party in the Family compound on Lake Tahoe and a munificent endowment for the local university. It all smacks of Hyannisport and the Kennedy compound—another conjunction of Catholics and dynasts.

Two aspects of *The Godfather Part II* illustrate more strongly than anything the contrast between the supremacy and the decline of the Corleone empire. One is the production design by Dean Tavoularis. For example, to demonstrate the idealism of the immigrants he uses recurring signs and visual idioms such as the Statue of Liberty (which is viewed in reality as young Vito enters New York harbor, then emblazoned on the stage curtain in the theater he attends in New York, and finally in the form of a bronze souvenir brought by Vito to Sicily for an aged relative). No comparable talisman of hope exists in the postwar episodes. Michael is located in soberly furnished rooms; the windows are crisscrossed invariably with steel ribs, lending such scenes a look of incarceration. Low ceilings accentuate the claustrophobic mood.

The other striking production element is cinematographer Gordon Willis's soft overhead lighting. De Niro's Vito relaxes in interiors that are flooded with sunshine, so strong that the windows cast a halo around the figure of the young Don. Even his return to Sicily, with the assassination of Don Ciccio as its main purpose, is bathed in a warm amber light. But Michael prefers murk and shadow, matching the malice he reserves for his enemies. His rooms are lit only by reading lamps; his own face is obscured more often than not, save for one memorable long-shot at the end when his features are caught in a spectral glare inside the boat house at Lake Tahoe, as he waits for the murder of his brother to occur far out over the water.

It is hard to believe that any major Hollywood studio would have permitted Coppola to narrate his film in such a complicated time framework had he not proved his popular appeal with *The Godfather.*

There is a good argument for preferring the straightforward chronology of the first picture, a case reinforced by the revelation in 1977 of *"The Godfather:* the Complete Novel for Television," which virtually shunned flashbacks (see page 113).

There are times in *Part II* when—certainly on a first viewing—the scenes involving Pentangeli are difficult to grasp and to relate to the duel with Hyman Roth and the duplicity of Fredo. And even after repeated viewings, the interjection of a brief scene from the Senate hearings still looks clumsy as it spoils the wintry tone of Michael's return to his home after learning that Kay has suffered a miscarriage. He enters the house silently, and observing Kay at her sewing machine, he turns away, unable to speak to her. As he puts his hand to his head in gloom, there is a cut to the Senate hearings room, where one of the Corleone "soldiers" is being questioned. This scene lasts only ninety seconds, but when Coppola returns unexpectedly to Michael, crossing the snow to his mother's house, we are puzzled. Is this a direct continuation of the silent episode involving Kay, or has there been a time lapse? As the film rejoins the Senate hearings right after the next scene (with Mamma Corleone), we may reasonably ask why Coppola found it necessary to fragment the order of things. Of course he was depressed and unnerved during the editing period; a rhythm refused to emerge from the mass of material to hand. On November 27, 1974, a sneak preview in San Diego convinced Coppola that he should improve the flow and logic of the final hour. He took a bold decision: there would be no intermission, even though *Part II* would run for more than three hours.

The film gives the illusion of an almost equal division of time between the early days of the Corleone saga and the postwar changes wrought by Michael. In fact, only just over one-quarter of the running time is allotted to the story of Vito, and almost two and a quarter hours focus on Michael's world. The film consists of ten parallel stretches of narrative, five for Vito and five for Michael. Reassembled, they would form two independent stories, two films. But Coppola bridges the episodes so imaginatively that the roving back and forth in time feels justifiable.

Six of the transitions are in the form of a dissolve from one image to another. Two are sharp cuts. One is a more profound interval—a fadeout to black from the ironically idyllic shot of Vito and his wife and three children just after he has shot Fanucci. No fewer than six of the time links involve babies and children, as though Coppola were eager to plant in the minds of his audience a subliminal acceptance of the family continuum. Vito as a boy of nine, in Ellis Island. Anthony Corleone, his grandson, in church for his first communion, and then again in bed being embraced by his father. Santino, Vito's first son, in his cot and then again, bawling on the new carpet that his father and Clemenza have stolen. Michael himself, first as a newborn baby and then being cuddled by his father on the stoop in Hell's Kitchen, and at last as a boy waving goodbye to his relatives as the train draws out of a station in Sicily.

The child thus becomes a living symbol of survival, and the nuclear family is like an ark against the assaults of a hostile environment. Nothing could be more Italian than that.

One of the hallmarks of Coppola as a filmmaker is his flair for montage. A keen admirer of Eisenstein, he loves to achieve counterpoint by leaping from one character to another, from one period to another, from one incident to another.

Behind the flamboyance of such a technique, however, lies a conviction that destiny fuses certain people and occurrences at certain times, like crystals drawn to one another. For example, Fanucci is doomed from the moment he leaves Vito in the café. Coppola cuts back and forth between the gangster's regal progress along Ninth Avenue, and Vito's nimble negotiation of the rooftops above until at last—and inexorably—the two men come face to face in Fanucci's doorway.

Striking the balance is the trick where this kind of montage is concerned, and the finale of *The Godfather Part II* excels anything Coppola has done in the idiom. As a coda, it is clearly inspired by the similar situation in *The Godfather*, but this time the cadence is more subtle and disturbing. As Michael waits alone in the boat house beside Lake Tahoe, three of his foes meet their end—Roth at Miami airport, Pentangeli by his own hand, and Fredo while fishing. The cutting between the separate incidents is formidable enough, but Coppola (and, one imagines, Puzo) enhances the elegiac tone of the finale by introducing a degree of religion and ideology. Roth proclaims with pride and defiance that he is a Jew and wanted to spend the twilight of his life in the State of Israel. Pentageli believes that his family will be cared for if he follows the honorable example of plotters against the Roman emperor. And on the verge of his assassination, Fredo recites his Hail Marys with the devotion of a child. So all three men contrive to transcend the grubby reality of their lives, and to meet death with dignity. Consequently, Michael endures not as a victor but as a loser, deprived of any inner belief whatever. Without enemies, without friends, his life is a void.

*   *   *

Variety sent *The Godfather Part II* off to a fast start with a bold-type summary at the head of its review: "Masterful sequel, broadening story scope of original blockbuster. Outstanding in all respects." But Vincent Canby, invariably condescending about Coppola's pictures, wrote in the *New York Times* that *Part II* looked very expensive but "spiritually desperate," and had the air of "a very long, very elaborate review sketch." The *Washington Post* all but dismissed the production as "fundamentally irrelevant." Theater owners had pledged almost $27 million prior to the December 1974 opening—a record advance in the annals of Hollywood—but soon after Christmas business died away. The film was too sophisticated to cater for the millions who had reveled in the blood and glamor of the original.

Part II dominated the Academy Awards, however, in the following spring. Nominated in twelve categories, the production secured the cov-

eted Best Picture Oscar previously claimed by *The Godfather*, and Francis
himself accepted three statuettes—for writing, directing, and of course
producing the picture. The Directors' Guild of America named him Best
Director, even as it gave John Korty the Best TV Director award for *The
Autobiography of Miss Jane Pittman*. Francis enjoyed a coincidence that
acknowledged the talent of the two pioneers of independent filmmaking
in the Bay Area.

On the nights of November 12, 13, 14, and 15, 1977, NBC presented
"Mario Puzo's *The Godfather*: the Complete Novel for Television." The
telecast was exciting because it included a total of about one hour's previously unused material. Together, the two films had run 6 hours and 15
minutes. On TV, the four segments amounted to 7 hours and 14
minutes—and of course a film loses 4 percent of its original length when
projected for the small screen at 25 frames per second.

"When you finish a movie," says Coppola, "even a movie that sounds
like a success at the time, there are many people pressuring you to cut
out scenes, make it shorter. You're in a very vulnerable situation and you
just want everyone to like the picture and you hope that if you cut a few
scenes out, maybe they'll like it better." The narrative structure of the TV
version of *The Godfather* developed by chance:

> I was in San Francisco with a couple of girls I was trying to impress, and I
> had just installed a new kind of television in my office, and I wanted to put a
> tape on—this was in the days when VCRs were not as common as they are
> now. All I could find to show off the system was a big box of the tapes of all
> *The Godfather* stuff. I fed in the first tape, and after a while I realized that we
> ought to cut the movie together just the way it was. So I called "Blackie"
> Malkin, and he came out to California, and I just showed him the reels, one
> after another in a row, and told him with notes and comments how to assemble
> it. Then I went back to the Philippines for *Apocalypse*, and "Blackie" worked
> on it, and came out to show me the assembly. We checked it everywhere, even
> on boats and things!

Malkin carefully excised some of the most explicit violent and erotic
shots from the original. The following did not appear in the TV version:
Vito's insertion of his pistol into Fanucci's mouth and pulling the trigger;
blood trickling down the face of Moe Greene after he has been shot in
the massage room; the corpse of Sonny Corleone being kicked by his
assassins after the ambush at the tollbooths; the medium-shot of the dead
prostitute "killed" by Senator Geary at the brothel in Nevada; and the
scene of Sonny screwing Lucy upstairs during the wedding celebrations
at Long Beach.

Coppola was, however, able to include several new sequences that fleshed out the narrative and enhanced some of the characters. For example, we now see Brando's Don Vito listening to a report from Tom Hagen after the latter's unsuccessful negotiations with Woltz in Hollywood. The ensuing scene, showing the producer waking to find the head of his stallion in his bedclothes, is slightly more convincing; in *The Godfather*, the transition from Tom's driving away from Woltz's mansion to the nighttime episode in the bedroom still seems too abrupt.

There is additional footage involving the young Clemenza in Hell's Kitchen, and Vito's own unequivocal attitude to bloodletting emerges in some new scenes in Sicily, when he disposes of two men who had been involved in the murder of his father (in *Part II* we see him kill only Don Ciccio). In contrast, the compassion of Brando's Don is underlined in a moving scene at the bedside of the dying Genco Abbandando. Michael Corleone also gains some exposure in the TV omnibus edition. During his days in hiding in Sicily he is shown talking to his bodyguards, and as Don he shares in a significant exchange of dialogue with a wealthy young man who wants to marry Sonny's daughter, Francesca. Michael urges him not to be ashamed of his fortune.

The telecast ends with Kay's lighting candles in church, whereas *The Godfather Part II* concludes with the telling close-up of Michael's face as he muses on his destiny in the garden at Lake Tahoe. Yet these images of Kay at worship coincide faithfully with the final lines of Puzo's novel, in which she prays for the soul of Michael Corleone.

At Christmas 1976, when there was a hiatus in the filming of *Apocalypse Now*, Malkin flew out to San Francisco to show Coppola the assembly. "We had to modify some of the Italian-Sicilian language exchanges," explains the editor, "because the network was worried about there being too much foreign-language material. So we had to put in some English phrases, mixed with Sicilian."

The impression remains that much more material lay on hand from *The Godfather* than from its sequel. Paramount had compelled Coppola to slice the original film down to less than three hours, but on *Part II* the director had been able to include most of the scenes that he shot.

The miracle is that when gathered in this new, chronological format, the myriad segments of both films constitute a persuasive whole. Only one part of the saga remains obstinately unbridgeable, and that is the twenty years that elapse between the last scenes involving Robert De Niro as the young Don Vito, and the first appearance of Marlon Brando at his daughter's wedding.

*   *   *

Although Francis had enjoyed more freedom in terms of time and money than he had with *The Godfather*, there were spells when his spirits touched rock bottom. He was working seven-day weeks without respite, often shooting *Part II* during the regular week, and then supervising the editing of *The Conversation* over Saturday and Sunday. The strain on his marriage was apparent. When he unexpectedly triumphed at Cannes festival with *The Conversation* in May 1974, the future looked brighter, but Coppola was so laden with commitments that he could not bask in the accumulated glory of such awards. When sneak previews like the one in San Diego mentioned above, and another at the Coronet in San Francisco, went badly, Francis reacted with impatience. "Francis, you can't win 'em all," someone scribbled on a rating card. Quoting the incident in an interview afterward, Coppola snapped, "But whoever wrote that was wrong. I can."

The profits from *The Godfather* found their way into an alarming spectrum of projects and properties. Advisers had urged Francis to pump money into tax shelter schemes. He preferred more original, more flamboyant gestures. He wanted his own vineyard, not the mobile retirement home in Albuquerque that those same advisers had purchased without consulting him. He wanted a headquarters with a difference in downtown San Francisco, and in 1973 he bought the sea-green Sentinel Building at the junction of Kearny and Columbus Streets. He paid $500,000 for this city landmark, built in 1905 by the notorious political grafter, Abe Ruef. The structure survived the 1906 earthquake and fire, and its Hungarian-style architecture is made even more conspicuous today by the absence of adjacent buildings.

Francis reserved the eighth-floor penthouse for himself, with a bedroom overlooking the Bay, a spectacular Japanese bath in red tiling, and, a few years later, a fabulous "frieze" of characters from his movies painted as a surprise by Alex Tavoularis around the inner walls of the cupola. Even in Zoetrope's darkest hours, after the calamity of *One from the Heart*, Francis refused to cede the Sentinel Building, and he still uses it for corporate offices, editing, and sound work.

He also bought the Little Fox Theater on Pacific Street, with a building alongside that accommodated *City* magazine, another Coppola acquisition of the period. Here space was earmarked for Zoetrope's postproduction facilities, as well as for KMPX, a Bay Area FM radio station. "I thought if we had a theater and a radio station, we could try out writing and ideas that might become the basis for films later," Coppola said. Referring to *City*, he maintained that "if there were a publication that tried to have its pulse on the people, that would be a tremendously healthy principle for the motion picture company [Zoetrope]."

In part, these acquisitions were motivated by a genuine desire to clean up the North Beach neighborhood, and to convert it into a sanctuary for artists and nonconformists rather than a drab quarter infested with strip joints and massage parlors. More insistent, though, was Coppola's belief in the need to control communications in the modern world. As he said in 1982, "In Napoleon's time, artillery was power, artillery was influence. Napoleon understood that. Today, communications is power and influence, and that is something *I'm* trying to understand."

Along with the Little Fox and *City* magazine, he owned a parcel of 72,000 shares, around 8 percent of the equity, in Cinema 5, Don Rugoff's New York–based distribution company specializing in foreign-language movies and which was then in danger of being absorbed by a major domestic exhibition group. Francis regarded Rugoff as a kindred spirit, someone trying to buck the system.

None of Francis's houses was on a scale commensurate with his enormous income. He had a modest home in Los Angeles, a twenty-two-room Victorian mansion on Pacific Heights in San Francisco, with its erstwhile ballroom soon converted into a regal screening room, a couple of apartment houses on Arguello Boulevard, and a hideaway in Mill Valley habitually reserved for friends, writers, and other colleagues. On the East Coast, he purchased an elegant apartment in the Sherry Netherland Hotel on the corner of Fifth Avenue and 59th Street. As his fame grew, Francis also arranged for a room to be at his disposal in the Algonquin Hotel in Manhattan, whenever he needed to do some uninterrupted writing.

Fame and wealth crept up on the Coppolas almost without their realizing it. Eleanor remembers walking out of the front door in her bathrobe to collect the morning paper, and a San Francisco tour bus passing, when the guide declared, "And this is the home of Francis Ford Coppola!" Once a screening room had been installed in the house on Pacific Heights, business and private life began to merge. "More and more people you didn't know were coming to screenings," says Eleanor, "walking around in your house. One morning I sat down in the breakfast room, and somebody came down the hall, sat opposite me, and said, 'I'd like an order of six bagels, please.' That's the point when I recognized that we had to make a division between our personal family life and our business existence." Now, in Napa, the Coppolas' house is off-limits to the business, which is conducted in separate buildings on the estate.

Nothing apart from his film work proved wholly successful for Coppola, however—save in recent years his wine, grown with loving care on his Napa estate. *City* magazine, marketed to the Bay Area, folded in 1976. The subscription blurb trumpeted a confident message: "You need *City*. It's full of news you can use week after week; it tells you inside stories; it lets you know where to go to have fun and where to get a great meal."

When his accountant warned him that the venture was bound to lose money, Francis retorted, "I earned it!" He began with an investment of just $15,000. Within a year his commitment had zoomed to close to a million dollars. "We tried to talk him out of it," his assistant Mona Skager told Judy Stone of the *San Francisco Chronicle*, "but I don't know anyone who's ever been able to change his mind."

For six months, Coppola came to the *City* office every day. Editors were appointed and dismissed. The last was Warren Hinckle, a true Bay Area eccentric who sprinkled the magazine with stories on everything from flying saucers to literary biography. The final issue proclaimed an exposé on "The Great Nipple Boom" and Francis hurled it aside in exasperation and disgust.

Even the Little Fox failed, dispelling the Coppola dream of an acting school from which a small company of players would evolve to the benefit of Zoetrope's movie ventures.

Much as Francis regretted these follies, he never complained about the loss of cash. In 1975 he confided to his associate Fred Roos, "I'll be broke and back to zero in a few years, so I might as well have fun."

Zoetrope pushed forward with an extensive lineup of film productions, but one by one they were postponed or aborted in the shadow of a juggernaut called *Apocalypse Now*. For Francis, the title would become appallingly relevant as the decade wore on.

The Conversation: *Harry Caul (Gene Hackman) with his cherished saxophone.*

The Conversation: *Francis discusses a scene with Gene Hackman in the big warehouse set in San Francisco* (above). *Gene Hackman and Elizabeth MacRae* (below).

The Conversation: *"The best bugger on the West Coast."*

The Conversation: *Harry Caul (Gene Hackman) in the opening sequence in Union Square* (above). *Harry "is manhandled by plainclothes guards"* (below).

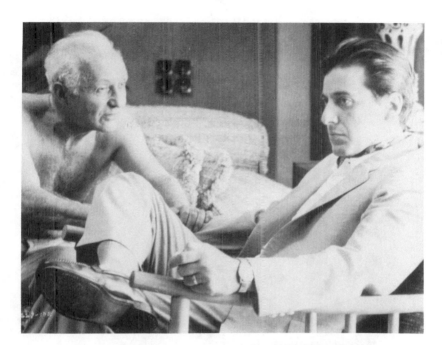

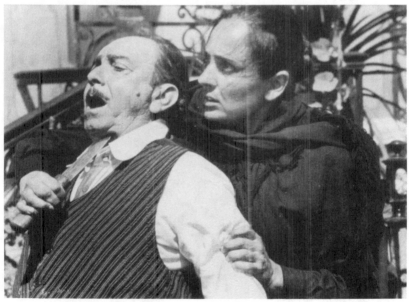

The Godfather Part II: *Hyman Roth (Lee Strasberg) and Michael (Al Pacino)*
(above). Violence in Sicily at the outset, as Vito's mother desperately
threatens Don Ciccio (below).

The Godfather Part II: *Francis confers with Al Pacino on location (above). Tom Hagen (Robert Duvall) counsels Michael during the Senate hearings. Diane Keaton as Kay sits behind them.*

The Coppola family on location for The Godfather Part II.

Apocalypse Now: *Francis on location with an Ifugao chief and a local helper* (above). *Francis discusses a scene with Marlon Brando (below). (United Artists)*

Apocalypse Now: *"The alien environment closes in on the men"*: Hicks *(Frederic Forrest) and Willard (Martin Sheen). (United Artists)*

Apocalypse Now: *Alfresco communion to the tune of an attack helicopter* (above), *and darkness and light at odds as the Playmates arrive to put on a show for the troops* (below). *(United Artists)*

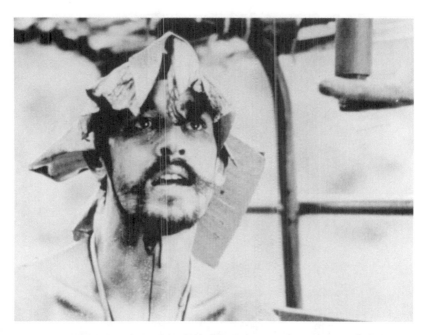

Apocalypse Now: *Hicks (Frederic Forrest) aboard the patrol boat* (above).
The craft glides into Kurtz's station (below). (United Artists)

Apocalypse Now: *Willard (Martin Sheen) "surfaces wraithlike from the oleaginous water" (above), and the end of Kurtz (below). (United Artists)*

Above: *Francis in his garden with Akira Kurosawa. (Photo: © Wim Wenders)*
Below: *Hans-Jürgen Syberberg and Werner Herzog with Francis in San Francisco.*

One from the Heart: *Leila (Nastassia Kinski) and Hank (Frederic Forrest)
on their night out (above), and Frannie (Teri Garr)
in optimistic mood (below). (Zoetrope Studios)*

One from the Heart: *"The playful suspension of reality"* as Frannie
walks down a studio street (above). (*Zoetrope Studios*)
The Outsiders: *Francis discussing a scene with* C. Thomas Howell (left), *Ralph
Macchio* (back to camera), *and Matt Dillon.* (*Pony Boy Inc.*)

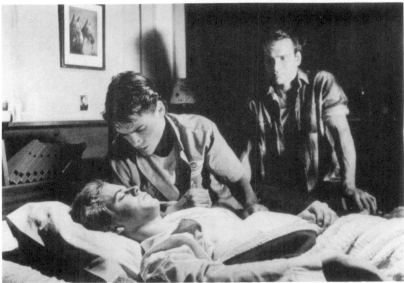

The Outsiders: *The Socs find Ponyboy (C. Thomas Howell) and Johnny (Ralph Macchio) alone and start a fight (above), and (below) Ponyboy is visited in the hospital by his older brothers, Sodapop (Rob Lowe) and Darrel (Patrick Swayze). (Pony Boy Inc.)*

CHAPTER SEVEN

Lost in the Jungle

The years 1976 and 1977 were probably the most fruitful of Coppola's career. To anyone reared on the lurid tales of the shooting of *Apocalypse Now* this statement may sound absurd. But although the *Godfather* films may be more controlled works of popular art, *Apocalypse Now* breathes the furnace heat of a personal vision, worthy to stand alongside Goya's *Disasters of War*. *One from the Heart* may have been made under less taxing conditions, but it lacks the heroic stature of *Apocalypse*. How ironic, too, that this monstrous, seemingly chaotic war movie should have succeeded against all odds in making a profit!

It was a profit achieved at great personal cost to Francis. The project sapped time, energy, and money on a prodigious scale. It almost wrecked the Coppola marriage. Production was so protracted that even close colleagues of Francis were doubtful if it would ever be completed.

Filming in the Philippines was the most savage and gruelling stage. "There were times," recalls Coppola, "when I thought I was going to die, literally, from the inability to move the problems I had. I would go to bed at four in the morning in a cold sweat." The postproduction phase may have been even more exhausting in psychological terms. The premiere was postponed from December 1977 to May 1978, then successively to the autumn of 1978, the spring of 1979 (when it was screened in an incomplete version at the Cannes festival), and at last to August 1979. United Artists, who had invested $7.5 million initially in exchange for U.S. distribution rights, had to answer Zoetrope's call for additional funds, and even discussed the grisly prospect of evicting Francis and his family from their home on Pacific Heights, repossessing the Napa Valley vineyard and other Coppola properties.

Where, then, were the seeds of this angry masterpiece? John Milius is customarily credited with the original screenplay and title for *Apocalypse Now*. Thirty years earlier Orson Welles had progressed to an advanced stage on a film of Joseph Conrad's *Heart of Darkness*. The project had foundered. In the late 1960s, John Milius transposed the plot of *Heart of Darkness* to the Vietnam arena. He had no ambitions to direct the movie himself, and regarded George Lucas as the ideal man to do so.

Carroll Ballard, however, takes exception to this. "*Apocalypse Now* started out as my idea," he says. "I wanted to do *Heart of Darkness* back in 1967, long before Milius. I had a deal cooking with Joel Landon, the producer of *Finian's Rainbow*. We scrounged around and tried to get the rights, and it came to a dead end. Then it was picked up by George Lucas without anyone telling me about it."

Milius remains adamant—and persuasive—in his claim to the heart of the matter. "My whole career is justified by having written *Apocalypse*," he says. "I wrote the screenplay in 1969, and based the Sheen character, and some of Kurtz, on a friend of mine, Fred Rexer, who actually experienced the scene [related by Brando] where the arms are hacked off by the Viet Cong. There were six drafts of the screenplay—well over a thousand pages. At one point Francis said, 'Write every scene you ever wanted to go into that movie.' " The title, he recalls, came from a button badge popular among hippies during the 1960s—"Nirvana Now."

When it comes to the Conrad connection the trail grows murkier. In 1982, Milius declared, "If it's based on *Heart of Darkness*, then *Moby-Dick* is based on the Book of Job." But in 1986 he freely admitted the literary source. "My writing teacher had told me that nobody could lick *Heart of Darkness*. Welles had tried, and nobody could do it. So, as it was my favorite Conrad book, I determined to lick it." Milius added that *Apocalypse* was also inspired by an article by Michael Herr entitled, "The Battle for Khe San," referring to drugs, rock 'n' roll, people calling airstrikes down on themselves and the like. He recognizes the ultimate credit for the film as belonging to Coppola. "Even had I written every line of every scene I could not have realized it on screen in the way Francis did."

*   *   *

When Warners recoiled with alarm at the prospect of Zoetrope's lineup of projects in the wake of *THX 1138*, they demanded that Coppola should buy back all the properties involved—all save *Apocalypse*. But Francis was intrigued by the Milius script, which he later termed as both "a comedy and a terrifying psychological horror story." He kept the rights close to his chest. Lucas signed a development deal with Columbia Pictures when he had finished *American Graffiti*. His friend and business colleague Gary Kurtz even traveled to the Philippines in search of suitable locations. Lucas and Kurtz intended to shoot the film in a low-key, documentary style, using 16mm cameras and real soldiers—for a mere $2 million.

Possession, though, is nine-tenths of the law of the jungle. Coppola owned the rights to *Apocalypse Now*. He even left a copy of the script with Dušan Makavejev in Paris, suggesting he might like to direct it. Of course all the original Zoetrope deals reflected the shoestring nature of the operation, but Coppola recalls, "I was anxious for George Lucas to do the picture on any basis at all." That deal may no longer have been attractive to Lucas, who was by then at work on *Star Wars*. He declined, and Francis himself pressed ahead, determined to get the project off the ground.

From the outset, Coppola envisaged the film as a definitive statement on many things: the nature of modern war, the perilous borderline between good and evil, the impact of American society on the rest of the world. The pyrotechnics were, in an appealing way, seductive. "I'd have done it in Cinerama if I could have, on a big, wide screen," he said later. "What I most hoped for was to take the audience through an unprecedented experience of war and have them react as much as those who had gone through the war."

Coppola's team at Zoetrope soon assembled $8 million from distributors outside the U.S. to add to the $7.5 million from United Artists—although admittedly on the assumption that Marlon Brando, Steve McQueen, and Gene Hackman would appear in the film. This grandiose casting did not quite materialize. McQueen was approached to play Willard, but demurred because he did not want to leave the country for seventeen weeks—and Coppola had selected the Philippines as an ideal location, with its access to American equipment and cheap labor. His production coordinator Fred Roos had already made two low-budget Monte Hellman films in the Philippines, and had friends and contacts in that country. Al Pacino was also concerned about the long absence from the United States, and feared the prospect of falling ill in the jungle as he had done in the Dominican Republic during the shooting of *The Godfather Part II*. Other major stars were offered the part of Willard or

Kurtz, among them Jack Nicholson, Robert Redford, and Coppola's old pal, James Caan.

By early 1976, Francis had persuaded Marlon Brando to play Kurtz, the American colonel who has established his own Montagnard army across the Cambodian border with Vietnam. Brando's fee was high— $3.5 million for a month's work on location in September 1976, for the actor wanted to enjoy the summer with his family on the South Seas atoll of Teiteroa. For the role of Willard, the captain who is dispatched by his superiors to terminate Kurtz "with extreme prejudice," Coppola chose Harvey Keitel.

On March 1, 1976, Coppola flew to Manila with his wife, their three children, his nephew Marc, his projectionist, a housekeeper, and baby-sitter. The shooting schedule amounted to five months, and the family rented a large house in the Filipino capital. Sound and photographic equipment had been flooding in from California since late 1975.

Less than three weeks after their arrival, shooting began, and within a few days the first problems were manifest. Coppola was disappointed with Keitel's characterization of Willard ("He found it difficult to play him as a passive onlooker"). The film stock was processed in Rome, so there was some delay before the rushes reached Manila. After viewing them, Coppola took a plane back to Los Angeles, and promptly replaced Keitel with Martin Sheen, who had made a stunning debut in Terrence Malick's *Badlands*.

Dennis Hopper was cast as a kind of Green Beret sidekick for Kurtz. When Coppola heard Hopper chattering away nonstop on location, he recognized in him the personality of the Russian in *Heart of Darkness*. "That day, right there, I put the cameras and the Montagnard shirt on him, and we shot the scene where he greets them on the boat."

Another inspired piece of casting was Frederic Forrest as Hicks, the cook from New Orleans who accompanies Willard on his mission up-country. Forrest had appeared in *Viet Rock*, one of the earliest off-Broadway plays about the war. "I'd lived in New York during the 1960s," Forrest says, "so I wanted to make an antiwar statement in *Apocalypse*."

With Sheen feeling his way into the role of Willard, the village of Baler and then the coastal area of Iba were used as locations for several further weeks. The logistics were hard to control. F5 jets had to scream over the jungle releasing canisters that would look like napalm, while special effects teams below ignited a vast fuel conflagration amid the densely crowded palms. Twelve hundred gallons of gasoline reputedly burned in a mere ninety seconds. "I had fifteen helicopters up in the sky," Coppola complained, "and no way to tell them that if they didn't fly another ten feet, they wouldn't be in the picture."

But Nature refused to kowtow to this American invasion. Rains of tropical intensity wrecked the sets at Iba, and on May 26 production was closed down. Fred Roos:

> A typhoon occurs over several days—it builds and develops . . . One part of the crew was stranded in a hotel and the others had small houses and were immobilized. The Playmate set had been destroyed, and about a month's shooting was scheduled for that set. So, most of us went home to the States for six to eight weeks. Dean Tavoularis and his team stayed on and new locations were scouted and the set rebuilt in a different place. The man who carried out most of the fiberglass construction work on *Apocalypse* happened to be a brother of Benigno Aquino . . .

Tavoularis recalls the bizarre circumstances of the typhoon.

> I was trapped for days in a house with the "Playmate of the Year," who had been flown out to appear in the show sequence. She didn't want to live in a hotel, so I took her to this little basement room, and told her there was just the one room because three or four of us were already crammed into the place. We sat around, and it started raining harder and harder until finally it was literally *white* outside, and all the trees were bent at forty-five degrees. A writer from the *New York Times* happened to be trapped there with us, along with my brother, my nephew, my driver, and a toothless old man who lived permanently in the house. The writer, Jonathan Reynolds, later wrote a play, *Geniuses*, about a kind of chauvinistic art director trapped with a Playmate!
> The typhoon eventually passed, and we went round surveying the damage. Everything was covered in mud. The insurance people arrived from Hong Kong and worked out this arrangement whereby we would stop shooting for a few months, reorganize everything at a single location, and then try to do the remainder of the film. We rebuilt down south, and in some degree when you have the chance to rebuild a set, it's a gift . . .

According to Eleanor Coppola, whose volume *Notes* forms a gripping diary of this phase in production, *Apocalypse* was already six weeks behind schedule and $2 million over budget. "More and more," she wrote, "it seems like there are parallels between the character of Kurtz and Francis. There is the exhilaration of power in the face of losing everything, like the excitement of war when one kills and takes the chance of being killed."

So in June 1976 Coppola flew back to the United States. At home in Napa, he read a book about Genghis Khan, presumably to focus his thoughts on the analysis of Kurtz's yen for sovereignty. It was at this crucial juncture too that Francis acknowledged the inadequacies of John Milius's original ending. From then on, he would rewrite the film, often working away in his trailer in the Philippines just before scenes were shot. Private jokes were sewn into the texture of the picture, like the name tag, Col. G. Lucas, on Harrison Ford's army shirt in the Nha Trang briefing sequence.

Coppola began to enumerate the aspects of the Vietnam struggle that were different to those of earlier wars. The use of helicopters. Drugs. The fact that blacks were always sent to the front lines. The extreme youth of the soldiers. "It was my thought," he wrote, "that if the American audience could look at the heart of what Vietnam was really like—what it looked and felt like—then they would be only one small step away from putting it behind them."

The director received aid from an unexpected quarter. Marlon Brando had arrived in Manila much overweight, despite submitting to a crash diet in a Los Angeles clinic. "I went with suggestions to him to rewrite the ending," recalls Coppola, "so that Kurtz's moral sickness is related to it. By dressing him in black, and photographing only his face and having another actor, who was quite tall, we'd try to give him [the stature of] almost a mythic giant."

At first, Brando wanted to disguise his obesity, but according to Michael Herr (author of the eventual narration for the film), the actor wrote a stream of brilliant lines for his character. "Brando's part was twice as long in the rough-cut as it was in the released movie," Herr confirms. It must have been during this phase in production that the balance tilted irrevocably in favor of a mythical tone, rather than naturalism. The rhyming of Kurtz's death with the slaughter of a water buffalo emerged almost from the environment in which *Apocalypse* was made. The Ifugaos were used as extras by Coppola in the sequences at Kurtz's jungle stronghold, and this tribe happens to kill the water buffalo as part of its ritual celebrations.

Coppola and Brando agreed that Kurtz should remain a mysterious figure. "The Kurtz in *Heart of Darkness* is sliced razor-thin. You build up a lot of anticipation . . . and when you get to him, he is literally a figure in the dark. Conrad never tells you what Kurtz says." He and Brando would talk over the material. Coppola would play back the tapes of their conversation, and dovetail some of the ideas into the screenplay.

In the days after Christmas 1976, Coppola viewed a rough assembly of the footage to date. Now there was the ending to improvise, and early in 1977 Francis returned to the Philippines. The final weeks of shooting proved arduous for all concerned. On March 5, alone in a mountain cabin, Martin Sheen awoke "feeling like there was a hot poker" on his chest. He had to struggle for a quarter of a mile to reach help. This heart attack was hardly surprising given the ordeals to which he was subjected—lying in mud in the cage where Kurtz holds him prisoner, covered with snakes, being spat upon, dragged through fetid mire. Miraculously, he was back on set on April 19.

A major sequence in a French plantation consumed hundreds of thousands of dollars, but was omitted from the film as it mutated month by month through the late 1970s. Aurore Clément and Christian Marquand flew from Paris to play a hostile French couple encountered by Willard and his escort team. Apart from containing dialogue apropos the French role in Indochina, this sequence would have been quite dramatic, with Clément being raped by American soldiers and Marquand then being executed.

This latter stage of filming became the source of most of the rumors surrounding *Apocalypse*. Coppola loathed the unremitting attention of the American press in the Philippines. "The notion of the film's not having an ending was true and not true," he says. "It was a film about morality, and there's not much place in America for those kinds of themes."

Richard Beggs, who worked on the film's sound elements, sets the record straight: "There were never *five* endings, but just the one, even if there were differently *edited* versions." The debate about the various finales blew up quite simply because Coppola departed so often from the original screenplay. Milius was never allowed to visit the Philippines ("I think Francis feared a coup!"), and Coppola was forced to improvise according to the dictates of circumstance. "He's on his way with another two pages," would crackle over the radio as his helicopter took off for the day's location. Milius concedes that Coppola did write one new scene in its entirety: the incident involving the sampan and the murder of the crew, but notes that "the finished movie is most like the first draft of all."

Coppola confesses that he struggled with the ending.

> I was really on the spot. I had no ending, but Brando couldn't play the scenes that were originally meant to form the ending. He was too fat. So, with the help of Dennis Jakob I decided that the ending could be the classic myth of the murderer who goes up the river, kills the king, and then himself becomes the king—it's the Fisher King, from *The Golden Bough*. Somehow it's the granddaddy of all myths. I was dealing with moral issues, and I didn't want to have just the typical John Milius ending, when the NVA attack and there's a gigantic battle scene, and Kurtz and Willard are fighting side by side, and

Kurtz gets killed, etc., etc. That's the way it was in the script. I wanted to explore the moral side, and in reading some of *The Golden Bough* and then *From Ritual to Romance* I found a lot concerning that theme. T. S. Eliot's *The Waste Land* also seemed so apt for the conclusion of the story.

Anyway, I was desperate. I was losing Brando in a matter of a week. So I shot all this stuff that I worked out in conversations with him.

Like many of the Zoetrope team, Richard Beggs was stunned by the phantasmagoric quality of those final months in the Far East. "For me, it was a mind-altering experience," he muses. "There were bodyguards watching constantly at night. One day the entire payroll was stolen. We used to swim by night in a naturally carbonated pool, surrounded by hundreds of candles just like the scene at Kurtz's headquarters."

Coppola snatched a few hours' sleep each night at the Pagsanjan Rapids Hotel, close to the location where the scenes of Kurtz's compound were staged and photographed. "It is scary," wrote Eleanor, "to watch someone you love go into the center of himself and confront his fears, fear of failure, fear of death, fear of going insane." Looking back from the perspective of 1988, Eleanor comments:

> Everybody I knew who cared about me, about us—everyone in the family who was aware of the conflicts that were going on in our experience—understood the situation. You go to the limits with your life and every possible aspect of it. You go to the heart of darkness in each of these different arenas, and why should I think I wouldn't go to the heart of darkness myself?

On May 21, however, Francis was in buoyant mood. The main shoot was at an end. Never in his life, he told the crew, had he seen "so many people happy to be out of a job." A private jet took him home the long route: first to Rome, where Storaro and his Italian colleagues deplaned, then to Cannes for a peek at the film festival, on to Madrid to see some bullfighting, and then back to New York via London.

In the summer of 1977, Walter Murch joined the production. Coppola told him that he had four months to assemble the sound. As Murch recalls:

> The script had been narrated, and yet when I came on the film the narration had been abandoned. I looked at it and said, well, if we have four months to finish the movie, and to get the ideas across—the script relied on narrative dialogue to convey certain ideas—there *is* a way of telling these ideas without narration, but it will take ten months to figure that out because it's a very sensitive area. So let's try narration again. I had just come off Fred Zinnemann's

Julia, and I was *used* to narration. So I put it back in, I recorded it myself, saying those lines of dialogue, and began to structure it around those ideas.

Coppola was dejected in September, telling his wife that he felt "there is only about a twenty percent chance [I] can pull the film off." By early November he had prevailed on Lehman Katz and other executives at United Artists to delay the premiere from May to October 1978. Privately, the Coppolas were enduring a crisis in their marriage. Francis, overwhelmed by the pressure of keeping *Apocalypse* on course, and infatuated with another woman, was far from home in many respects.

Michael Herr received a call from Zoetrope in January 1978. His dazzling, profoundly troubled journal about Vietnam, *Dispatches*, had just appeared and was attracting ecstatic notices. "In the great line of Crane, Orwell, and Hemingway," wrote the *Washington Post*. "He seems to have brought to his book the ear of a musician and the eye of a painter, Frank Zappa and Francis Bacon."

Herr arrived in the Bay Area in February, and found Coppola and his colleagues exhausted and depressed, staring at 1.5 million feet of film. "The narration written thus far," Herr maintains, "was totally useless. So, over a period of a year I wrote various narrations. Francis gave me very close guidelines. It was a new experience for me and, I must say, a great experience."

Murch, meanwhile, was striving to address the problem posed by the requirement to make a quadrophonic film about Vietnam when the libraries were devoid of *any* stereo recordings of *any* weapons, much less weapons used in Vietnam. Compounding the difficulties was the inadequacy of the sound material brought home from the Philippines. The small location crew had apparently lacked both time and resources sufficient to record jungle sounds, or any ambient noises whatever. "So when they came back," comments Richard Beggs, "we had essentially to fabricate the mood of the jungle on the soundtrack."

Ironically, *Apocalypse Now* would establish a benchmark in sound technique for the movies. Murch's fastidious insistence on recording the most up-to-date gunfire, for example, created a sense of authenticity lacking in most contemporary war films. "Split surrounds" were used so that the audience would enjoy a measure of directionality in place of the old mono sound. "Actually it was a *quintuphonic soundtrack*," emphasizes Murch, "because there were three channels of sound from behind the screen and two channels of sound emerging from behind the audience—a left rear and a right rear."

Each new deadline seemed to dissolve in a mist. Eleanor recorded in her diary on May 10 that Francis had "decided that it will not be possible to finish the film for a December release and will have to postpone the opening until spring of 1979."

Melodrama pursued the production even in the comparative peace of the Sentinel Building. Fred Rexer turned up while they were looping the film, and regaled the sound engineers with stories of how, as a CIA operative, he had executed Viet Cong chieftains by squeezing his fingers through their eye-sockets and literally tearing their skulls apart. This colorful individual had presented John Milius with a rifle as a mark of respect for *The Wind and the Lion*, the film that had established Milius as the standard-bearer of the new machismo in Hollywood. In the basement studio he produced a loaded .45, handed it to Martin Sheen and said: "You could shoot anyone in this room. You have the power of life and death in your hands." Sheen was stunned, and Coppola gaped in horror through the glass of the control room. The specter of the war continued to haunt Zoetrope long after *Apocalypse* was completed. One veteran tried to reach the upstairs offices, insisting that Coppola should make a film of his experiences and that if he would not, well, then he'd blow him away.

Coppola's relationship with Jim Harvey, chairman of United Artists and boss of its parent company, Transamerica, remained good. The Transamerica pyramid building overlooked Coppola's eyrie at the junction of Columbus and Kearny Streets in San Francisco. Francis had given Harvey a telescope, inscribed with the words, "To Jim Harvey, from Francis Coppola, so you can keep an eye on me." (It was also an in-joke, because a similar telescope stands in the offices of the ominous "Director" in *The Conversation*.) But by September 1978, even this friendship was under stress. Money was still being poured into *Apocalypse*, and it was obvious that the picture would not be ready for the Christmas season. *The Black Stallion*, a Zoetrope production for UA release, was also more than a year behind schedule.

Confidence had been eroded by bad vibrations from a "work-in-progress" screening Coppola had held for 900 people in late April. Yet such daring runs through Francis's personality; without this gambler's impulse he could never have achieved many of the most stirring scenes in his work. The "sneak preview" is part and parcel of Hollywood's marketing strategy, just as a new play or musical opens its doors for previews prior to the first night. Coppola has enhanced the significance of such screenings. The two most trumpeted "public previews" in his career to date have been at Cannes in 1979 (with *Apocalypse*; and at Radio City Music Hall in 1981 (with *One from the Heart*). United Artists shrank from the idea of presenting an untidy version of *Apocalypse Now* at such a prominent event as the Cannes festival. Over a thousand members of the press would be gathered together, ready to destroy the picture in a moment unless it proved to be a masterpiece. But, although UA had advanced funds to Zoetrope for finishing the production, the company in fact possessed only domestic rights to the title. So Coppola could determine for himself what tactics would be pursued outside the United States. Remembering the warm reception accorded *You're a Big Boy Now*, and the unexpected Palme d'Or for *The Conversation*, Coppola was tempted by the invitation to screen *Apocalypse* at Cannes. The final commitment to enter the festival was made in mid-April 1979, less than a month before the Riviera event was due to unfurl.

In the week prior to Cannes, Coppola arranged three sneak previews —each a slightly different version of the movie. He foolishly allowed critics to attend the screenings, believing they would honor the embargo Zoetrope had placed on reviews. But on May 14 Rona Barrett, in her infinite wisdom, told millions of TV viewers that *Apocalypse Now* was "a disappointing failure." *Variety*, realizing that the embargo had been broken, went ahead and reviewed the film.

Murch and his colleagues worked under intense pressure to produce a quadrophonic soundtrack in time for the festival screenings. At Cannes, Zoetrope technicians worked during the night to install additional speakers on the theater walls and in the corners of the auditorium (and this would be the sole major occasion on which *Apocalypse* opened in darkness with a medley of jungle sounds and cries on the track).

Francis spent the night on board a yacht moored off Cannes. Early next day, the Palais des Festivals was congested with critics and others trying to see the morning projection. The response proved better than Coppola could have anticipated, and prolonged applause greeted the final fadeout to blackness. Those present were puzzled by the indistinct logic of the ending, with Martin Sheen apparently either trapped forever by the spirit of Kurtz or sailing downstream to salvation. But Coppola had outflanked the press by proclaiming beforehand that this was a "work in progress." He almost lost the goodwill he had gained when he emerged from the wings of the Palais for his press conference, and gave vent to his frustration where the media were concerned. To be accorded the entire

Palais for a press conference was an enormous privilege; only Ingmar Bergman, for *Cries and Whispers*, had been granted such an honor during the 1970s.

Coppola relished the chance to strike back at his tormentors. He harangued those journalists who, he claimed, had taken every opportunity to castigate him and his film during the months of misfortune in the Philippines. He veered from the practical detail ("as of May 1979, the budget is $30.5 million") to the magniloquent pronouncement, saying that *Apocalypse Now* was "about the precarious balance between the choices between good and evil, light and darkness." He even admitted his own recklessness. "We had access to too much money, too much equipment. We built villages in the jungle and the weather destroyed them, and we went insane. Eventually I realized I was not making the movie. The movie was making itself—or the jungle was making it for me." Today he acknowledges that his anger had overcome his better judgment. "I shouldn't have spoken that way. The press had been hounding me, slipping people into the Philippines, and kept emphasizing the financial aspects. It was *my* money, so if I was being brave enough to continue, why hurt my picture by laying stress on an out-of-control budget?" The newspaper critic Rex Reed took umbrage, and stalked out of the Palais.

When, on the final day of the festival, word leaked out that the Palme d'Or had been shared between *Apocalypse* and Volker Schlöndorff's *The Tin Drum*, fortune seemed at last to be turning in Francis's favor again. True, the award carried little weight at the American box-office—as the precedent of *The Conversation* had established—but it certainly improved the prospects for *Apocalypse* in the international market, and reconfirmed Coppola as the prime American director of his generation.

Back in San Francisco after the festival, Murch, Beggs, and others continued to fine-tune the picture for a late summer release. Michael Herr recalls that at one stage Coppola wanted to present the film with an interval. This would have occurred after the dramatic shooting-up of the sampan. "Then, coming out of the intermission, we would have heard Sheen for some thirty seconds—no image, just voice-over—giving vent to his thoughts about the sampan incident, while he cleans his .45."

The final release version runs to a minute or two less than two and a half hours. To the surprise of many industry observers, not least executives at United Artists, *Apocalypse Now* performed well at the box-office when it opened in August 1979. Hy Smith and others at UA had produced a stoutly bound book, tracking the campaign strategy for *Apocalypse* through its summer opening all the way to Academy Awards night the following spring. The TV commercials emphasized the drama and mystery of the movie, with one forty-five-second spot using the spectacular *Ride of the Valkyries* music. Joseph Farrell and his National Research Group had convinced Coppola that the film should be marketed around the name and image of Marlon Brando, and had dismissed the Zoetrope plea for a $10 admission tag to emphasize the "special event" quality of *Apocalypse*. For all his rejection of traditional Hollywood methods, Francis Coppola remains a born showman. It was he who forced through the concept of adding "II" to the title of a hit movie, creating a compulsive interest among devotees of the original picture. It was Coppola who—perhaps inspired by the example of Hitchcock—gave his blessing to films in which he personally believed, so that the credit above the title, "Francis Ford Coppola Presents," added luster and credibility to a film's marketing campaign. Steven Spielberg has since adopted these tactics with conspicuous success. And it was Coppola who cheerfully and courageously hired the 6,000-seat Radio City Music Hall in order to present Abel Gance's silent film masterpiece, *Napoléon* (see Chapter Eight).

A majority of critics praised the ambition and confident visual sweep of *Apocalypse Now*, although several expressed dissatisfaction with the finale. Most scathing was Frank Rich in *Time* magazine. He branded the film as "emotionally obtuse and intellectually empty. It is not so much an epic account of the grueling war as an incongruous, extravagant monument to artistic self-defeat."

Vincent Canby, in the *New York Times*, criticized the film as regards *Heart of Darkness* for expressing "no feeling for literature, for how the written word operates on the mind, and no sense of history, of how these events connect with war." He granted that individual scenes and images possessed "tumultuous life," but declared that "the end effect of the film is of something borrowed and not yet fully understood." As so often in his career, Coppola received the most sympathetic notices from the West Coast. Charles Champlin, in the *Los Angeles Times*, admitted that "Some ultimate and flawed perfection may have been narrowly missed. But as a noble use of the medium and as a tireless expression of a national anguish, it towers over everything that has been attempted by an American filmmaker in a very long time."

United Artists' massive, and patiently constructed campaign brought dividends. In its first five days at the Ziegfeld in New York, the University Theater in Toronto, and the Cinerama Dome in Hollywood, *Apocalypse Now* grossed $322,489. The picture ran exclusively at these three locations for four weeks. Then it opened at a further dozen theaters on October

3 before fanning out to several hundred the following week. Printed credits were distributed to audiences during the exclusive engagements. But for the general release, on 35mm prints, Coppola played the end credits over footage he had shot of Kurtz's stronghold being blown up. "I don't know who it was who said that if you cut the titles off the front of all movies, you wouldn't be able to tell the difference between them," reflects Coppola.

> *Apocalypse* was always intended to have no titles, and it's wonderful without titles. But when we did it in 35mm, we had to have titles, and I was going to put them on a black background when someone suggested that as we had all that footage of the explosion, why not use that? The closest thing I can reconcile titles with is curtain calls. When I was in school, I was famous for not having curtain calls. We would do a play like *Streetcar Named Desire*, and Blanche DuBois would be taken off to the insane asylum, and the people would clap and the lights would come on, and no one came out for a bow. There was an uproar. The audience got upset. The faculty got upset. And I said, they took Blanche off to the asylum, and I don't feel right about interrupting that.

The final tally for domestic rentals exceeded $40 million. Revenue from overseas release meant that *Apocalypse Now* had come home a victor, bloody but unbowed, with over $100 million in box-office takings. "I know," laughs Francis, "because we pay Brando on percentage!"

Late in 1979, Eleanor's diary of the production, *Notes*, appeared. She had written the notes without any intention of publishing them but when she read them aloud to Francis, he told her they were good and urged her to seek a publisher. He felt that her comments had a universal touch, that they referred not just to her story but to the experience of anyone who had ever been sucked into the logistics of making an epic movie on location. After the book came out, however, many reproached Coppola for "letting" his wife do such a thing. "Francis became embarrassed, and angry," recalls Eleanor. "I myself was a little shocked; people saw the diary only in terms of the gossip aspect."

*   *   *

Michael Herr needed seven full years to write *Dispatches*, his scarifying account of life under fire during the Vietnam War. So the three years or so that Coppola required to produce *Apocalypse Now* seems not unreasonable in a creative (if not financial) context.

Like some mighty hawser, the film consists of various tightly braided strands—the psychological plot from *Heart of Darkness*, the traumatic ordeal of an entire generation in the Southeast Asian conflict, Francis's own odyssey, and the melodramatic, pop-opera idiom so accurately reflecting time and place.

The many affinities between Coppola and Orson Welles might have become more unmistakable had the Mercury production of *Heart of Darkness* not been abandoned in 1940 in the face of daunting technical problems and a soaring budget. Both men are obsessed with the abuse of power, on a personal rather than national level. Welles, throughout his career, scarcely touched on contemporary political issues by name. Joseph Conrad had been fired by the impact of Belgian imperialism in the Congo during the nineteenth century; but so stripped of any specific geographical reference is the narrative that *Heart of Darkness* might as well unfold in the Far East or Latin America. Cinematographer Vittorio Storaro claims that in *Apocalypse* he "wanted to express the main idea of Joseph Conrad, which is the imposition of one culture on top of another culture. I was trying to express the conflict between natural energy and artificial energy."

Coppola has been rebuked for not analyzing the ideology that brought the United States into the war. But other films, mostly documentaries, had already done so—*In the Year of the Pig* and *Hearts and Minds* are just two examples. Even the widely applauded *Platoon* makes no reference to the strength of antiwar sentiments in the United States.

Both *Apocalypse Now* and Welles's *Heart of Darkness* were conceived on a metaphorical scale, although Coppola's film deploys the sights and sounds of modern warfare to an extraordinarily plausible degree. Welles intended the camera to represent the point of view of Marlow, the narrator of Conrad's novella, perhaps producing a claustrophobic mood that would have forced the spectator to confront Kurtz's evil with no means of psychological escape. Coppola's continual concentration on close-ups of Willard serves a similar purpose. These close-ups are sometimes so intimate that Martin Sheen's eyes fill the screen, their smoky blue irises and bloodshot whites reflecting the candor of Willard's attitude and the stress of his mission. Such shots, plus the equally revealing close-ups of Kurtz in his somber hideout, impart a private dimension to a film that deals so effectively with the large-scale theater of war.

In other respects, to judge by the surviving documents and storyboards concerning the Mercury production, Welles would have remained more faithful to his source in terms of period and structure (the book appeared in 1902). *Apocalypse Now*, for instance, contains no role for a woman, and

Kurtz's fiancée (who would have been played in Welles's film by Dita Parlo) is reduced to a silent native girl who wanders in and out of a scene or two at the close of the movie.

The two directors are tightly linked, however, by their fascination with the exotic and the diabolical, the notion of Man as a fallen angel. Their villains all arouse a tantalizing sympathy in the audience. Willard in *Apocalypse Now* not only resembles Marlow; he has a distinct kinship with Leland in *Citizen Kane*, van Stratten in *Mr. Arkadin*, and Vargas in *Touch of Evil*: he finds himself implicated in Kurtz's monstrous guilt, contaminated by the force of his personality. Speer's relationship to Hitler is a real-life equivalent—and according to Charles Higham, Kurtz would have referred specifically to Hitler in the dialogue of the Welles film.

* * *

By all accounts (those of Robert Stone, Michael Herr, Stephen Wright, Tim O'Brien, and others), most GIs in Vietnam spent their days and nights lodged in a ghastly spectral zone between waking and sleeping. All dreams were nightmares. Paranoia fused with a degenerate loathing of the Viet Cong, the North Vietnamese Army, and finally that most chilling of nominal abstractions for the jungle foe, "Charlie."

The My Lai massacre became the most extreme image for this desperate assertion of firepower. A crawling insecurity, bound up with a self-loathing that few soldiers could ever articulate, triggered the indiscriminate killing that occurred under stress in Vietnam. "There must be a temptation to play God," as a general says by way of explaining Kurtz's dementia. This overwhelming sense of nightmare pervades *Apocalypse Now* to an extent barely noted when the film appeared. Having been temporarily deceived by *The Deer Hunter* less than a year earlier, critics tended to bracket Coppola's film with Cimino's, excoriating both men for sidestepping the true controversy and lessons of the war. *Apocalypse Now* eschews any direct discussion or dissection of the Vietnam disaster; its very idiom, its cinematic language, precludes philosophical debate.

Only one other film, *Platoon*, has approached the authenticity of mood captured by Coppola in *Apocalypse*. When Oliver Stone's requiem for the grunt took America by storm in the winter of 1986–1987, critics were quick to mock *Apocalypse* by comparison. Stone, after all, had served on the ground in Vietnam; he knew the landscape and the soldiers' argot. There is no denying the visceral savagery of *Platoon*, but Coppola too had shown the sweat and the tears. His approach was altogether more operatic than Stone's. *Platoon* is a *little* film, over so quickly that one wonders if the end is only an intermission. With each passing year, Americans have felt more able to confront the hideous facts of the war in Southeast Asia, and it is doubtful if *Platoon* could, or would, have been made ten years earlier. The greatest strength of *Platoon* is its *pain*, its frustration and fury in the face of ignorance and a hostile terrain. Coppola, instead, goes for the high ground of objectivity. In this respect, he clings to Conrad. Kurtz's tormented gasp, "The horror! The horror!" was chosen by T. S. Eliot as an epigraph for the original version of *The Waste Land* long before Brando utters it at the end of *Apocalypse Now*. Like Eliot, Coppola regards *Heart of Darkness* as a metaphor for the black soul of our era. Even such an extrovert director as John Ford gropes for a similar effect when he shows John Wayne emerging from the Comanche tent at the close of *The Searchers*, his face clouded with a dreadful disgust after scalping the Indian chief who abducted his niece.

Time and locale are fixed with supreme precision in the opening seconds of *Apocalypse*. The edge of a distant jungle. Helicopter gunships flitting back and forth across the frame like irritant insects. Then the blooming incandescence of a napalm attack on the lushness of those remote palms, accompanied by what Herr called the "distant, icy sound" of the Doors —Jim Morrison singing "The End." The absence of realistic noise from the airstrike establishes at a stroke Coppola's determination to focus on the glamor and intoxicating tints of modern technological warfare. Less thoughtful directors have perverted this approach in films like *Commando* and *Rambo*.

By degrees the dreamlike torpor of this introduction gives way to more naturalistic shots of Captain Willard waking in his room in Saigon, realizing that the fan in the ceiling had stimulated his recurrent thoughts of helicopters. Willard talks to us almost seductively, the intimacy of his voice beckoning us into his state of mind, proffering a shared confession. Bored, frustrated, haunted by God knows what atrocities in the past, Willard waits for a mission. Already at this early stage, Coppola switches, as it were, from DC to AC; when the captain suddenly smashes his fist into the bedroom mirror, and collapses screaming, the sound of his anguish is unheard. This rotation between subjective and objective, collusion and repugnance, will continue throughout the movie.

Apocalypse Now calls on the essentials of opera, myth, and melodrama more even than those of the 1960s drug culture. The conversation in the General's quarters at Nha Trang, when Willard's mission is revealed to him, reeks of the uneasy realism of a recitative The camera crawls over mundane objects like plates of food, packs of cigarettes. The balance of this scene is wrought with painstaking care by Coppola. There are three voices—the general's, Kurtz's on the tape recording, and Willard's, enunciating his anxiety at the prospect of the river "snaking like a main-circuit cable into the heart of the war, plugging me straight into Kurtz." The delicate synthesis of these verbal declarations transcends the usual formula exposition of most war movies, and contrives also to evoke the spirit of *Heart of Darkness*. Conrad's Kurtz may not have dreamed of a snail crawling along the edge of a straight razor (as Brando's Kurtz does), but in most other respects he is reflected in Coppola's vision and description.

Colonel Kurtz's exploits with the Green Berets are a latterday equivalent of the "universal genius" label accorded by Conrad to his character. Kurtz, in the words of the general briefing Willard, is "one of the most outstanding officers this country has ever produced." He lurks at the head of a serpentine river, as in Conrad's description, "resembling an immense snake uncoiled, with its head in the sea, its body at rest curving over a vast country, and its tail lost in the depths of the land." To reach this "Chief of the Inner Station," Marlow—Conrad's narrator and an obvious model for Willard—must negotiate a primeval forest and suffer dangers comparable in spirit and detail to those experienced by Coppola's officer. The avid search for ivory in the novella has been replaced by Milius and Coppola with a more abtract power complex. The Americans stayed in Vietnam not so much for fiscal gain as for the maintenance of sovereign influence in their imperial struggle with the Soviet Union. In an otherwise sympathetic review of the film, Washington-based Margot S. Kernan wrote with feeling: "*Apocalypse Now* mystifies the facts: that Vietnam was the longest war in American history; that it was undeclared and unpopular; that we grossly misunderstood the Vietnamese, enemies and allies alike; that opposition to the war finally drove President Johnson from office."

Apocalypse Now, like *Heart of Darkness*, amounts to a journey, a quest the ramifications of which emerge from the gloom only as each step is completed. Willard's brief is to "terminate the colonel's command—with extreme prejudice." For Marlow, "it was written I should be loyal to the nightmare of my choice." For both travelers, the discovery of Kurtz will lead to a confrontation with their inmost self. It is a journey from sanity to insanity, dream to nightmare, and finally to deliverance and enlightenment. Nor is the personality of Kurtz so removed from actuality. Michael Herr in *Dispatches* refers to similar spook deities. "There had been one man who 'owned' Long An province, a Duke of Nha Trang, hundreds of others whose authority was absolute in hamlets or hamlet complexes where they ran their ops until the wind changed and their ops got run back on them."

Even more familiar a Vietnam figure is Lt. Col. Kilgore, the manic officer encountered by Willard on the first stage of his long, arduous trip. This archetypal Southern bullshitter bears the name of a real Texas town. Kilgore struts around in black-felt stetson, a yellow Flying Corps scarf at his throat. His principal obsession in life is surfing; strafing and murdering the Vietnamese appears subordinate to the size of the waves on a particular beach. Willard lights on him in the aftermath of a punitive airstrike. Kilgore marches past the dead, flipping a playing card atop each corpse —"A message for Charlie," he announces. Michael Herr recalls that, after an ambush that had killed several Americans, the Viet Cong "covered the field with copies of a photograph that showed one more young, dead American, with the punch line mimeographed on the back, 'Your X-rays have just come back from the lab and we think we know what your problem is.' "

If *Apocalypse Now* is a voyage from sanity to madness, then the Kilgore episode marks a crucial port of call. This officer is consumed with delusions of grandeur, but can still function with ruthless discipline in the eye of such surreal scenes as a cow being borne aloft by a Chinook while in the foreground a padre celebrates alfresco communion. Coppola himself enjoys a cameo role, as a newsreel director shouting to Willard that he should "go on through" the chaos, "just like in the war." In Willard's startled expression resides the manifest question, If this isn't the war, what is?

Kilgore offers to airlift Willard's boat and literally drop it into the river in the heart of enemy territory if he can be rewarded with a glimpse of a "really good six-foot break" in the water.

A bugler sends them on their way at dawn and the ensuing sequence is one of the most inspired and breathtaking in the Coppola canon. The helicopters sweep in like locusts, and as they approach the placid village Kilgore snaps on a tape of Wagner's *Ride of the Valkyries*, until the sky rings with the whooping, arrogant chords, and the villagers quail. Willard is appalled by the indiscriminate slaughter. But he is part of the remorseless machine. He must press on with his mission. Not so a young grunt who cringes inside one of the gunships. "I'm not going!" he screams, "I'm not going!" before being dragged out along the sand by a fellow soldier.

Kilgore comes across as all the more alarming for his calmness under fire. Others panic when their machine is hit; Kilgore realizes immediately that it is just a flare. Ordering his men to strip and surf while the battle still booms on, he watches with satisfaction as some U.S. jets lay down a mass of napalm over the treeline. "I love the smell of napalm in the morning," he declares. "It smells like . . . *victory!*"

Some of the virtues of the old cavalry run in Kilgore's blood, but in demented form. He gives his canteen to a wounded South Vietnamese man who cries for water. The instant he sees some of his own soldiers wounded during the attack, he demands over the radio that they be kept out of the fighting and back in the hospital inside fifteen minutes. Kilgore embodies the Westmoreland brand of commander whose efficient manipulation of men and materials should have been sufficient to win the war in Southeast Asia. By presenting Kilgore's exploits in operatic terms, Coppola suggests the self-conceit and the fascination with pyrotechnics that kept the Americans from challenging the Viet Cong successfully at a guerrilla level. Like Orson Welles's Harry Lime in *The Third Man*, Kilgore can gaze down from his Olympian heights and regard all men as scurrying ants. Robert Duvall acted the part with a particular person in mind, an officer at West Point, "whose life only made sense if there was a war." One is reminded of a comment by John Milius to the effect that war is "unspeakably attractive. People enjoy intensity. The human animal seems to be drawn to it like a moth to a flame."

As Willard continues his journey, however, even this control of resources and weaponry begins to ebb. The alien environment closes in on the men. In a bizarre sequence, Willard and Hicks "the Chef" (Frederic Forrest) leave the boat to search for mangoes in the encroaching jungle. Their clumsy movements among the huge trees and clotted vegetation verge on the ludicrous. In Conrad's words, "Going up that river was like traveling back to the earliest beginnings of the world, when vegetation rioted on the earth and the big trees were kings." Hicks, though, chats with incongruous affability about his training to be a *saucier* in New Orleans.

Suddenly some weird sound alerts Willard. Guns cocked, he and Hicks move stealthily forward. But this time Charlie is not around. A tiger bursts into sight with a snarl, and sends Willard and the Chef flailing back to the boat. Like Pavlov's dogs, the soldiers aboard start firing in all directions. The tiger was a real, tamed one called Gambi. A stuntman tied a pig to a piece of line and dashed away with it to make the tiger run across camera. But Forrest and Sheen panicked, and flew for their lives. Emilio, the focus-puller, scaled a palm tree in seconds.

In one brilliant scene, Coppola has unleashed the frustration and terror that tremble just beneath the well-armored surface of these conscripts. "Never get out of the boat," repeats Willard like a litany as the panic subsides and the voyage proceeds. The boat becomes an ark, sheltered and sheltering, full of talk of home, and booze, and the consolation of dope.

Kurtz, though, left his boat. And Willard, sifting through the dossier, starts to empathize with the renegade colonel. The blurring of identities moves on a stage. So too does the ambiguity of Coppola's and Milius's attitude to the war. Kurtz's persistence in joining the Green Berets at the age of thirty-eight is viewed as a plus for his personality, ruling out any eventual revelation of him as a routine pacifist or conscientious objector.

Women, for these men, exist only in photographs. In the sequence at the supply depot, Willard witnesses the arrival by helicopter of some Playmates, who put on a provocative show for the soldiers. Above the crowded bleachers rises a row of phallic tubes, each blazoned with a regimental coat-of-arms. The dancers taunt their audience, bringing them to a rowdy climax of enthusiasm and frustration. One is reminded of Willard's earlier remark, "The more they tried to make it like home, the more they made [the soldiers] miss it." The entertainment symbolizes the colonial mood prevailing in even such a desperate conflict as Vietnam. The R & R at this supply station is merely a glitzier, more garish version of the English club with its tiffin at 4 P.M. and gin-slings at sundown. In contrast, according to Willard, Charlie is "dug in too deep, or moving too fast. His idea of great R & R was cold rice and a little rat-meat. He had only two ways home: death—or victory."

The screenplay still adheres to Conrad. The steamboat in *Heart of Darkness* has become the navy patrol boat of *Apocalypse Now*, but the nature of the trip remains identical. Willard, like Marlow, lies below deck and speculates on the character of Kurtz. The last-known photo of Kurtz shows only a bulky black shadow, fringed with a halo of light. Kurtz has slipped his official moorings, escaped illegally into Cambodia beyond the official reach of the generals.

The chaos aboard the patrol craft seems like a microcosm of the entire war situation. Drugs have fermented a spiritual claustrophobia, ready to explode at the slightest excuse. Shooting off a few rounds at a stray tiger may be a humorous aside, but the sampan incident comes as a sobering jolt to the men as much as the audience. Two of the young soldiers are so trigger-happy that when an unfortunate Vietnamese woman aboard a junk makes a spontaneous movement toward a covered basket, they open fire.

Hicks breaks down yet again, screaming and sobbing at the crazed pity of it all. Willard finally puts a bullet into the head of the wounded woman, extinguishing her agony as the hero of a Western kills his wounded horse. Lance, probably the youngest member of the team, his face daubed with outlandish camouflage, contains the crew's spasms of guilt by taking aboard the puppy that had lain concealed in the basket. Offscreen, Willard notes with rancor, "It was the way we had over here of living with ourselves. We'd cut 'em in half with a machine gun and give 'em a band-aid. It was a lie, and the more I saw of them, the more I hated lies." Frederic Forrest recalls how the first take of this scene "knocked everyone out. Vittorio Storaro was very moved. They just let the cameras roll."

They come by night to the last outpost on the Nong river, a bridge being bombarded by the enemy in a lurid inferno of flares and mortar fire. "You're in the asshole of the world, Captain!" yells a soldier who delivers a pack of orders to Willard.

Grunts are firing at random, listening to the taunts of the Viet Cong beyond the wire. Willard crawls through the Stygian dugouts, searching in vain for a commanding officer. The collapse in morale and discipline is complete. For Coppola, the apocalypse will always occur in the blackness, "as on a darkling plain . . . /Where ignorant armies clash by night," to quote Matthew Arnold. The reason for this film's rhyming so well with Conrad's book lies in the persistent triumph of darkness over light. And in that sudden extinction of light, Coppola perceives a more profound truth.

As the boat surges upstream, the crew revels in mail from home. Someone has sent a clipping about the Manson murders, a sharp reminder that insanity rules at home too. Lance sets off flares for fun, clothing the craft in a purple haze and quickly attracting the attention of Viet Cong hidden along the river bank. In the exchange of fire, another member of the crew dies. But, shielding himself from the truth, Lance cares only for the dog he has coddled since the sampan incident. The voice of the dead man's mother reading the letter that has just arrived contributes an incongruous touch of sentimentality. It is an arbitrary and unrealistic moment, at odds with the rest of the film.

The one specific incident in *Apocalypse Now* that belongs both to the earliest Milius screenplay and also to *Heart of Darkness* occurs as the boat emerges from a fog-bank to come under attack from tribesmen. Chief Phillips, driving the boat, is struck by a spear. In Conrad's story the helmsman is also black, and foolishly leaves the shelter of his housing to fire a Martini-Henry in indiscriminate response to the fusillade of arrows.

Coppola reproduces the texture of that moment exactly as Conrad wrote it, with the chief looking at Willard "in an extraordinary, profound, familiar manner, and fell upon [his] feet." But he adds a macabre touch. The dying chief seizes Willard around the throat as the captain bends over him. For several seconds, Willard fights to free himself, but not before recognizing, surely, that the chief regards him as the villain for pressing on with this insane mission.

The final phase of *Apocalypse Now* fuses with *Heart of Darkness* to a remarkably precise degree. It also remains faithful to the realities of the Vietnam War. Michael Herr, in *Dispatches*, describes the Montagnards as "a kind of upgraded, demi-enlightened Annamese aborigine, often living in nakedness and brooding silence in their villages . . . Their nakedness, their painted bodies, their recalcitrance, their silent composure before strangers, their benign savagery and the sheer, awesome ugliness of them combined to make most Americans who were forced to associate with them a little uncomfortable over the long run."

When at last Willard's boat glides into Kurtz's "station," the Montagnards awaiting it appear livid in their white paint, and mesmerizing in their silence. The American photographer (Dennis Hopper), who comes aboard, echoes Conrad: "You don't talk with that man—you listen to him," adding that Kurtz is a warrior poet in the classic sense. As Willard wanders up the incline that surrounds Kurtz's temples, he sees human heads arrayed and ensconced in the walls, as though the place were a set from Puccini's opera *Turandot*. In *Heart of Darkness* the heads are dried, and impaled on posts. In Welles's storyboard for his aborted 1939 feature, the interior of Kurtz's temple would have been festooned with skulls.

Kurtz's appearance, after such a long wait, has a thrilling mystery to it. He addresses Willard from the shadows of a large, faintly sacred room. The dome of his bald head steals partially into the light, looking for some seconds like the sunstruck quarter of an alien planet. Conrad's Kurtz was bald too, as bald as an ivory ball. But although the slumbrous tone of Brando's speech is reminiscent of the book, his corpulence is not. Kurtz is described in *Heart of Darkness* as thin and lanky. In context, however, Brando's massive girth fits the role better. He looms like a predator out of the darkness. "You're an errand boy, sent by grocery clerks to collect a bill," he murmurs scornfully to Willard. Conrad's character makes a similar accusation: "You with your little peddling notions—you are interfering with me."

In the novella, Kurtz dies aboard the steamboat. There is no duel between him and Marlow. Coppola and Milius have altered the fundamentals at this juncture. Kurtz imprisons Willard in a cage, has Hicks killed, and then tosses his bloody head at Willard.

Willard cannot now escape a personal loathing of Kurtz's diabolical misuse of power. Willard must indeed terminate his quarry, "with extreme prejudice"—if only to expunge his own guilt at participating in the excesses of the war.

Coppola uses dissolves more and more, slowing the passage of time and blurring the divisions between night and day. Vittorio Storaro's cinematography in these scenes alone must have earned him the Academy Award he so richly deserved.

Kurtz recites lines from *The Waste Land*. The light-headed photographer snatches his cue like a Shakespearean fool, and exclaims to Willard, "This is the way the world ends, not with a bang—but a whimper!"

Kurtz's bookshelf is instructive: a Bible, copies of Sir James Frazer's seminal work on primitive religions and magic, *The Golden Bough*, and *From Ritual to Romance*, by Jessie Weston.

Apocalypse Now has often been charged with failing to come to any conclusion. But this long coda in Kurtz's domain houses the core of the film's meaning, and Kurtz's speeches alight unerringly on the reasons for the American predicament in Vietnam. He tells Willard that one must make friends with horror and moral terror. "If they are not [friends], then they are enemies to be feared; they are truly enemies."

He recalls an incident during his spell with Special Forces, when the Viet Cong had hacked off the arms of children whom Kurtz and his men had inoculated a short time before. He tells Willard how he suddenly recognized the superior strength of the enemy. "If I had ten divisions of those men, then our troubles here would be over very quickly." He admires their ability to "utilize their primordial instincts to kill, without feeling, without passion, without judgment—because it's judgment that defeats us."

Then Kurtz, in soft, veiled tones, bids Willard to be his executioner. He asks him to go to his home in the States and tell his son everything he has witnessed "here" (a word that seems to embrace all Vietnam rather than just the grotesque rituals of Kurtz's stronghold), "because there is nothing I detest more than the stench of lies."

"And if you understand me, Willard," he adds, "you will do this for me."

As the tribespeople inhale their drugs, and prepare for the sacrifice of the buffalo, Willard leaves the sanity of his boat and surfaces wraithlike from the oleaginous water; grasps a long machete; kills a guard without a sound; and slips into Kurtz's inner sanctum. On the soundtrack, Jim Morrison sings "Baby, Take a Chance with Us." Kurtz is dictating a final indictment of U.S. army policy as Willard gathers the strength to dispatch him.

Coppola spares us the realistic horror of the murder. Instead, with his remarkable gift for the montage climax, he alternates it with the death of the buffalo in the clearing below. Willard's machete rises and falls, but the blows are not heard, and the violation of Kurtz's body is suggested in the mortal strikes delivered to the buffalo's shoulders. The assassination obeys a dreamlike cadence, while the delicate chorus offscreen provides a contrapuntal effect. The buffalo slumps beneath the attack, but like Kurtz it takes an agonizing few moments to expire. In a final effort of will Kurtz—his face in horizontal profile, flecked with blood—utters the words that Conrad's Kurtz bequeathed to Marlow: "The horror! The horror!"

Moving as though underwater, Willard lurches through the camp. He pauses at Kurtz's desk, flicks through a manuscript. "Drop the Bomb. Exterminate them all!" has been scrawled in red across one typed page. Outside the crowd waits for him. As one man, the people kneel like acolytes, accepting Willard as their new god. With hair slicked back and his face smeared with livid shades of warpaint, Willard bears an uncanny resemblance to Kurtz. The "guilt" has been transferred to him, in the way that Hitchcock's and Welles's characters suffer from contact with evil.

But Willard lets the machete fall with a clatter, and the men stand yet again, moving docilely aside to let Willard pass. They drop their own weapons in unison. Willard leads Lance out of the throng and back to the boat.

Coppola closes the film with a haunting cluster of dissolves, evoking Willard's initial dream of helicopters and reprising Kurtz's oath, "The horror! The horror!" There is no progression into light, no easy release, no catharsis. Willard may be sailing back to civilization, may indeed be promoted to major for terminating the renegade Kurtz, but the murky, coagulating images reflect the final lines of Joseph Conrad's masterpiece: "and the tranquil waterway leading to the uttermost ends of the earth flowed sombre under an overcast sky—seemed to lead into the heart of an immense darkness."

CHAPTER EIGHT

Blows to the
Heart

In April 1979, Francis Coppola was asked to present the Academy Award for Best Director. *Apocalypse Now* had still not been released. Yet this was an opportunity chosen by Coppola for speculation. Startling an audience unaccustomed to lengthy declarations by Oscar presenters, he saluted the future: "I can see a communications revolution that's about movies and art and music and digital electronics and satellites but above all, human talent—and it's going to make the masters of the cinema, from whom we've inherited the business, believe things that they would have thought impossible."

Then, opening the envelope and reading the name of Michael Cimino for *The Deer Hunter*, he must have felt a pang of irony in the triumph of another director of Italian stock who had completed a movie about the Vietnam experience before *Apocalypse Now* had seen the light of day. Still, he hugged Cimino, calling him *paisan*, and looking for all the world like the patriarch of the 1970s. This probably marked the peak of Coppola's reputation, the moment when his aura of benevolence and brilliance was at its most bright. Ever since, the American critics and audiences have confessed to a feeling if not of betrayal then of frustrated expectation where Coppola is concerned. Little by little, month by month, he would have to fight harder to achieve credibility in the eyes of his audience.

A few days after the Oscar ceremonies, Francis's sovereignty among those he loved and with whom he worked was celebrated at a lavish party in Napa for his fortieth birthday. "This was an unbelievably spectacular party," recalls Francis, "that went on for days and days!" More than a

145

thousand guests put in an appearance, and the birthday cake, borne in on a stretcher, measured six feet in length.

Coppola had been fortunate in that his first disaster—the so-called Black Thursday when Warners had canceled all Zoetrope projects after seeing *THX 1138*—had occured at a point in his career when he was still far down the ladder. Before *The Godfather*, failure was permitted, even admired. After *The Godfather*, even the slightest shortcoming became a fiasco. "I have an ability like a pied piper to get everybody's dream going," he said later of the collapse of American Zoetrope in 1970, "but in the end I was vulnerable and got wiped out."

Now, at the tail end of the decade, he was determined to rebuild the ideals of Zoetrope by harnessing them to the new technology. But before plunging into the mysteries of video, he wanted to gather a team of talented individuals in San Francisco even as he planned to expand his studio activity in Los Angeles. While still engrossed in *Apocalypse Now*, he found time to give his name and blessing to friends and apostles. Carroll Ballard's *The Black Stallion* was bankrolled in effect through United Artists because of the company's involvement with Zoetrope on *Apocalypse*.

Fred Roos had been filleting book after book in a quest for suitable properties. One of his first acquisitions was *Hammett*, a novel that focused on the phase in Dashiell Hammett's life when he left the Pinkerton detective agency and set up as a mystery writer in downtown San Francisco. Nicolas Roeg, the English director of *Don't Look Now* and *The Man Who Fell to Earth*, was signed by Zoetrope to make a movie from Joe Gores's screen adaptation of his own novel. The script was delivered in mid-1977. But the search for a plausible star in the title role of Hammett proved fruitless. Roeg abandoned the project. Truffaut was approached, and found to be lukewarm about it all. Then in early 1978 the assiduous Roos caught a screening of *The American Friend*, and immediately contacted its German director, Wim Wenders, with a view to his taking the helm on *Hammett*.

Back in April 1977, however, Coppola had circulated a long memo to his staff. It was leaked to the *San Francisco Chronicle* and *Esquire*, and painted a picture of Francis as a man under siege in his own redoubt; as a man, indeed, resolved to concentrate on his own projects. "Once Carroll Ballard finishes *The Black Stallion*," he wrote, "and Nick Roeg finishes *Hammett*, there will be no future productions by any other directors. This will be a one-client studio and the sooner that we are able to gear ourselves to that fact, the better the company will run." This defensive stance has always been reflected in Coppola's insistence on absolute loyalty from his staff. As the financial crunch of the early 1980s approached, this loyalty became even more mandatory. Some could not last the pace, and quit Zoetrope. Others, like John Peters and Tom Luddy, came aboard just as Francis was running out of the big-time loot, and had to help steer Zoetrope through turbulent waters.

Part of the problem resides in Coppola's divided aims. On the one hand, he stands willing to risk all for his work. "I am cavalier with money," he says in the memo, "because I have to be, in order not to be terrified every time I make an artistic decision." On the other, he claimed as late as 1975 that all he "really wanted was to be a living member of *La Bohème*. My idea is to go up and write for three hours, then sit down in the café and tell funny stories about Proust to Mauriac, who is sitting next to me, then go over and see what's happening at the theater, drop down and see what the guys at the magazine are doing, have another *caffè* . . ."

This combination proved, in certain circumstances, fatal. *One from the Heart*, Francis's pet project after *Apocalypse Now*, led to the collapse of Zoetrope's Hollywood facility primarily because Francis's own money was sunk into it. Bernard Gersten, former vice-president for creative affairs at Zoetrope Studios, remarked in 1981: "The very qualities that attract the banks and their financial resources to Francis in the first place—that he's an exciting, classy director, that he makes profitable films, that he's a great showman—also put them off in time."

It would be unfair, however, to dismiss Zoetrope's non-Coppola films as mere satellites to his bright star. The artistic shortcomings of most of them are not connected to Coppola's dominance or interference in individual projects. Besides, with each passing year he was eager to give support to films and presentations over which he could, in practice, exercise no artistic control. During 1979 he helped James Caan re-edit *Hide in Plain Sight*, his first film as a director. More publicized was the crusading zeal with which he joined George Lucas in fighting for 20th Century–Fox to save Akira Kurosawa's epic, *Kagemusha*, by urging them to commit for an advance purchase of rights outside Japan. Such a spontaneous gesture was natural in a man who had screened *Seven Samurai*, Kurosawa's masterpiece, in the basement of his home in San Francisco. *Kagemusha* performed spectacularly in Japan, becoming the most popular of all domestic films ever released there.

And the enthusiasm for Kurosawa led to other things. When, at Kurosawa's invitation, Francis visited Tokyo for the premiere of *Kagemusha* in April 1980, he joined Tom Luddy in meeting the executor of the literary rights in Yukio Mishima's work—all because Paul Schrader had visited Coppola on the top floor of the Sentinel Building the previous month and told him of his dream of making a movie about the Japanese novelist. Francis called Luddy, his director of special projects, upstairs and said, "Look, Paul has this great idea and although we've set up the studio in LA to have things go through Lucy Fisher at the story department, this is one for you. I want you to produce it."

This little anecdote hints at the division of power that marked the brief period when Zoetrope functioned in both Los Angeles and San Francisco. Francis had begun renting space at the old Goldwyn Studios in 1972. By 1975 he was spending several days each month at the studios in LA, while continuing to initiate and supervise most projects from the Bay Area. "Francis had a dream of re-creating the 'old studios,' " says Fred Roos, "with writers and actors staying under contract. Everyone helped out. Caleb Deschanel did some uncredited photography on *Apocalypse* and some insert work was done by Carroll Ballard. We'd all be there helping, with Walter Murch a key figure, who had a hand in almost all the projects." The climax to all this activity was Coppola's acquisition of the former Hollywood General Studios for $6.7 million, in early 1979. In June of the same year, Tom Luddy was engaged by Zoetrope as a consultant in the research and development department. Soon he would be appointed director of special projects.

The arrival of Luddy in the Sentinel Building typified Coppola's abiding devotion to film-as-art. Tom Luddy had been friends with Francis for more than a decade, and attended the party to launch American Zoetrope in 1969. He was one of the most energetic film buffs in the United States. He had made the Pacific Film Archive in Berkeley a mecca for directors and critics from all over the world. Luddy screened hundreds of films a year, preserved hundreds more. His arch skill lies in introducing one talented person to another. When Kurosawa was eating dinner at the Chez Panisse restaurant in Berkeley in 1977, Luddy presented him to Coppola. In 1975 he had rented a large theater in San Francisco to screen Abel Gance's fabled *Napoléon* with a Wurlitzer organ and special projection that allowed Gance's triptych technique to be appreciated to the full. Francis was there in the first row, and adored the film. "One day," he told Luddy, "this thing should be done with an orchestra in Radio City Music Hall. It's incredible. This mustn't be just for the archives."

So Luddy, whose friends included everyone from Jean-Luc Godard to Dušan Makavejev, fostered Coppola's artistic kinship with non-American directors. If Zoetrope could not afford to finance their motion pictures, well, it would at least strive to have them shown in the United States. In late 1979, Zoetrope bought the U.S. rights to Hans-Jürgen Syberberg's *Our Hitler: A Film from Germany*. The critic Susan Sontag had alerted Luddy to the film. He screened it for Coppola, who was impressed. "This was really our first personal project," Luddy recalls. "We decided to put it on at Lincoln Center, in the 2,700-seat Avery Fisher Hall, and charge $10 to $12 a seat. People thought we were nuts. But it was a sell-out in twenty-four hours, and we repeated it several more times in New York, then took it on to various cities where it packed out theaters and became a kind of phenomenon."

Coppola wanted Zoetrope to initiate theatrical film events outside the realm of the normal commercial movie, proving that there was not merely an archive audience for productions that broke the rules.

Funding was generous, considering that the risks were so high. Zoetrope signed a deal at the turn of the decade, for instance, with Jean-Luc Godard. The French director had dropped out of fashion during the 1970s, and now had only a minority following even among film buffs. Although he had never ceased to be an innovator in his use of technology, his political preoccupations had drained his work of its early wit and sophistication. So when Coppola gave him $250,000 to help with the production of his film on the life of Bugsy Siegel, he was being courageous beyond mere philanthropy. Godard wanted to star Robert De Niro and Diane Keaton, but soon abandoned the project. He nurtured another idea, tentatively called *The Story* or *The Audience*, but this too was shelved. Godard, though, acted equitably in the circumstances. To cover Zoetrope's original investment, he offered Coppola and Luddy the U.S. rights to a new, recently completed feature film, *Sauve qui Peut (La Vie)*. Zoetrope accepted the arrangement, and released the picture through New Yorker Films in October 1980.

Godard, with his misanthropic view of the world, and his resolute rejection of traditional studio methods, fascinated Coppola. Back in the 1970s, Godard had started coming frequently to the West Coast. In July 1980 he assisted Coppola on background process plates of the Las Vegas settings for *One from the Heart*.

*   *   *

Even during the shooting of *Apocalypse Now*, Coppola had been giving thought to fresh projects. He planned, for example, to direct *Brotherhood of the Grape*, a novel about an Italian-American bricklayer in his seventies, living in California with his family. The book had been serialized in *City* magazine, and Robert Towne was set to write the screenplay.

Nothing came of it.

He was reported as being signed to direct a science fiction drama for NBC-TV during the 1976–1977 season. It would deal with earth's response to a first contact with creatures from another world. Carl Sagan, installed at Cornell University if not yet the guru he would become after *Cosmos*, would work on the script, and the movie would be produced by the Children's Television Workshop.

Nothing came of it. And with Steven Spielberg making *Close Encounters of the Third Kind*, it was hardly surprising.

By the time Coppola took his family to Moscow to attend a screening of *Apocalypse* at the film festival on August 24, 1979, he knew that the picture would in all likelihood recoup the huge investment he and United Artists had made in it. He began to concentrate on the re-creation of Zoetrope Studios. John Levin and Dan Cassidy, two Bay Area writers, were commissioned to produce an original screenplay entitled *South of Market*, about an Irish dry docks worker in San Francisco. A screen version of Jack Kerouac's bible of the Beat generation, *On the Road*, was in development. Godard toyed with the idea of directing it.

The acquisition of the studios in Los Angeles in mid-1979 gave the green light to several Zoetrope projects. Coppola now had a ten-and-a-half acre lot at his disposal. There were nine sound stages and thirty-four editing rooms. Francis added a touch of class wherever possible. "I'm trying," he said, "to create a film studio that really makes sense—not a place where lawyers and businessmen make deals with independent artists. Rather, a family or a large repertory company engaged in making movies." By February 1980, the studio was staffed up and running. Between two and three hundred people were on Zoetrope's books at the peak of its activity early the following year.

Zoetrope Mark II failed because of a fatal misjudgment of the public taste. On the one hand, Coppola wanted to exploit the dazzling new technological facilities that were emerging from Japanese and American labs. On the other one, he was convinced that audiences wanted old-fashioned, traditional genre movies. As Lucy Fisher, who worked as the industry's first woman head of production at Zoetrope until 1981, put it: "People are sick of watching actors walking around New York talking about their personal relationships"—a clear dig at the world of Woody

Allen. But Allen's productions, for all their Manhattan elitism, have still outgrossed the majority of the Zoetrope efforts.

Coppola, a fan of magazines like *Popular Mechanics* and *Scientific American*, sincerely believed "that the medium was about to undergo a big transition, that it *was* about to become electronic, and that possibly if you had a studio of the future that enabled you to take advantage of the great illusion-making quality of television, that we would be able to make serious writing and shows of all types with dimensions that you had never really done before." And on another occasion, he declared:

> I don't believe that talented people today have less gifts than their artistic ancestors. The *times* are exhausted—stories come from the structure of ideas, ethics, beliefs, actualities of the times. Our *times* are exhausted—not our artists. Technology, however, is one aspect of today that is truly fresh and brimming with new tunes and story turns ... So there is and can be *content* in technology—new tunes we've never heard before because they've never been possible before.

Accordingly, no expense was spared in equipping the Zoetrope Studios in LA. Location-shooting appeared to be anathema. Zoetrope's movies would celebrate the artifice of filmmaking, the ideals of Georges Méliès rather than those of Louis Lumière.

The slate was packed with new productions. According to Steven Bach in his book *Final Cut*, Coppola wanted to develop Gay Talese's *Thy Neighbor's Wife* as a Zoetrope project, but United Artists owned the rights and the decision not to turn the property over to Coppola was a corporate one, not governed by "aesthetic judgment." Martha Coolidge saw her Zoetrope production, *Photoplay*, fall victim to intractable script difficulties. Shooting on *Hammett* began in February 1980, and Coppola himself was preparing *One from the Heart*. Caleb Deschanel, a lighting cameraman of some brilliance (*The Black Stallion*, *Being There*), began blocking out a film of David Wagoner's novel about a precocious magician, *The Escape Artist*.

Still other directors had development deals going with Zoetrope, among them Franc Roddam, who had touched a cult chord with *Quadrophenia* and the avant-garde, quasi-underground figure, Scott Bartlett. David Lynch, fresh from *The Elephant Man*, turned down the opportunity to direct *Return of the Jedi* for Lucasfilm and came to Zoetrope to work on *Ronnie Rocket*. Had the studio not run aground, one wonders if Lynch's future might have been significantly changed.

Week by week, month by month, Coppola's movie Parnassus embraced new luminaries. The four lead actors in *One from the Heart*, Frederic Forrest, Teri Garr, Raul Julia, and Nastassia Kinski, signed contracts along the lines of the old studio deals that kept Gable at MGM and Bette Davis at Warners. Forrest's contract ran for two years, and for a spell he was working simultaneously on *Hammett* and *One from the Heart*. Despite the collapse of Zoetrope, Forrest remains gung-ho about Coppola. "Francis is a maverick, almost a Fellini of America," he says. A neophyte actress like Rebecca De Mornay received equal encouragement. Attending Lee Strasberg's Theater Institute in Los Angeles, she responded to a Zoetrope ad for "unusual people" and found herself in the restaurant scene of *One from the Heart*. Coppola even gave her one throwaway line—"Excuse me, those are my waffles!"

Gene Kelly was accorded an office, and concentrated on choreography for *One from the Heart*. Veteran English director Michael Powell, then still out of fashion, was revered by Coppola and appointed "senior director in residence" in November 1980. Powell gazes back with affection, tinged with sorrow, at his brief time in the sun at Zoetrope. "I told them to scrap *Hammett* and *The Escape Artist*, but they were too far advanced."

Hammett was becoming a minor *Apocalypse*, accumulating horrendous problems with each passing day. Wim Wenders wrestled with around a dozen versions of the screenplay before turning a camera. The first scriptwriter had been Joe Gores, author of the novel *Hammett*. Then Thomas Pope, a young writer, labored for nine or ten months. According to Wenders, this script "wasn't at all bad, but the plot was too complicated." A third screenwriter, Dennis O'Flaherty, was brought in to simplify and condense the story. Wenders joined him in writing a definitive version, and this was the script from which the film was shot.

Wenders argued with Zoetrope over the title role. He lamented the fact that Montgomery Clift was not alive to play Hammett, but liked the idea of Sam Shepard taking the part. Shepard, though, had shone only in *Days of Heaven*, and Zoetrope wanted a star. At least Frederic Forrest resembled Dashiell Hammett to an extraordinary degree.

Wenders, accustomed to shooting on location in Germany, filmed for two weeks in the streets of San Francisco (much of the movie takes place in Chinatown), and then for eight further weeks in Los Angeles. Joseph Biroc, one of the most respected of Hollywood cinematographers, was behind the camera for all this period.

Suddenly, Coppola's people began worrying about the end of *Hammett* as well as the ever-expanding role being written for Wenders's wife, Ronee

Blakley. Wenders assembled a rough cut of the material already shot, and showed it to Coppola. Uneasy about this problem, and increasingly preoccupied with *One from the Heart*, Francis ordered a halt to production while he and Wenders each tried to write a new ending. Don Guest, coproducer of *Hammett* with Fred Roos and Ron Colby, remembers that "Francis wrote an ending which was awful, Wim wrote one which was pretty poor, and the ending in the script wasn't much good either."

When *Hammett* closed down in the late spring of 1980, it was just seven to ten days short of completion. The budget was already overheating. Orion, the company that had put up most of the money, could see no glimpse of a reasonable picture. They urged Coppola to fire Wenders. But Francis remained loyal to his director (even going so far as naming his café on the ground floor of the Sentinel Building "Wim's"). Instead, he promised to make Wenders shoot and reshoot until the result was satisfactory to all concerned. A fourth screenwriter, Ross Thomas, joined the effort to save *Hammett*.

Wenders learned that he could resume principal photography in February 1981. But in January Ron Colby called him from the Coast to say that things were difficult at Zoetrope. He thought it would be April before shooting could resume. So Wenders trekked to Portugal and made another movie, *The State of Things*, which was destined to carry off the Golden Lion at Venice in 1981. In November, he at last embarked on what amounted to a virtual remake of *Hammett*, with a new director of photography, Philip Lathrop, and without the characters played in the first shoot by Brian Keith, Sylvia Miles, and Ronee Blakley (whose brief marriage to Wenders had broken up in the interim). Peter Boyle replaced Keith as Hammett's old pal from the Pinkerton agency. Shooting in the studio proved much more economical. Ninety pages of screenplay took just four weeks at Zoetrope. The same number of pages had required ten weeks in the first version. According to Wenders, that first version was modeled closely on the rhythm of Hammett's life as a writer. The second caught the whiff and rhythm of his fiction.

In May 1982, the film surfaced at the Cannes festival, and failed to excite the arbiters of taste. Ten million dollars had been spent on an incorrigibly slight period piece. Hammett's curious blend of melodrama and hard-boiled film noir sat uneasily with Wenders, whose forte from the beginning has been an understanding of the pressures of contemporary life. Pastiche—and that is what *Hammett* amounts to—lies both beyond and beneath him.

Later in the year, the film opened in Seattle and San Francisco, to pale business. Warners, who had rashly committed to distribute the Wenders picture, shelved it for a while, and then staged a new release campaign starting in LA on May 20, 1983.

But nothing could quite save *Hammett*.

* * *

While *Hammett* was lurching slowly to defeat, Coppola himself was in deep trouble. He continued to adopt a bold stance wherever he could. He basked in the prestige of presenting Gance's *Napoléon* at Radio City Music Hall, with a live orchestra playing a new score by Carmine Coppola, in January 1981. Kevin Brownlow, who had reconstructed this silent masterpiece with fanatical devotion since his early teens, admired Francis's "reckless and flamboyant gesture" in underwriting and presentation (advertising the event cost $100,000 alone). As early as 1979, Tom Luddy had negotiated an agreement for Bob Harris's distribution company, Images, to partner Zoetrope in staging the Radio City screenings. Carmine was given a full year to prepare his score. He had to work from scratch, because the original music by Arthur Honegger had been lost.

Some of the harmony of the occasion vanished, however, when the British Film Institute and Thames Television, without informing Luddy, commissioned their own score from Carl Davis, in order to present *Napoléon* at the London Film Festival in November 1980.

The London screening received an ecstatic response, and the film enjoyed the same kind of affectionate approval in New York two months later. Coppola's gamble was justified.

Luddy explains the rationale behind the effort and money expended by Zoetrope. "Francis and George Lucas always used to say that video and TV will ultimately take over movies as we know them, and that to get people into the theaters you'll have to stage *very* theatrical, almost operatic film events. So, start paving the way for those audiences *now*."

Down at the sound stages of Zoetrope Studios in Los Angeles, Coppola luxuriated in the freedom accorded him by MGM, who had proposed that he should make a personal movie for them to release. "I told myself, rather slyly," concedes Coppola, "that I was going to use their money to make an experimental work. Then they dropped out and I was too involved in the film to be able to give it up. So I produced it."

This begs several questions. First, the background to what by common consent is the least successful fiasco in Coppola's career.

One from the Heart is an everyday fairy story, the commonplace and the cliché exalted and enhanced by some of the most imaginative special effects ever seen in a Hollywood movie. A glittering Fabergé egg of a film, its emotional range is not so much broad as condensed. "I wanted to do a story told all by song," he declared to Christopher Frayling in a BBC-TV profile. "It was really basically stagecraft and a kind of musical parable about a couple being together, breaking apart, each having another affair, getting back together again—it was no more complex than that and it had a beautiful score and songs—t was a little musical Valentine."

Coppola's wistful tone of justification echoes the sentiments of the film itself. *One from the Heart* possesses a quivering, vulnerable quality not found in the traditional Hollywood musical. Hank's anguish at the prospect of losing his live-in girlfriend of five years, Frannie, is as genuine as her romantic confusion when faced with the flamboyant Latin affections of Ray, the waiter-cum-singer in a Las Vegas restaurant. "The city is a metaphor for the state of love itself," says Coppola. "I'm interested in films that *are* what they're *about*."

After the perils and frustrations of making *Apocalypse* on location, Coppola had decided to create his next film wholly within the confines of a studio, where he could exercise undiluted control. Where the sun would rise and set to his command. Where the rain could be turned off at a second's notice. And where he could edit on the spot, without waiting days if not weeks for rushes to return from a distant lab.

He assembled a hand-picked crew. Vittorio Storaro, who had won an Academy Award for *Apocalypse Now*, came to Los Angeles as cinematographer. Union leaders protested at a foreigner working in Hollywood. Coppola retorted that he would take the entire film to Italy if need be; seizing a chair, he smashed several windows in his office. The union officials, all neat in business suits, were shocked, and Storaro was accepted.

Richard Beggs was named sound designer which meant a great deal on *One from the Heart*. Dean Tavoularis took charge of production design, with his brother Alex painting many of the lush backdrops that illustrate the film. Kenny Ortega received final credit for choreography, but his mentor Gene Kelly offered numerous suggestions to him. Thomas Brown and Murdo Laird headed the "electronic cinema" unit, backed up by experts from the Sony Corporation.

Storaro, one of the most thoughtful and articulate of cinematographers, claims that he "had the idea to use the physiology of the color itself to establish the mood of the film." He points out that when the body is exposed to yellow, we feel active, and when it is exposed to blue we need to rest. So the ceaseless incandescence of Las Vegas, where the gambling hotels do all they can to mask the barriers between night and day, stimulates the characters in the movie, charging their emotions as though under the influence of amphetamines.

Zoetrope's Lucy Fisher felt that Coppola wanted to make *One From the Heart* inside the studio in order to test his new electronic equipment, but also to create "a Las Vegas of the mind—it doesn't have litter, it isn't ugly or vulgar, it's a dream city where the reality falls short of the dream, which is what the film is about."

Much of the technology still needed in-flight testing. In March 1980, Francis had directed a half-hour live video address by California Governor Jerry Brown, during the Democrat's campaign in the Wisconsin primary. By all accounts the evening had degenerated into a chaotic series of technical hitches and pratfalls. Everyone made light of the situation, but certainly when Coppola began work on *One from the Heart* there was much at stake and much unknown territory to explore.

Already in the preparatory stages, computers such as the Xerox Star (ancestor of the Macintosh) were brought into play. The entire screenplay, composed in individual paragraphs, in by no means chronological order, was keyed onto floppy disk. This made the arrangement of scenes much easier to modify. Then a storyboard of some five hundred drawings was committed to video, and this would serve as a prime resource for several departments.

The cast recorded their lines and these, along with various initial pieces of music and sound effects, were synchronized with the video storyboard. As rehearsals got under way, Polaroid pictures of each scene gradually replaced the rough drawings on the storyboard. Coppola maintained that this "previsualisation" gave him the opportunity to rewrite or even omit certain scenes, and thus reduce the editing schedule.

He took the actors to Las Vegas for two days, using a video camera to get a sense of the real settings and atmosphere. Then they returned to LA for three weeks of technical rehearsals on the sound stages, while Dean Tavoularis supervised the final construction of the sets. The models reproduced the outrageous architecture of Vegas with three-dimensional fidelity. Greg Jein constructed neon lights only a couple of millimeters in diameter, as well as brightly spangled hotel signs that Coppola used for the credit sequence.

Everyone was working on top of one another in a beehive of activity. Francis's portable headquarters, "The Silver Fish," was packed with Sony Betamax recorders and monitors. Cables snaked out like umbilical cords from the van, leading to video cameras attached to movie cameras on the seven sound stages where scenes were being rehearsed and shot. Coppola often preferred to remain in the Silver Fish, booming his comments and orders out over a loudspeaker on the sound stage. He cherished the great days of television, where the director would sit in the booth and monitor the action.

> I was seeking a compromise method where I'd rehearse the show with the cast for weeks, and then I staged it on the set, but when they were ready to do a take, I would *then* go into the trailer in order to watch it. I was always on the floor for the preparatory stuff. The control-room method is used in live TV and the recording industry, so why wouldn't it be applicable to films?

This method enabled Coppola to define each scene, each image, to a degree of accuracy previously unheard of in Hollywood. He could forge a preliminary cut of the video pictures reaching the van, while Richard Beggs, squeezed with his colleagues into one end of the Airstream trailer, contrived to mix the eight-track dialogue recordings into an audio composite.

Not surprisingly, the pressure affected everyone. Francis tried to compensate for the cramped space by equipping the Silver Fish with a kitchenette and espresso machine—even a hot-tub. He actually directed one scene while immersed in the tub. On another occasion, furious with co-producer Gray Frederickson, Coppola let fly a bombardment of costly china plates. Frederickson ducked most of them. At night Coppola would go home the few blocks to his house on June Street, purchased for him by Zoetrope from the entertainer Lindsey Buckingham of Fleetwood Mac.

Once shooting began, on February 2, 1981, Coppola was plagued by financial problems, just as he had been on *Apocalypse Now*. MGM had balked at providing a "completion" agreement for Zoetrope. Quite why is hard to establish. Perhaps Metro did not believe in the strength of the screenplay by Coppola and Armyan Bernstein (who had written the story for *One from the Heart*). Without such a completion guarantee, Zoetrope could not obtain from the Chase Manhattan Bank the loan required to fund the production.

So Zoetrope signed a distribution deal with Paramount. The studio offered no cash in hand but did promise to spend $4 million on advertising the film, to release six hundred prints throughout the States on February 10, 1982, and to take a below-average distribution fee.

It all seemed too good to be true. It was. The budget for the production had swelled to $23 million by September 1980, much of it dictated by

Coppola's decision to do all filming inside the studios. Even before a video camera rolled, *One from the Heart* looked like costing more than two-thirds as much as *Apocalypse*. The precarious funding structure would prove disastrous in a matter of months. Zoetrope raised the $23 million from Chase Manhattan (an initial $8 million, followed by a further $4 million, and finally by $7 million more against foreign presales), from Canadian real-estate tycoon Jack Singer ($3 million), and from various other sources (Paramount, Norman Lear, Security Pacific Bank).

By April 1981, the studio recognized that the budget would rise still further. Thirty-two days of additional shooting, plus an increase in the cost of the title sequence and the special effects, meant that by October Zoetrope required a further $4 million.

Paramount reacted coolly. Coppola had broken his contract, it claimed, by shooting longer than agreed. Chase Manhattan gave Zoetrope the crucial $4 million, but like all banks it demanded collateral. At this juncture, Coppola must have felt he was reliving the nightmares of the late 1970s, when United Artists had contemplated evicting him from the Napa estate. This time he had to pledge his personal property again, as well as the studio facility in Los Angeles.

Despite the unrelenting monetary pressure (the weekly bills ran to half a million dollars), the mood among Zoetrope staff was loyal, even optimistic. Everybody agreed to take a reduction in salary for a six-month period. The chairman of Paramount, Barry Diller, and the president, Michael Eisner, combined to extend a personal loan to Coppola as well as buying a $500,000 slice of a Zoetrope project entitled *Interface*. (This, the story of a government test pilot who survives various accidents and whose brain is linked to a TV camera so that scientists can observe him and he the world, was never made.)

Fans of Coppola and his work sent in a stream of donations to aid the cause. "Actual money has come in the form of cash in envelopes," said Zoetrope's Anne Schwebel, "which we are sending back, every penny." Calls were received from all over the world, offering help. In the first week of February, when Zoetrope could not meet its payroll, union officials agreed to let members work for nothing. It was an extaordinary gesture, and a tribute to Coppola's charisma as a filmmaker. It sprang also from an awareness of Francis's readiness to invest his own money and belongings. As he had written in the 1977 memo to staff, "I know that the amounts of money I deal in seem unreal to most people—they do to me as well; but please always remember that I work in these amounts because *I am willing to risk everything for my work*" (Coppola's italics).

When shooting was at length completed in June, Coppola made a brief visit to the Sony headquarters in Japan, to examine the latest electronic goodies. After stopping over in Europe, he returned to a taxing bout of doing pick-ups for *One from the Heart* as well as re-editing *The Escape Artist*, which had been shot from the late summer of 1981 in Cleveland and completed at Zoetrope Studios on sets built originally for *Hammett*.

On August 19, 1981, Paramount held a "blind bidding" screening of *One from the Heart* for exhibitors in the Bay Area. The reaction was appalling. Worse still, the fact was publicized in the *San Francisco Chronicle* by Judy Stone. She quoted one exhibitor as refusing to bid on the picture and saying, "I almost think the film is unreleasable. How can these very talented Big People be so wrong . . . Does Francis have people all around him mesmerized so that they can't even tell him the truth?"

Coppola, taking a few days off in New York flew into a rage when he heard the news.

> Paramount required the print from me, saying that they must comply with blind-bidding laws. Technically, such screenings can only take place in blind-bidding states, of which there are thirteen, but Paramount, in order to be goody-goody with all its friends, showed it to everyone. The studios literally take your movie out of your hands, and they show it . . . If it's legally binding on us filmmakers to have blind-bidding screenings, then the press *must* be discreet about it—but they're not.

Zoetrope had hoped to launch the movie to the trade at the Northpoint Theater in San Francisco only when a 70mm print became available, with the music score properly in place. A sneak preview in Seattle on March 15 had produced mixed reactions. Coppola had been trying to sign Bette Midler to sing the lyrics. When that came to nothing, Crystal Gayle was hired instead. The version screened on August 19 was bereft of most of Tom Waits' off-screen songs.

Coppola, ever the perfectionist, flew to Rome to pore over the film with Vittorio Storaro in the Technicolor lab there. On New Year's Eve, remembering the spectacular success of the *Napoleon* showings at Radio City Music Hall the previous winter, he called his office and urged executive producer Bernard Gersten to hire Radio City for a single evening. On January 15, 1982, the public at last had a chance to judge *One from the Heart*, at just two evening screenings. The cost of the theater plus a full-page ad in the previous Sunday's edition of the *New York Times* set Zoetrope back some $51,000. Coppola spent further funds on posters, programs, and split-pea soup for the lines of spectators shivering in freezing temperatures around the block.

Although the five thousand or so spectators at each performance applauded respectfully, the tumultuous ovation Coppola had hoped for was missing. He had finished mixing the sound at dawn that day, and he reacted irritably to the often crass questions at a press conference following the first show. He announced that he had "terminated Paramount's release of the film." The news came as a shock, and hit the headlines the following day.

One from the Heart charmed many talented figures that night. Martin Scorsese, Norman Mailer, Joseph Papp, and Andy Warhol all congratulated Francis at the lively party after the screenings. But too few reviewers shared the enthusiasm. The influential if lightweight Rex Reed called the film "Hogwash!" and the even more arbitrary Vincent Canby in the *New York Times* condemned the picture as "unfunny, unjoyous, unsexy, and unromantic," when it opened a month later.

The one unreserved rave came from Sheila Benson in the *Los Angeles Times*, and she tapped the true virtue of *One from the Heart* when she extolled its cherishing of "surfaces even more because of the hollowness they cover." She accepted the superficial characterizations and said, "The picture comes from the same artistic impulses that inspire airbrush art, three-dimensional pop-up greeting cards, and the deliberately beautiful new neon that illuminates LA shops."

After dallying with the idea of distributing *One from the Heart* directly to theaters himself, Coppola accepted an offer from Columbia. To the astonishment of industry observers, Robert Spiotta, president of Zoetrope Studios, admitted that no upfront money was involved. Zoetrope preferred to retain as many rights as possible in the picture, as it had done in *Apocalypse Now*, and to gamble on the long-term success of the new film. And it was a bold gamble. Coppola told the *Los Angeles Times* that if *One from the Heart* bombed at the box-office, "our studio couldn't survive it."

Bomb it did. According to figures from Columbia, the first twenty days' gross (from nineteen theaters) amounted to a dismal $804,518. Lillian Ross, who wrote an enthralling account of the entire affair for the *New Yorker*, discovered that on April 1, 1982, only one cinema in New York City was screening the picture. There were forty-three people in the audience at the late evening session. Next day, *One from the Heart* vanished from sight, which the director had wanted to happen for some weeks.

Coppola shielded his defeat by declaring a moratorium. The film would be rereleased—by Zoetrope itself—during the autumn, in selected cities. *One from the Heart* opened in Europe to rather less disparaging reviews, and in France, where Coppola has always been appreciated for his Wellesian flair, it performed respectably. Coppola was fascinated by the popularity of the film in Stockholm. "In Sweden," he told a friend, "they really seem to *like* the movie."

The brutal fact confronting him, though, was Chase Manhattan's insistence that Zoetrope Studios in LA be sold to help repay the $31 million owing the bank in respect of *One from the Heart*, *Hammett*, and *The Escape Artist*. Coppola placed the facility on the market. The value of the real estate had tripled during the previous thirty months. By the time Zoetrope was finally sold in desperation, in February 1984, it realized only $12.3 million. The purchaser was none other than Jack Singer, the Canadian magnate who had invested in *One from the Heart*. Today, the lot is known as Hollywood Center Studios.

As he sat in the Silver Fish in Tulsa, making his next film, *The Outsiders*, Coppola may have remembered the quote he used to sign off his memorandum to Zoetrope staff in 1977. It paraphrased Euripides: "Whom God wishes to destroy, He first makes successful in show business."

*   *   *

It is tempting to join the majority and damn *One from the Heart* with faint praise. It is also difficult to refute those who find obscene *any* movie budget in excess of, say, $10 million. But the film is so unpretentious in its emotional content, and the mind behind it so incurably romantic that it eventually seduces you. The enterprise is a perfect example of form colliding with content. Coppola may have been correct in believing that audiences wanted a return to old-style movie stories. But he was off course in thinking that he could present such stories in a blaze of state-of-the-art pyrotechnics. Those who have seen *One from the Heart* on video may have noted how much more intimately and affectingly the love story plays. Many of the film's most flamboyant touches are lost, but do not therefore distract us from the plaintive on-off relationship of Hank and Frannie.

The first half of the film breathes a domestic warmth and *verismo*, a lack of constraint that many would dismiss as triteness. Hank (Frederic Forrest) and Frannie (Teri Garr) have been living together for five years. Tomorrow is their anniversary, which also happens to be the Fourth of July. Each brings home a gift for the other. Hank has committed their savings to acquire the deeds to their modest home. Frannie, who works in a travel agency, surprises her lover with plane tickets for a vacation in Bora Bora.

From the outset, Coppola and Bernstein offer metaphors that need no explanation. Owning one's home, flying off to paradise, celebrations on the Fourth of July—these codes are within the grasp of everyone. Not for Coppola the fiendish and pretentious match-game of *Last Year at Marienbad*, which might mask the pain of the tiff that develops between Hank and Frannie. The insecurity of their relationship surfaces quickly when Hank fails to react with sufficient excitement to the air tickets.

"Like everyone, I've experienced a story similar to the one told in *One from the Heart*," confessed Coppola.

> Everyone knows that this kind of situation is no joke. Love can kill . . . So I made the film in this particular way because I couldn't talk directly about a break-up, having lived through it myself. The days or nights of twelve hours of crying, the suicide attempts, were still present in my memory, and I wasn't interested in tackling them. I preferred—in the religious manner—to locate an equivalent of this experience in the form of a ritual. There's no doubt I selected this type of distanciation because the real story was still so fresh in my mind.

Our loyalties keep shifting throughout *One from the Heart*. At first, Hank acts like an insensitive oaf, well suited to his work in a body shop. Then Frannie strikes us as too obstinate in her pique, flouncing out of the house despite Hank's trading insult for insult along the way. This long opening sequence boasts no technological rhetoric; in fact it is a model of classic screenwriting. The dialogue sounds plain and unsubtle, but it divulges all the emotional preoccupations on which the film will hinge: Frannie's conviction that life has to add up to more than this; her recognition that Hank wasn't, isn't, and never will be her Prince Charming; her resentment at being treated condescendingly ("Trust me, honey, I know best," soothes Hank) without even the compensation of being married. On Hank's side, we see an obsessive macho jealousy, fueled by Frannie's disclosure that she had been kissed by his partner Moe at a New Year's Eve party; a fondness for domestic peace and dreaming allied to small-time business savvy (he has bought out Moe's share in the house—committing Frannie's funds in the process); a craving for music and the reveries it induces.

Coppola counterpoints all this without the least flamboyance, in ways that are unmistakably his, and unmistakably cinematic: the protective darkness, for example, that envelops the scene of Hank and Frannie making love, so that the act becomes a ritual, with just a single reading lamp left to burn like a candle of commitment.

The verbal exchanges are never too forced or bathetic. Hank accuses Frannie of not shaving her legs; she replies that while he once had a pretty good build, he now looks like an egg. Outside the house, as they have the first of their stand-up fights, there is a gutter tang to the language that would sound out of place in a classical Hollywood musical.

Unfortunately, as the story expands to include Hank's partner Moe (Harry Dean Stanton), the Latino, Ray (Raul Julia), who makes a successful pass at Frannie, and Leila, the high-wire dancer (Nastassia Kinski), Coppola loses the intensity that distinguishes the opening section of the movie. We grow more aware of the mechanics behind the camera. The artificial backdrops begin to intrude (one, of a sunset, is as embarrassingly distracting as the notorious "harbor painting" in Hitchcock's *Marnie*). The more Coppola lingers on the glitter of Las Vegas, the less persuasive the mood; like Welles, he is at his best when using his visual verve to drive forward a narrative.

The second of the arguments between Hank and Frannie demonstrates this point. She has come home, with an all-new perm, to change and pack for her dream trip to Bora Bora with Ray. Hank is there, too, shaving and readying himself for his rendezvous with Leila. The house stands quiet and in semidarkness. The homespun conversation, dwindling into a weary coda of despair, seems wholly natural in the circumstances, and its poignancy is accentuated by Tom Waits singing, "I'm just a scarecrow without you/Baby, please don't disappear" on the soundtrack. Critics have not given enough credit to such songs in *One from the Heart*, which enhance the movie's mood indigo.

The cross-cutting between these two couples, Hank/Leila and Frannie/Ray, proceeds in conventional form, although the electronic editing facilities available to Coppola allow him to blend images from time to time that include both Hank and Frannie, physically apart yet emotionally linked. The almost equal time accorded Hank and Frannie on their one-night stands cannot disguise the fact that *One from the Heart* is a man's film, told from the man's point of view. Hank is able to play out his fantasy encounter with Leila, out on the edge of the desert, while Frannie's moment of oblivion is all too brief. In her best scene with Ray she looks on amazed as he sits at her table instead of waiting on customers, and has a blazing row with his boss (Allen Garfield, alias Allen Goorwitz in the credits and alias Bernie Moran in *The Conversation*).

The French critic Christian Viviani has observed that *One from the Heart* proves that you are never alone in a crowd, a point illustrated also in *The Conversation*, when Frederic Forrest and Cindy Williams choose to hold their clandestine meeting in the midst of a crowded Union Square. Hank and Frannie are surrounded by people whenever they go to the center of Vegas. Nothing is private. When Ray starts talking to Frannie as she dresses the window of the travel agency, it is as though he were chatting through the glass wall of her bedroom. Later, caught up in the zest of the moment, both Frannie and Ray dance uninhibitedly through the teeming streets. They become part of what seems like a huge, spontaneous number—a gimmick Coppola introduced as far back as 1968, in *Finian's Rainbow*.

The difference in personality between Hank and Frannie becomes more pronounced as the night wears on. Frannie's most exhilarating moments occur in the heart of the neon-spangled city, mingling with cheerful people. Even when Ray makes his most ardent proposal to her, they are in a crowded elevator (with Coppola's father and mother having fun as extras) and the scene is played for public laughter, not private tears.

Hank seeks a more introverted kind of fulfilment. He nurses a drink and watches Leila do her act in a gigantic champagne glass, and soon enters the film's one contrived flight of fancy, where Leila's features loom over him and blend with the glitzy signs of the city as she tells him in *Sprechgesang*, "Little Boy Blue . . ." When they drive out to the garage Hank runs with his partner Moe, there isn't a soul in sight. "This is where I come to think," Hank tells Leila. Gradually, his fantasies unfurl. Leila does her circus routine for him against the backdrop of illuminated signs and the distant silhouette of mountains. Perhaps Hank's finest moment comes when he "conducts" the headlights of the cars on display in the showroom. "I call this 'Usedcarlotta,' " he says with a wry grin worthy of either Carmine or Francis Coppola.

Poor Frannie never quite escapes the regular surroundings she knows all too well. Even when Ray takes her to his place, she finds the rooms uncomfortably like the home she shares with Hank. It's a long, long way to Bora Bora.

Each wakes with a feeling of guilt and panic after the night of love, although Frannie sends a defiant message to Hank as she lies atop Ray —"It's nothing—just a little somethin'," mimicking his earlier nonchalance about the occasional one-night stand. And Hank, true to his chauvinistic self, is set on retrieving Frannie from the arms of her lover rather than wanting to ask her forgiveness. He also lacks the courage to treat Leila as anything other than a sex object. But Leila, a runaway from her European circus family, has been around. "All you gotta do is close your eyes," she warns him, and she'll disappear, "like spit on a griddle." Hank doesn't listen, but he discovers too late that she's right. Leila does vanish into thin air, most conveniently for him, as he concentrates on the search for Frannie and Ray.

Some slapstick enlivens Hank's "crashing" Frannie and Ray's tryst in a motel room, but the final third of the picture, like all awakenings, is an anticlimax. Coppola gleefully defies logic and airline schedules by letting Frannie return to Las Vegas and be reunited with Hank after her plane has taken off for LA and the South Pacific. But it hardly matters; the whole point about *One from the Heart* is its playful suspension of reality, which of course is also the point about Las Vegas, where the casinos have no windows lest gamblers be aware of the passage of night and day. "I never wanted the decor to look artificial as such," Coppola has explained. "I wanted it to be built up in sections, but still it should be as real as possible, even if you know it isn't real. My story lies at the heart of this contradiction."

Besides, the reunion of Hank and Frannie contains a lovely visual touch, when all the lights in the living room suddenly come up like the lights on a stage; Hank has finally made it out of the darkness.

As in a theater too, curtains swing across to close the film, and superimposed upon them is a proud admission: "Filmed Entirely on the Stages of Zoetrope Studios." *One from the Heart* has been a little night music, an *opera buffa* or even perhaps, as Jean-Loup Bourget has suggested, something in the style of Puccini where *Apocalypse Now* was Wagner. (Early in 1981, indeed, Coppola had mulled plans for directing *La Bohème* for Joseph Papp, and Carmine had arranged a chamber version of the score.)

Nowhere in his career does Coppola indulge more elaborately his fascination with the cinema as an illusionist's medium. *One from the Heart* offers a voyage into dreamland, a flirtation with the glitter of showbiz, and the prospect of bliss beyond the uncertainty and the diffidence that identify nearly every Coppola character.

Back to Back
in Tulsa

Every movie director receives a deluge of mail from admirers, but most of the fan letters addressed to Francis Coppola reach his offices in San Francisco. By sheer chance, Francis was in New York when Paramount forwarded a package containing a paperback of *The Outsiders*, by S. E. Hinton, and a letter begging Coppola to make a film from this book.

Dated March 21, 1980, the letter was written by Jo Ellen Misakian, the librarian at Lone Star School, Fresno County, "on behalf of the students and faculty." A petition had been drawn up at the school, demanding that *The Outsiders* be filmed, and Coppola had been selected as the director most suited to tackle the project. "We have a student body of 324," wrote the librarian. "I feel our students are representative of the youth of America. Everyone who has read the book, regardless of ethnic or economic background, has enthusiastically endorsed this project."

Coppola glanced through the letter, and handed the slender paperback to his producer, Fred Roos. "I bet kids have a good idea of what should be a movie," he said. "Check it out, Fred, if you want to." Roos took it on a plane trip. "I said to myself that I'd give it ten pages. I ended up reading it from cover to cover, and I agreed with the kids. I thought it was a movie."

Susie Hinton, who had written *The Outsiders* at the age of just fifteen, and had it published by Viking Press two years later, in 1967, asked Zoetrope for an option of $5,000. Although not an unreasonable sum by Hollywood standards, this was too much cash for Zoetrope to find at that grim juncture. Hinton was persuaded to accept a down payment of $500 and a screenwriter began work on the project.

Even so, *The Outsiders* might well not have reached the screen. Successive scripts were regarded by Coppola as too mawkish, and the spiraling fortunes of *One from the Heart* were sapping his time, energy, and will to direct fresh movies. "When the crisis had hit at Zoetrope," he said some years later, "there were two ways for me to go. One was just to shed it all and let go of everything and basically quit the film business . . . and the other was to fight back to being as productive as I could be and make one film after another." He had enjoyed being a camp counselor in his youth, and relished the prospect of traveling to Tulsa (where the novel is set) and working independently as he had done on *The Rain People*.

Despite the disastrous losses on *One from the Heart*, Coppola raised money for *The Outsiders*. Chemical Bank gave Zoetrope a loan on the strength of a distribution contract with Warners (Columbia having withdrawn from a possible deal) and a completion guarantee from Britain's National Film Finance Corporation.

So in March 1982, Coppola and his crew flew to Tulsa and established a working base there, with all essential equipment on hand. Casting was crucial and, in retrospect, accomplished with remarkable astuteness. Most of the fifteen- and sixteen-year-olds who appeared in the film have become stars or heartthrobs since 1983: Matt Dillon, Diane Lane, Tom Cruise, Ralph Macchio. Coppola thought highly of Matt Dillon—"One of the best young actors to emerge since the Brando-Dean era"—and asked him to stay on in Tulsa for *Rumble Fish*, which he shot back to back with *The Outsiders*.

Rumble Fish had been Susie Hinton's third novel, and Coppola read it while on location. He decided without hesitation to prolong his stay in Oklahoma and use the same technicians, and some of the same cast, to make *Rumble Fish*. Both productions were in the can by the last week of September 1982. *The Outsiders* found a responsive audience across the country, helping Zoetrope to survive its leanest spell ("We made many, many millions on that picture," states Francis), but *Rumble Fish*, although costing much less to make, never prospered at the box-office. This strange, bizarre production would, however, be lauded by critics in France and Scandinavia.

The production of two full-length films in seven months owed much to the sophistication of Coppola's electronic equipment. His facilities enabled him to make *The Outsiders* and *Rumble Fish* in wholly contrasting styles. The first film is lavish and succulent, shot in 'Scope and glowing *Gone with the Wind* colors. The sound is crisp and sensual, abetted by Carmine Coppola's music score. *Rumble Fish*, by comparison, is photographed in monochrome. Dean Tavoularis, the production designer, recalls that Coppola "wanted a stark-and-brutal look, the kind of thing you find in old German expressionist films." The sound, too, had an unearthly weight to it; almost disembodied. "It was ninety-nine percent looped," says Richard Beggs, "which gives you a great deal of latitude in terms of intelligibility."

The Outsiders follows the grand tradition of luxurious Hollywood entertainment. *Rumble Fish* looks to the European art film as its prototype, and has an intriguing feel to it that is ultimately more satisfying than the naïve candor of its companion piece, *The Outsiders*. "One is the antidote of the other," thinks Beggs.

The "Silver Fish" was pressed into service for the Tulsa productions. Michael Powell believes that the mobile center was more suited to this form of location work than to the studio environment of *One from the Heart*. Francis waxed enthusiastic about his technological breakthrough. "Movies have always been thought of in three stages," he told the *San Francisco Chronicle*. "There's preproduction, production, and then postproduction, where you actually put the movie together. The whole point of our system is to make it possible to do all that at once—cheaper, faster, and better. Someday, for example, we'll be making movies with no sets at all. We'll work with only a stage. And it will look totally realistic."

Visual realism, though, was not what Coppola wanted on *The Outsiders*. The aim was to catch the spirit of Robert Frost's poem, "Nothing Gold Can Stay," which Ponyboy quotes in the Hinton novel. To have opted for a tough, seamy version of *The Outsiders* would have been to betray the unashamed sentimentality of the book. Writing at fifteen, Susie Hinton had not acquired even an incipient cynicism. Her story of the rivalry between two classes of kids in Tulsa, the "Greasers" and the "Socs," is shot through with an idealism unfamiliar in the 1980s. In 1967 things were different. Coppola, honoring his commitment to the freshness and vitality of youth, steers a dangerous course. The borderline between the cute and the cloying is a slender one.

But *The Outsiders* does not suffer from the patronizing flavor that would make the whole fiction intolerable. From the very first close-up of Ponyboy starting his story with the words, "When I stepped out into the bright sunlight from the darkness of the movie house . . . ," Coppola establishes a genuine warmth and disarming simplicity of expression that take us back to the days of our earliest youth and optimism.

Although the film throbs with violence, it takes place at one remove from reality, disconnected from the adult world. Grown-ups do not figure in *The Outsiders*. We see a couple of parents fighting through curtained windows from a distance, but otherwise everyone seems forever young —even Ponyboy's parents appear only in a dream sequence, happy in the golden, shimmering landscape of the countryside before dying in a blazing auto wreck.

Susie Hinton had been frustrated by the lack of literature concerning kids running their lives without the reassuring, patronizing presence of their elders. This, more than anything, spurred her to write *The Outsiders*.

The plot makes no claim to originality. Dallas (Matt Dillon) is attracted to Cherry (Diane Lane) in the tradition of Romeo and Juliet or *West Side Story*. He is a Greaser, she a Soc from the prosperous South Side of the city. Their love is doomed, of course, because not enough of the kids are as sensitive as Johnny (Ralph Macchio), who longs for a place away from the warring Socs and Greasers, or even as Ponyboy the narrator himself, with his instinct for reconciliation toward the end.

Both *The Outsiders* and *Rumble Fish* hinge on the relationship between brothers. The tensions belong to Susie Hinton's books, but Coppola accentuates them to a point at which it is obvious he is discussing his own feelings towards August Coppola—to whom, indeed, *Rumble Fish* is dedicated: "My first and best teacher." The family links grow more intense in the second movie, but already in *The Outsiders* Ponyboy's flight from home is triggered by a row with his domineering elder brother, Darry. This in turn unleashes the film's central incident—when the Socs find Ponyboy and Johnny alone at night and start a fight. Ponyboy is almost drowned in a fountain, and in desperation Johnny kills one of the Socs.

Panicking, the two friends locate Dallas at a party. He gives them a gun, and they take off for the hills. They hide in an abandoned church and make clumsy attempts to dye their hair to avoid being caught. But this is also a charmed interlude. Johnny brings Ponyboy a copy of *Gone with the Wind*, which serves as a kind of talisman in Susie Hinton's book, and Ponyboy in his turn quotes Robert Frost and notes with a writer's eye the changing patterns and colors of clouds and sunsets. Broad, spacious landscapes dwarf and envelop the boys.

Johnny and Ponyboy become unlikely heros when they rescue some children from a burning schoolhouse. Dallas, who has come to visit them in their hideout, reluctantly joins in. Johnny gets badly burned. The weakest section in *The Outsiders* follows this dramatic event. The energy drains from the Greasers. They sit around, wallowing in a "boys will be boys" camaraderie. Johnny, in the hospital, utters his lament for doomed youth: "Sixteen years ain't long enough." He laments the things he has not yet seen or done. He personifies the conscience of even the most hard-boiled members of the Greasers gang. Dallas, who has also suffered in the blaze, miraculously rises from his hospital bed and enters the climactic "rumble" between the rival groups almost as though he were bearing a standard for Johnny.

The big fight is more than just another Coppola exercise in montage. The light is lurid, apocalyptic. Smoke from a bonfire obscures the struggling figures, and when a storm breaks, the boys' movements become sluggish and animalistic, like the soldiers' at Shrewsbury in Orson Welles's *Chimes at Midnight*. The Greasers triumph in the mud, and the Socs retreat in disarray. Ponyboy is wounded, and Dallas drives him to the hospital where, in the true tradition of melodrama, Johnny is about to die. "It's useless," he whispers when he hears the news of battle. "Fighting ain't no good." He leaves a message for Ponyboy "Stay gold, stay gold."

Dallas, distraught, robs a local supermarket (Coppola uses the same store in *Rumble Fish*), and then willfully dies in a hail of police bullets. Ponyboy, leafing through Johnny's copy of *Gone with the Wind*, finds a letter from his dead friend. Johnny has no regrets about saving the schoolkids from the blaze. He has grasped the message of the Frost poem. "That guy that wrote it, he meant you're gold when you're a kid, like green. When you're a kid everything's new, dawn."

The tale may be trite, especially to European eyes, but Coppola has never looked upon sophistication as a virtue. The corruption of innocence and the yearning for a lost paradise run like a current of anguish through his work. *The Outsiders* brims with nostalgia not just for everyone's adolescence but for a particular period, when Mustangs were in vogue and *Beach Blanket Bingo* and *Muscle Beach Party* might make up a double bill at the local drive-in. On Long Island, at the age of fifteen, Francis himself had belonged to a mild little street gang called the "Bay Rats." The film is also a celebration, like *American Graffiti*, of life in the anonymous American city, where aspirations are not entirely blunted as they would be in the slums of the metropolitan centers; and where, moreover, the status quo is in a curious way accepted. As Randy the Soc says to Ponyboy before the rumble, "No matter if you whip us, you'll still be where you were before, at the bottom, and we'll still be the lucky ones, at the top, with all the breaks."

When the film was screened on American TV in 1985, some five and a half minutes were restored—mostly a courtroom flashback where Cherry admits that "I could have made it simple for the fight not to have happened in the first place," and Ponyboy is acquitted as a result. There is also a poignant rap session among the surviving Greasers.

For Coppola, the death of Dallas carries more weight than that of Johnny—not because he is a hood and Johnny a saint, but because he is the character most admired by Ponyboy. He, much more than Ponyboy's real brothers Darry and Soda, is an ambivalent idol for the younger kid, the coarse-cut predecessor of the Motorcycle Boy in *Rumble Fish*.

The Outsiders is an excellent ad for Coppola's mobile technology and the mysteries of the "Silver Fish." The soundtrack is alive with offscreen snatches of pop music, the *sostenuto* purring of crickets, and the long withdrawing wail of freight trains. There are moments, too, of visceral impact, such as the fight by the fountain, with a final shot from above of bodies frozen like statuary beside a pool of spreading blood, or the head-on terror of Dallas suddenly pulling his gun on the storekeeper.

Many reviewers wrote about the film in disdainful terms. David Denby in *New York* magazine said that *The Outsiders* "is heartfelt, utterly humorless, and shockingly banal." Vincent Canby of the *New York Times* accused it of being "spectacularly out of touch, a laughably earnest attempt to impose heroic attitudes on some nice small characters." Michael Sragow in *Rolling Stone* concluded that "Coppola has aimed for the poetry of youth and achieved mere doggerel." But John Engstrom in the *Boston Globe* hailed it as "a small, sincere and nearly perfectly realized film about adolescence in Oklahoma," and praised Coppola's "cool restraint," while *Variety*, often a down-to-earth judge, regarded the production as being like a 1950s drama about problem kids.

*   *   *

It is a paradox that *Rumble Fish* should have emerged as Coppola's most pretentious and also most intimate film. Pretentiousness has a perjorative ring to it, but in its literal sense it can be equated with unorthodox artistic ambition, and in *Rumble Fish* lies more technical experimentation (and more visual imagination) than in any American movie of the decade.

At times the production is also pretentious in the modern meaning of the word, with high-flown dialogue, and images so underlit that they become indiscernible. The huge clockface with no hands that is hitched to the side of a truck looks like a clumsy attempt at symbolism. The outrageous dream sequence, showing Rusty-James (Matt Dillon) levitating after being mugged in an alley comes across as bathetic, even if it may be a compliment to Victor Sjöström's silent classic, *The Phantom Carriage*, where David Holm's body rises from his corpse in a graveyard.

As a meditation on brotherhood, however, *Rumble Fish* is more personal than any of Francis's films. Rusty-James has been at odds with himself and everyone else since his elder brother, "The Motorcycle Boy" (Mickey Rourke), took off for California. When the brother returns, to save Rusty-James's skin in a gang rumble, both young men start to analyze their shared past and to drift toward a tragic if also liberating destiny.

The film amounts to a kind of exorcism, or purgation, of Francis's relationship with his brother August. In real life the bond between them seems to have been positive and fruitful. It was Augie, after all, who introduced Francis to the movies, and who has served as counselor on many Zoetrope productions. But on screen the elder brother represses the younger, intimidating him with his command of philosophy and the inner meanings of life. Even when a blood kinship does not exist, this notion of a disciple seated at the feet of an elder marks a film like *Apocalypse Now* (with Brando's Kurtz lecturing Willard). In *The Cotton Club* and both *Godfather* productions, a fierce, coiled tension exists between the brothers.

In the words of August Coppola, *Rumble Fish*

> marks the closing of a phase—so there is regret. There's a recognition of the fact that, okay, I *was* the one he looked up to, but that he achieved things in the eyes of the world and of the others around him. The dedication was a recognition of my importance in his life, both good and bad. It's a poignant film in that Francis has often had regrets because I was supposed, in his mind, to achieve what he achieved. Our family was consecrated to success.

As usual, these family references are woven unostentatiously by Coppola into the film—Rusty-James wears Augie's old club jacket ("The Wild Deuces"), and Francis's daughter Sofia plays Diane Lane's younger sister while Augie's youngest son, Nicolas Cage, scores as Smokey. Cage's later rise to stardom, though, has been accomplished on his own brash, swaggering terms, as *Birdy*, *Raising Arizona*, and *Moonstruck* demonstrate—not forgetting his likable performance in his uncle's *Peggy Sue Got Married*.

So strong, though, is the expressionist imagery of *Rumble Fish* that it threatens to overwhelm the characterization of Rusty-James and his brother. The grainy black-and-white photography of Stephen Burum evokes two essential sources—German cinema of the 1920s, and the middle period of Orson Welles. The film opens on a vision of racing clouds in a somber sky. The soundtrack tinkles hypnotically. On a wooden signboard, and then also on a wall, are scrawled the words, "The Motorcycle Boy Reigns," where in Lang or Murnau the message might have read, "Dracula Lives." Each shot arrives at a rakish angle, creating the disorienting, bilious effect familiar from Welles's *Mr. Arkadin* or *Touch of Evil.*

A nattily dressed black man comes to the poolroom to warn Rusty-James that Wilcox, a rival gang-leader, is threatening to kill him. The tone is altogether tougher and less mawkish than in *The Outsiders*, which had its saccharine theme tune by Carmine Coppola to mitigate the loss of life and dreams. In *Rumble Fish*, four-letter words sprinkle every exchange of dialogue. Lines are tossed off as gutter rhetoric, some audible, some incoherent. Coppola plunges us into the depths of a vision, a surreal trip eons removed from *The Outsiders*. Offscreen sounds and bursts of music (in part composed by Francis himself while on location) overlap the dialogue, serving to distort the perspective in which we view the movie.

As Rusty-James walks along the street, past the local pet store, the Siamese fighting fish from which the film takes its title are isolated in color against the surrounding monochrome. It is no more than a conceit, even if the fish represent the spirits of Rusty-James and his pals, who fight each other and themselves within the confines of the city. The fish, says the Motorcycle Boy later, would surely not fight if they were set free in the river, and this longing for deliverance courses through the writing of Susie Hinton. The countryside in *The Outsiders*, for instance, beckons like a paradise.

The magic brother's presence is felt at every turn. Rusty-James gets uptight when someone asks what will happen if his brother comes back after his two-month absence. He tells his girlfriend Patty that his brother is "cool" and "sharp." Then, during the fight with Wilcox, the Motorcycle Boy makes a dramatic entrance.

"I thought we had a treaty," he calls softly to Rusty-James over the din of battle.

Rusty-James swivels to glance at him and in that split-second his opponent stabs him in the side. The Motorcycle Boy takes immediate revenge, hurling Wilcox into the air with the force of his bike at full throttle.

But the incident underlines the ambivalent relationship between the Boy and the disciples he left behind. "You know we'd all be better off if you'd stayed gone," says the local cop, Patterson, as he surveys the scene after the rumble.

Even before being wounded, Rusty-James has experienced life at fever-pitch. Restless, chain-smoking, he suffers from the loneliness that has infected him since his brother's departure. Now the Boy is back, whispering enticing words about California. He leafs through one of Rusty-James's books and finds a cherished photo of the two of them in childhood, his arm grasping the infant Rusty-James in a protective embrace. Later in the film, he explains to Rusty-James how, "when you were two years old and I was six, your mother decided to leave. She took me with her." Ever since, Rusty-James has felt choked when he's abandoned. His brother reproaches him in the lugubrious strains of a litany: "Why, why are you fucked up all the time, one way or another?" Perhaps the Motorcycle Boy knows the answer, for toward the end of the film he mutters a defense of Rusty-James: "Loyalty's his only vice."

The boys' father (Dennis Hopper) took up liquor when his wife went home with her elder son. Now he lurches from bar to bar and back to his miserable bed. But he has moments of clarity, and will defend the vanished mother, saying that someone who has a different view of the world is not necessarily crazy. "Nor," he goes on, "contrary to popular belief, is the Motorcycle Boy crazy. He's merely miscast in the play. He was born in the wrong era, on the wrong side of the river." The other youths also idolize the Boy. He's referred to as a prince. "He's like royalty in exile," comments one guy. "Isn't there anything he can't do?" asks Steve in a tone of reverence as the Boy casually pockets a pool ball.

Throughout *Rumble Fish*, Rusty-James struggles against his brother's personality, against "the living legend" by whom he measures himself. "You ain't never gonna look like him," says a fellow drinker. "You ain't got your brother's brains," sighs Smokey. In the eyes of Rusty-James, his brother is as old as Methuselah, even if he is a mere twenty-one. The tragedy of the film is that the Motorcycle Boy cannot match up to such expectations. Rusty-James ignores the cop's snide comment, "He's no hero," but listens when his brother chides him for following him around like a lost puppy. "You never gave me a chance," complains Rusty-James. "I wish I were the big brother you always wanted," comes the weary response, "but I can't be what I want, any more than you can." The Motorcycle Boy urges him to take the bike and leave, and "follow the river clear to the ocean."

Rusty-James, remembering this advice, and perhaps also an earlier line of his brother's—"If you're gonna lead people, you've gotta have somewhere to go"—roars out of town, his silhouette racing across the livid wall with its graffiti-scrawled refrain, "The Motorcycle Boy Reigns." The Boy has been gunned down (like Dallas in *The Outsiders*), at the hands of his nemesis, the cynical cop Patterson who has the icy air of an Angel of Death. The fish that the Boy has stolen (rescued?) from the pet store lie floundering on the grass, and Rusty-James takes them down to the river.

In the final shot, Rusty-James gazes out at the Pacific, with gulls wheeling and fluttering like black specks against the ocean's glitter.

Rusty-James has supplanted his brother, traveled "clear to the ocean," but may have forgotten the Motorcycle Boy's earlier description of California as "a beautiful wild girl on heroin, who's as high as a kite, thinking she's on top of the world, but she's dying . . ." The family, too, is finally dismembered, the Boy dead, the father in Tulsa, the mother living somewhere in LA with a movie producer, and Rusty-James at the fringe of the Pacific, confronting the solitude that awaits a majority of Coppola's characters.

When Mickey Rourke signed to play the Motorcycle Boy, Coppola gave him some books by Albert Camus, and a biography of Napoleon. "There's a scene in there when I'm walking down the bridge with Matt [Dillon]; and I'd try and stylize my character as if he *was* Napoleon." Although he had registered a modest impact in films like *Heaven's Gate*, Rourke established himself as a formidable actor in *Rumble Fish*. He glides through the movie wearing the smile of the victor—Napoleon, indeed. His sophistication has not yet ripened into cynicism. He is able to mock his own other-worldliness, and when Steve asks why no one has blown his head off, Rourke replies, "Even the most primitive society has an innate respect for the insane." He can see in perspective the insignificance of teenage triumphs in the rumbles of yesteryear, when he was the leader whom Rusty-James worshipped.

Coppola told Judy Stone that he saw the Motorcycle Boy as "a character out of Tennessee Williams or Carson McCullers, a kind of rat who can't find his way out . . . His flaw is his inability to compromise, and that's why I made him color-blind. He interprets life in black-and-white."

The Boy is convinced that the rumble fish will not destroy one another if they are released. When the cop growls, "Someone oughtta get you off the streets," the Motorcycle Boy responds, with a knowing smile, "Someone oughtta put the fish in the river." It is the plea of a generation. In

Coppola's words, young people "have no room to grow; our institutions only want to control them."

But the Motorcycle Boy, with his ability to invoke classical references that baffle Rusty-James, himself suffers from hubris as well as a fatal narcissism that Coppola suggests by placing his face hard up against the camera, as though the lens were a mirror in which Rourke were admiring himself.

Compositions of this kind give *Rumble Fish* a distinctly Wellesian look. People loom into close-up and linger there while other characters talk in the far background, recalling the deep-focus of *Citizen Kane* and *The Magnificent Ambersons*. Another little nod to Welles is the crane shot that soars up behind a departing bus, creating a sense of space and vertigo at the same time.

The fight between Wilcox and Rusty-James might well have been shot by Welles himself, with its giddy angles and syncopated cutting; the violent swinging of overhead lamps is a particular Welles trademark (cf. the whipping scene in *The Trial*). Like the Old Master, Coppola captures the *visual* properties of heat. Youths loll in languid poses, trapped in a torpor by the summer temperatures. Faces glisten with sweat, alleys glitter with water, much more effectively in monochrome than in color. During the orgy sequence, bodies writhe like gleaming fish in the semidarkness. Even the blood oozing from Rusty-James's wound looks more sinister and oleaginous in black-and-white. The structures in *Rumble Fish*—fire escapes, bridges, and so on—are as deliberately exaggerated as those in *Metropolis* or *The Cabinet of Dr. Caligari*.

Despite the premeditated aspect of every shot in the film, Coppola refuses to lose sight of the vivid immediacy of the performances. In the scene, for example, where Matt Dillon comes up to Diane Lane in front of the house and finds her unpacking groceries, a stream of sprocket-holes runs across the film for some twenty-five to fifty feet. "It was damage to the negative in the lab," recalls Richard Beggs "There were five or six other takes, but Francis *liked* that particular take."

CHAPTER TEN

Playing
The Cotton Club

The period 1982 to 1984 was turbulent and distressing for Coppola. It was a time for retrenchment and loss. Closures abounded, from "Wim's," Francis's restaurant in the Sentinel Building, to the entire Zoetrope Studios facility in Los Angeles. Even the Sentinel itself was saved only by a whisker when Coppola paid off a loan of $1.7 million from Security Pacific Bank at Christmas 1984, just days before the property was due to go under an auctioneer's hammer. Eleanor was prepared for the worst by Zoetrope's lawyers. Seventy-five hundred dollars was about the maximum one could retain if one declared bankruptcy, and so on.

Some successes, though, were recorded. Zoetrope signed a deal with Godfrey Reggio for the worldwide distribution of *Koyaanisqatsi*, a controversial if lyrical documentary on American life and iconography, with a riveting score by avant-garde composer Philip Glass. *Koyaanisqatsi* had been edited by Alan Walpole and Ron Fricke with the aid of Dennis Jakob from the Zoetrope stable. The movie, blazoned with the now familiar headline, "Francis Ford Coppola Presents," met an enthusiastic reception at festivals in Telluride and Berlin, as well as at Radio City Music Hall.

Then there was *The Grey Fox*, a Canadian production about Bill Miner, an aging outlaw who had been inspired by Edwin S. Porter's 1903 movie, *The Great Train Robbery*, to become a great train robber himself. Zoetrope agreed to represent the film for global distribution and Fred Roos signed its first-time director, Philip Borsos, to develop a second feature, *Father Christmas*, for Coppola's organization.

The Black Stallion Returns, with a lot of input from Zoetrope even though it was financed by MGM/UA, failed to spark the same fervor as its original. Carroll Ballard was not involved; instead the film was directed by Bob Dalva, a contemporary of Lucas and Murch at the University of Southern California. He had edited *The Black Stallion*. The action in the sequel was lively, but the emotional quality could not match that of Ballard's movie. It was not quite such a disaster as *The Escape Artist*, which sank without trace after a thrashing from the New York critics in May 1982.

Reviewers were slightly less scathing when *Rumble Fish* finally played at the New York Film Festival in October 1983. Vincent Canby raised a grudging salute to its grandiose aspirations. "There's something almost Promethean about its wrongheadedness," he wrote in the *New York Times*, "as there was with *One from the Heart*." Jack Kroll, in *Newsweek*, hailed *Rumble Fish* as "a welcome reach for beauty and honesty by an artist who won't surrender." But the film bombed, and its espousal as a cult movie by *Cahiers du cinéma* and other coteries in Europe proved scant consolation for a Coppola hard-pressed by creditors.

Francis abhorred the idea of abandoning Zoetrope to earn his keep as a journeyman director. He could hardly refuse an offer to direct *The Pope of Greenwich Village*, an Al Pacino vehicle about gangsters in Manhattan. But Pacino's schedule prevented him from starring, and the production stagnated. Eventually it emerged with Eric Roberts in the part earmarked for Pacino.

So by early 1983, the situation looked desperate. John Peters, the bright young lawyer from Yale, had helped Coppola to wriggle and then bulldoze a path through the problems. Merely servicing the colossal debt was a daily nightmare. Zoetrope employees were never sure if they would still have a job at the end of the week. Coppola had mortgaged everything. Even individual floors in the Sentinel were hived off. The Zoetrope headquarters shrank to Francis's own eyrie atop the building, and a couple of levels beneath. Liquidity had proved to be Zoetrope's abiding weakness. Back in 1981, Coppola had said in conversation with Gay Talese, "I could be worth $100 million. That doesn't mean I can meet my payroll . . . It's one thing to be wealthy and quite another to be liquid."

Residual income from *Apocalypse Now*, plus heartening receipts from *The Outsiders*, provided a lifeline for Coppola during this critical spell. Either from vanity or sheer obstinacy, he maintained all too large a staff at the studio in LA, preferring to sacrifice his Zoetrope premises in San

Francisco. But the selling of the Pacific Street facility, for example, was like cutting the heart out of Zoetrope. The dubbing stage and the editorial rooms there had come to represent the physical core of the movie industry in the Bay Area, and with their disappearance went a whole phase in film-making on the West Coast. Saul Zaentz's Fantasy Films across the Bay Bridge, and George Lucas's San Rafael hideaway functioned as alternative bases for postproduction work, but the spiritual appeal of Zoetrope was irreplaceable.

Among those to whom Coppola turned for professional advice in his financial crisis was his sister Talia's second husband, Jack Schwartzman. In return, Francis acted as unpaid and uncredited script doctor on *Never Say Never Again*, the film that tempted Sean Connery to enjoy a final fling as James Bond, and that Schwartzman was setting up for production in 1984. "My approach," says Francis, "was to go back to the original book, *Thunderball*, and I did a real adaptation, building up the romance between Bond and the girl, Domino. But what I wrote was never used."

In February 1983, a more substantial project had arrived on the horizon. It began with a phone call to Coppola from Robert Evans, who sounded distraught. He needed help with the script of a new film about Harlem's legendary Cotton Club. In his heyday as head of production at Paramount, Evans had backed Coppola on *The Godfather*.

The six-year saga of this film, *The Cotton Club*, is sleazier and more fascinating than the movie itself. Michael Daly, in an exhaustive, relentless exposé in *New York* magazine, revealed how Evans was forced to sup with real-life gangsters, gamblers, and the wealthy of many races and persuasions in order to finance the production. Ultimately, Evans would lose all control over his dream project and would have to be content with a credit line above the title and a percentage of net profits that seemed light-years away.

Bob Evans had paid $350,000 for the screen rights to a nonfiction book about the Cotton Club. When Arab arms dealer Adnan Khashoggi agreed to invest $2 million in the film, Evans commissioned a script from Mario Puzo, author of *The Godfather*. Khashoggi pulled out, ostensibly because he disliked Puzo's screenplay. Evans then sought a star to add luster to the package. Pacino, Stallone, and then Richard Pryor were all approached. Stallone and Pryor escaped by demanding $4 million.

Richard Gere proved more amenable to Evans's overtures, however, and when substantial investment was forthcoming from Ed and Fred Doumani, who owned hotels and casinos in Las Vegas, the project began to motor. Richard Sylbert was set to design the production, and Evans decided to shoot at the Kaufman Astoria Studios on Long Island. That was in January 1983.

Over the next month, it dawned inexorably on Evans that the script for *The Cotton Club* left much to be desired. So he called Coppola and sent him the material. Without a moment's hesitation, Coppola replied that the screenplay was worthless, "a futile gangster story devoid of any zest"—harsh words about the work of Puzo, his partner on the script of *The Godfather Part II*. Coppola's monetary predicament was so grave that he agreed with alacrity to rewrite the script, for a tidy $500,000.

Coppola became engrossed in the mystique of the Cotton Club—a place where some of the greatest jazz musicians (Duke Ellington, Cab Calloway, Fats Waller) had excelled, and where gangsters hung out alongside show biz celebrities like Charlie Chaplin, Fanny Brice, Cole Porter, and James Cagney. The audience was exclusively white, the performers almost without exception black. Coppola glimpsed a means of interweaving these two worlds, black and white. He also wanted to examine the hoodlums of the period, small-time purveyors of crime who came of German, Irish, and Jewish descent, and who throughout the early 1930s would cede power to the rapacious Italian mafiosi.

In early April, before flying to Santa Fe with his entourage to attend a festival tribute to "The Spirit of Zoetrope," Coppola gave Evans his first draft of the screenplay. Nobody liked it. The Doumanis and their partner in the venture, Denver millionaire Victor Sayyah, halted financing. Not for the first time, the project looked doomed.

Somehow, a team was forged of Coppola, Evans, Gere, and two black performers: Gregory Hines (who had been desperate for the part of Sandman) and Marilyn Matthews. They huddled for ten days on Coppola's estate in Napa. From the protracted sessions, which usually ended with Francis's cooking a vast dinner around 10 P.M., came a script that seemed altogether more coherent. At this point, Coppola agreed to direct *The Cotton Club*. He envisaged the Harlem nightspot if not quite as a *Cabaret*-style microcosm of an age, then certainly as "a plantation, with black talent, white owners, white patrons. I, being a hired hand, was probably attracted to a scenario that sees all its characters as hired hands of one sort or another." He felt the subject concerned different forms of servitude, and happily abandoned himself to almost a year of chaotic improvisation.

Since the mid-1970s, Coppola had expected a fee of $2.5 million for directing a picture. He also demanded outright control of the production

Rumble Fish: *Francis with Matt Dillon, Vincent Spano, and Mickey Rourke on location in Tulsa* (above). *The Motorcycle Boy (Mickey Rourke) and the Siamese fighting fish that give the film its title* (below).

Rumble Fish: *Rusty-James (Matt Dillon) stabbed by Wilcox (Glenn Withrow)* (above), *and* (below) *"the structures are as deliberately exaggerated as those in* Metropolis *or* The Cabinet of Dr. Caligari." *(Hot Weather/Universal)*

Rumble Fish: *Rusty-James (Matt Dillon) and the Motorcycle Boy (Mickey Rourke)
remember simpler, happier times (above), and Francis's nephew Nicolas Cage plays
Smokey (below) in a scene with Matt Dillon. (Hot Weather / Universal)*

Above: *Francis with Paul Schrader and George Lucas* (circa 1983).
(Photo: Lucasfilm)
Below: *Dixie (Richard Gere) and Vera Cicero (Diane Lane) in* The Cotton Club.
(Orion / Adger W. Cowans)

The Cotton Club: *Sandman (Gregory Hines) does his a cappella tap.*
(Orion/Adger W. Cowans)

The Cotton Club: *Irving Stark (Tom Waits) shows Gregory and Maurice Hines the wonders of the club* (above). *Francis on location for* The Cotton Club (below).
(Orion / Adger W. Cowans)

The Cotton Club: *Dixie (Richard Gere) shows he can play piano too, with Diane Lane as Vera and James Remar as Dutch Schultz (above), and "a world of overwhelming blacks and whites, tuxedos and starched evening shirts, damson eyes and powdered faces" (below).*

Peggy Sue Got Married: *Peggy Sue (Kathleen Turner) meets her two closest chums of yesteryear, Maddie (Joan Allen) and Carol (Catherine Hicks) (above). The reunion in* **Peggy Sue Got Married,** *with Kathleen Turner and Barry Miller (below). (Tri-Star Pictures)*

Peggy Sue Got Married: *Peggy Sue and Charlie Bodell (Nicolas Cage)*
(above), *and (below) Francis discusses a scene with Nicolas Cage.*
(Tri-Star Pictures)

Above: *Francis with his father Carmine and James Caan* (second from left) *on* Gardens of Stone. *(Tri-Star Pictures)*
Below: *Eleanor visiting her husband during the shooting of* Tucker: The Man and His Dream. *(Photo: Lucasfilm)*

Above: *Francis with cinematographer Jordan Cronenweth on* Gardens of Stone.
(Tri-Star Pictures)
Below: *George Lucas, producer of* Tucker, *confers with Francis. (Photo: Lucasfilm)*

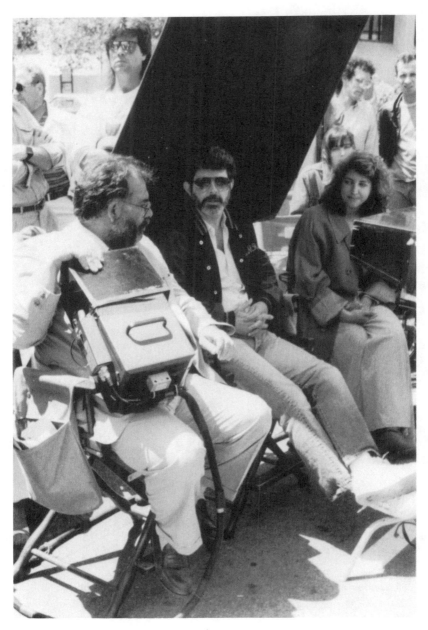

Francis with George Lucas on location for Tucker. *Note the video monitor held by Coppola—"it's my bomb site." (Photo: Lucasfilm)*

Tucker: *Preston Tucker (Jeff Bridges) outside his new factory (above), actually a disused plant in Richmond, California, and (below) with his spanking new automobile. (Photos: Lucasfilm)*

Jocular exchange (above) between real-life father and son, Lloyd (at right) and Jeff Bridges, with Martin Landau (at left). (Photo: Lucasfilm)
Below: *Francis in pensive mood while shooting* Tucker. *(Photo: Lucasfilm)*

Preparing the sound mix for Apocalypse Now at Zoetrope Studios. State-of-the-art equipment has always appealed to Coppola. (Photo: Zoetrope Studios)

Francis with daughter Sofia during the shooting of Tucker: The Man and His Dream. *(Photo: Lucasfilm/Ralph Nelson)*

The Godfather Part III: *Francis Ford Coppola directs Al Pacino*
(Michael Corleone) and Andy Garcia (Vincent) (above).
Connie (Talia Shire) offers the poisoned pastry to her godfather,
Don Altobello (Eli Wallach).

Bram Stoker's Dracula: *Jonathan Harker (Keanu Reeves) is confronted with one of Dracula's (Gary Oldman) distinctive incarnations (above). Van Helsing (Anthony Hopkins, right) wards off Lucy Westenra (Sadie Frost), one of Dracula's latest victims.*

down to final cut and approval of the release prints. When, in June 1983, he reiterated these terms to Bob Evans, he must have hoped in some secret corner of his heart that they would be rejected. However invaluable the money would be in his fight to stave off bankruptcy, Coppola knew that the project was seriously flawed.

But Evans accepted—and even agreed to give Coppola a slice of the gross. With six weeks to go to the scheduled start of principal photography, the pace accelerated, as did the spending. Preproduction work at Kaufman Astoria Studios was consuming $140,000 a week. Cinematographer John Alonzo was fired, with $160,000 as a golden handshake. So too was music producer Jerry Wexler, whose compensation amounted to a mere $87,500. Coppola's Silver Fish trailer traveled across the country and would serve as a mobile headquarters for the director while shooting was in progress.

Coppola now began supervising everything, from casting Fred Gwynne as a doleful gangster, a cross between Boris Karloff and Leo G. Carroll, to employing his son, Gio. daughter Sofia, and nephew Nicolas Cage to work on the production. His most significant appointment was that of William Kennedy, as his partner on the ever-mutating screenplay. Without Kennedy's contribution, *The Cotton Club* would most likely have lacked its period detail and clipped vernacular. Kennedy, who relished long dialogue scenes, began to recognize the idiom that Coppola was searching for. The internal rhythm of the finished film derives from the terse, fast-forward flavor of classical jazz. Most important of all, Coppola respected William Kennedy as the author of *Legs* and *Ironweed*, novels set in Albany in the 1920s and 1930s. *Legs*, tracking the flamboyant career of gangster Legs Diamond, almost came to the screen in 1986 with Coppola at the helm.

Together, the men screened old gangster movies like *Scarface* and *Public Enemy*. Apart, they churned out hundreds of variations of individual scenes, and between forty and fifty versions of the screenplay. In the first draft, for example, Dixie Dwyer was a regular gangster. But Richard Gere insisted on displaying his modest talents as a cornet-player on screen, so Dixie changed into a musician as time and drafts went by. Coppola pinned long strips of paper on the walls of his workroom, each representing a reel of finished movie. According to Kennedy, "great chunks of story" were lifted and moved from this immense storyboard.

"Francis was constantly trying to reduce the cost, and bring everything to the Cotton Club," Kennedy recalls. It was an impossible struggle. The production had been up and running for six months before Coppola took over the reins. "The Tiffany concept of the production was made before I got there," said Coppola, who would break his own cardinal rule of always having the definitive script on hand prior to shooting.

The cast chemistry seemed promising. Gregory Hines's grandmother had been a showgirl at the original club, and Hines responded to the prospect of a film that "black people could be proud of—something that would show them as *special*." Diane Lane, who had impressed Coppola with her acting in *The Outsiders* and *Rumble Fish*, landed the potentially plum role of Vera Cicero, the calculating moll who charms Dixie Dwyer. Still only nineteen years of age, Lane saw Vera as "a very manipulative, goal-oriented woman." British cockney actor Bob Hoskins, with a stunning performance as a London gangster in *The Long Good Friday* to his credit, was cast as Owney Madden, proprietor of the Cotton Club. Idiosyncratic personalities like Joe Dallesandro, erstwhile Warhol star of *Flesh* and *Heat*, and Julian Beck, the foremost exponent of the Living Theater, joined the production in small but feisty roles.

On July 25, 1983, the actors met Coppola for rehearsals on the first major draft of the screenplay. Revisions multiplied. According to Michael Daly in *New York* magazine, Coppola and Kennedy produced four drafts in a single weekend. Richard Gere grew restless, and vanished just as principal photography was about to begin. The star's anxieties concerning the script were mollified by Bob Evans's agreeing to pay him $1.5 million for his 10 percent of the gross. This meant that Gere would clear $3 million all told, pushing him into the Brando league.

Five weeks' shooting took place outside the studios, in locations such as the Plaza Hotel in New York City. Somebody reassured Coppola that as a director he enjoyed ultimate control of the picture. Francis laughed: "In this case, the director is ringmaster of a circus that's inventing itself." He tried to retain some sense of perspective by retreating as often as possible to his home in Napa. He invited a group of the actors up to the house and asked them to contribute ideas. Gregory Hines found it "a very open way of working. Things came together right before your eyes and I liked that." He told Coppola at one of these sessions in Rutherford that he wanted to perform his closing tap dance "without any music, just a cappella . . . If I could do that, I could do something special." Coppola agreed. Several weeks later, the scene was due to be photographed and Hines, feeling apprehensive, suggested that he be given just a little bass, and then piano, accompaniment. "No," said Francis. "You told me if I gave you this opportunity you could do something special. Now do it."

Hines was startled, but soon appreciated his director's confidence. He also admired Coppola's casting of his real-life brother, Maurice Hines, as his screen partner on the stage of the Cotton Club. Gregory and Maurice had danced as a team for two decades before Gregory quit in a fit of pique. Coppola took advantage of the feelings involved and restaged that quarrel in the movie. Besides, he liked Maurice's inventiveness as a dancer.

The early days of shooting in the Kaufman Astoria Studios saw Coppola assailed by financial panic on all sides. The Doumani brothers, now too deeply involved to escape, found themselves short of ready cash. Costs had to be cut. But instead they mounted. Coppola himself was not being paid. All the while he was haunted by personal debt. Not for the first time, American Express withdrew his card-member facilities. Francis was talking as much with personal lawyers as he was with his actors. Cinematographer Stephen Goldblatt noted how morose and bitter Coppola would become after such wrangles. "Sometimes he could be very unpleasant, and it was necessary to keep your head down until the crisis was over."

The tension finally snapped after six weeks of filming. "Who needs this?" Francis stormed at Evans. "It's not my picture. You need me; I don't need you." He flew to London, in what may be seen as a reckless bid to duck the pressure. This forced the producers into offering to purchase some of Coppola's points in the film's gross. They also began to pay his basic fee, even if cast and crew could never be certain if wages would be forthcoming.

Despite protestations to the contrary, Coppola seems to have relished the improvisational atmosphere of *The Cotton Club*. As he had done in the Philippines on *Apocalypse Now*, he rewrote pages of screenplay on a daily basis. According to Gregory Hines, "We would rehearse a scene and be ready to shoot and [Coppola]'d come on the set and say, 'We don't have a scene here.'" Furniture would be arranged, lines amended, and Coppola would tell his actors what to *feel* rather than say. "But then you'd see the scene come together," asserts Hines. "We just trusted him."

Not all such scenes survived. Characterization suffered—gangster boss Dutch Schultz's relationship with his mother, and then with Vera, had been developed and illustrated on paper, as had the family background of the Hines brothers' characters of Sandman and Clay Williams, on the one hand, and of Dixie and Vincent Dwyer on the other. It was in-depth observation of this sort that had made *The Godfather* different from the routine gangster movie. But Coppola did not have Paramount behind him on *The Cotton Club* even if, in their desperation, Bob Evans and Ed Doumani tried to switch from Orion to Paramount (whose chairman, Barry Diller, was ready to invest $3 million in the production).

Instead, the race was on to complete principal photography by December 23. The crew dashed up to Harlem for one sequence, and back to Astoria for another. Bob Evans lost control of the production during these final hectic days, when Orion agreed to advance further funds only if he waived his right to oversee distribution and advertising. Coppola met the deadline, by a matter of hours, and was able to head west for Christmas with his family.

Long after the last scenes had been photographed, however, the legal struggle for ownership of *The Cotton Club* raged through the courts. In a ruling in July 1984, U.S. District Court Judge Irving Hill compared the imbroglio to Kurosawa's film *Rashomon*, "in which every event is reported entirely differently by every person who saw it."

Bob Evans ceded not only essential controls over the production, but also his home in Hollywood, as well as suffering the familiar humiliation of canceled credit cards. He gained the consolation of a credit above the title—"Robert Evans Presents"—but stood little to gain from the film in the immediate future. The credits themselves betrayed the elaborate nexus of proprietorship, with no fewer than nine individuals listed as "producers" or the like.

Coppola laments the death of *The Cotton Club* through a kind of "slow poisoning." The producers, he recalls, would preview the picture, "and the young audiences would say, 'Too much tap-dancing,' and so we'd cut out another number. We eliminated about twenty minutes or so that probably should not have been cut out."

When it opened on December 14, 1984, *The Cotton Club* surprised pundits with its performance at the box-office. It by no means flopped, as had been predicted with such relish by the industry; nor did it break any house records. Business, like the notices, was mixed but everyone agreed that Coppola had contrived to drag the white rabbit out of the hat and survive to fight another day, his reputation intact as the man who could marshal immense logistics and still produce an entertaining experience.

With the first weekend's gross reaching $2.9 million, the fate of the production looked uncertain. As of December 31, 1986, it had reached $12,931,284 in domestic rentals, and did respectably in numerous overseas countries. Home video and TV income now serves to cushion even an extravagant film like *The Cotton Club* against punitive losses. *The Out-*

siders, though, earned almost the same amount and cost a fraction of *Cotton Club*.

Sheila Benson in the *Los Angeles Times* once again defended Coppola's faith. She called the film "a glorious celebration of an era that at the same time feels like a masterly maker of movies having one whale of a wonderful time." *Variety* hedged its bets, saying that for enthusiasts of Coppola, "the latest effort may be a bit of a letdown, but it is by no means a disaster, nor is it a film lacking commercial appeal." The reviewer shrewdly blames Diane Lane for the failure of the Dixie-Vera romance to ignite, saying she appeared "incapable of throwing off her exterior."

Vincent Canby, in the *New York Times*, felt that the best things in the film were its musical numbers, and compared it to *Cleopatra*, another production that was somewhat better than expected even if also worse than its supporters claimed. The most ecstatic notice came from Jack Matthews in *USA Today*, who hailed *The Cotton Club* as "fabulous," asserting that while Coppola's recent sin had been to concentrate on style at the expense of substance, "with *The Cotton Club*, style *is* substance—the style of the place, its people, its time, and its music." Matthews preferred the scenes inside the club itself and even if he echoed the common dissatisfaction with the Dixie-Vera relationship, he accorded Coppola's film his highest rating, four stars.

*   *   *

Like *One from the Heart*, *The Cotton Club* remains an exercise in craftsmanship rather than a profound analysis of character. Both movies seem on the verge of being musicals, their narrative interwoven with bright threads of song and dance. Richard T. Jameson has made the astute observation apropos *The Cotton Club* that "like jazz itself—one beat imposed over another, teasing towards temporary congruence and then diverging—the movie at times weaves its storylines together, at other times allows them to separate and run more or less parallel." This homage to jazz traditions is allied to a theatrical flamboyance that Coppola had already indulged in *One from the Heart*. The whole film is much less intimidating than *The Godfather*, even if certain ingredients (the montage of newspaper headlines and gangster shootouts, for instance) match. *The Godfather* carries the authority and coloratura of grand opera. By comparison, *The Cotton Club* amounts to a jam session.

A succinct summary of the story might go as follows. Dixie Dwyer happens to save gangster boss Dutch Schultz from an assassination attempt in the Bamville Club in Harlem. The year is 1928, and Dixie, good-looking and naïve, is appointed musician in residence by Dutch, who also instructs him to guard his latest moll, Vera Cicero.

Meanwhile, tap dancers Sandman and Clay Williams succeed in getting their act accepted at the Cotton Club, where the sinister figure of Owney Madden holds sway. When Madden witnesses Dutch's savage knifing of a rival bootlegger, all these characters become entangled with one another. Dixie's incipient glamor attracts the attention of Gloria Swanson during a visit to the Cotton Club, and he winds up in Hollywood playing gangsters in the Cagney mold. Sandman falls in love with black singer Lila Rose Oliver and pursues her from club to club.

The years pass. Prohibition. The Wall Street crash. The numbers racket war. A climax in which Dutch meets his death, Owney Madden is escorted to jail, and Dixie and Vera depart for Hollywood on the "Twentieth Century" from Grand Central Station. Fantasy wins the day.

This complex, diagrammatic mesh of relationships is the worst handicap of *The Cotton Club*. Each of the principals adopts his or her favorite acting stance. Richard Gere oozes complacency and flashes the smirk of a star earning millions of dollars per part. As Dixie Dwyer, he never looks vulnerable or threatened. Each of the others works in an individual idiom, so that the film becomes more a series of acts than a coherent saga. This in turn is a consequence of the movie's unholy alliance of genres: musical, gangster film, comedy, farce, melodrama, romance, thriller and—in the performance of Diane Lane—even film noir.

But *The Cotton Club* cannot be accused of being arch or frivolous. Coppola's personality peeps through in every scene, especially in the dialogue, with its tongue-in-cheek verve. Teaching Dixie how to pronounce her name, Vera Cicero asks him if he ever studied Latin. "I was an altar boy," he grins. Julian Beck, playing a button man in the pay of Dutch Schultz, delivers a series of ghoulish lines. "I didn't have a mother. They found me in a garbage pail," he says with deadpan candor. Later, he recalls racing rats for fun in his youth.

Even Richard Gere's uninspired performance cannot quite destroy the pleasure of certain exchanges. "If I didn't like you," Dutch tells him outside the Cotton Club, "you'd be dead."

"It's nice to be liked," answers Dixie with an awkward smile.

In another scene, Owney Madden feeds his pigeons on the club roof and exacts a bribe of $25,000 from Dutch. When the gangster hands over the cash without a quibble, Owney tells him, "Sometimes you're a big man, Dutch," to which Schultz replies, "You know how I got that big? I ate pigeon every day when I was a kid."

Contempt, though, governs the film. There is contempt in the club bouncer's treatment of "niggers" like the Williams brothers. There is contempt in Dutch Schultz's murder of Irishman Joe Flynn, ramming a meat-knife into his throat on the spur of the moment. There is contempt in Vera's opinion of Dixie Dwyer and his slavish obedience to Dutch. And there is contempt in the blood of nearly every minor personality in the film, from Vincent "Mad Dog" Dwyer, who rebels against Dutch's forcing him to keep the blacks in their place, to suave black lawyer Bumpy Rhodes, with his remark that there are only two things in this world for him and his race to do—"Stay black and die."

Everybody in sight is on the make. Dixie is wooed first by Dutch and later by Owney Madden, who wants him to be his "face" on the West Coast. Sandman woos Lila, the singer who is always a little ahead of him in public esteem. Dixie himself woos Vera, even if that includes slapping her around on the dance floor.

This bass line of patronizing scorn is tempered by Coppola's insistence on the glittering lights of the city's nightspots. They displace the grim, sordid reality of everyday life, as they do in both *Apocalypse Now* and *One from the Heart*. Shadows prevail in moments of failure, sadness or loss, as in the seduction scene between Dixie and Vera in the shrouded darkness of an apartment, where a lace curtain dapples their faces and bodies with undulating light. This duel between light and darkness runs through the film, reminding us again of Coppola's similarity to Orson Welles. In a conspicuous tribute to *Citizen Kane*, Coppola sets one scene in a Hollywood viewing theater, with a studio boss's head surrounded by a spill of light from the projector carbons, as he watches Dixie's screen test. Another Wellesian touch is the frequent use of subjective camera movements following characters up flights of stairs, along sidewalks and across streets, although as far back as *The Rain People* Coppola had shown a penchant for this.

The rhythm, however, belongs to the Jazz Age, as do the sleek, glossy looks of Dixie and Vera and just about every hoofer in sight. It is a world of overwhelming blacks and whites, tuxedos and starched evening shirts, damson eyes and powdered faces. In turn this counterpoints the conflict between black and white characters in the movie, and the parallel romances involving Dixie and Vera, and Sandman and Lila. White eventually becomes the color of death, as Sandman performs the climactic dance, dazzling in the merciless glare of a spotlight, his twinkling feet tapping faster and faster until—almost in mid-step—he stops, and Dutch Schultz is seen dying from gunshot wounds in a public toilet.

This final montage sequence is one of several in *The Cotton Club* that were directed by Francis's son Gian-Carlo Coppola and mimic the 1930s gangster picture. Lila sings "Ill Wind" over a montage depicting the Harlem numbers racket war, with explosions, slayings, and piles of dollar bills being counted. Another sequence condenses the impact of the Wall Street crash and the early months of the Depression. After Vincent has gunned down Sol in the street (photographed in similar style to the attempt on the life of Don Vito in *The Godfather*), Coppola uses a montage to chart the outcry and manhunt that follow. And the same device tracks the passage of time covering Dixie's success as a movie star, and the relaxation of the "whites only" rule at the Cotton Club.

For all its fancy wipes and irises, though, this production is no mere pastiche of a much-loved genre, in the vein of Alan Parker's *Bugsy Malone* or Billy Wilder's *Some Like It Hot*. The killings, for example, are carried out with Coppola's customary, operatic bravado. Dutch's murder of Flynn in the hotel comes as a visceral blow, and the blood that drips from a chandelier on to the delicate cheek of Vera Cicero carries a tangible, macabre *frisson*. Equally savage is the vengeance enacted by the club's blacks on their chief tormentor—the huge, rebarbative bouncer. An iron bar is flung across his throat from behind, and he is bundled into the toilets, to have his head thrust down the urinal. Murder and mayhem acquire a kind of glamor, which we accept because the costumes and comportment of the era insulate us from the sordid fact of crime. Coppola is more convincing in such scenes than he is when trying to underline the social importance of the Cotton Club. The scene when "Chaplin," "Fanny Brice," and "James Cagney" are introduced to the crowd is the most inept and embarrassing in the film. These lookalikes are not so much larger, as smaller, than life.

Fantasy and escapism were the stock-in-trade of the Cotton Club on 142nd Street, and Coppola's film functions best when indulging them. In fact the audacious fusion of dream and reality so common to the Hollywood musical provides *The Cotton Club* with a delightful ending. As the train carrying Dixie and Vera draws out of Grand Central, the camera pulls back also, revealing not an extension of the railroad track but the crowded tables of the Cotton Club itself. It is a cheat, but it sends the audience out of the theater in a good mood, to the strains of Duke Ellington's "Daybreak Express." It also underlines the conceit that the

Cotton Club was a symbol of its age, assimilating jazz and crime on a daily basis just as the movies did on the screen.

Neither *Finian's Rainbow* nor *The Cotton Club* were projects close to Coppola's heart. It is interesting, though, that in both movies he tried to express outrage at the treatment of blacks in American society, and yet finally bowed to commercial pressures and allowed the frothy side of the story to triumph over social indignation. What stays intact is the sense of an intolerant, prejudiced epoch in U.S. history. Jews and "niggers" are abused in practically every bout of dialogue. Flattery ensures survival for Sandman. "Listen, you white folks are *so smart!*" he exclaims in delight after learning that he has made the next show. And survival was the name of the game.

From Rip van Winkle
to Peggy Sue

Throughout the early weeks of 1984, Coppola fought a losing battle to retain the studio in Los Angeles. On Friday, February 10, the property was sold to Jack Singer for $12.3 million. Ironically, it was Singer who had come to Zoetrope's aid during the filming of *One from the Heart*. An agreement worked out with a bankruptcy judge and the principal creditors would permit Coppola to continue operating Zoetrope Studios as a production company in San Francisco. For month after month, week after week, seemingly day after day, Francis and his advisers had forestalled the auction. A dream, after all, was at stake. Long afterwards, the company stationery would still include "San Francisco" and "Hollywood" below the familiar Zoetrope logo. In the words of his associate John Peters, Francis bade farewell to his "utopian society of filmmakers. The other losses were mere appurtenances."

Although his predicament was splashed over the pages of the Hollywood trade papers, Coppola continued in the eyes of the outside world to promote and initiate projects. Tom Luddy's production of *Mishima* for Zoetrope was on location in Japan that year, with the names of Coppola and Lucas above the title. Since *One from the Heart*, Zoetrope had been unable to fund any project off its own bat. When George Lucas approached Warners, however, with a request for $5 million for this new film by Paul Schrader about the Japanese author, the studio agreed with alacrity. Lucas had given his *Star Wars* series to Fox, and his *Indiana Jones* movies to Paramount, so perhaps next time he had a bright idea he might pick up the phone and call Warners—if they financed *Mishima*.

193

Coppola took a keen interest in the project, but with constant fiscal emergencies bombarding the Sentinel Building, he could spare little time. Each March 20 he had to pay out almost $1 million in interest charges on the outstanding debt. In addition, postproduction work on *The Cotton Club* sapped his energies. Somehow he found time to develop his ideas for an "electronic cinema" of the future.

Coppola and Luddy admired a Japanese designer, Eiko Ishioka. She had prepared a spectacular poster for *Koyaanisqatsi*, and a coffee-table book of her drawings, sets, and costumes had been published in English. Eiko Ishioka produced some striking sets for *Mishima*, and during one of their meetings Coppola asked if she could help him with a TV movie he had been commissioned to make for Home Box Office (HBO).

Rip van Winkle would be one of several films in HBO's "Faerie Tale Theater" series, introduced by Shelley Duvall. As usual, Coppola converted what was a trivial, fifty-minute kids' movie into a major challenge for himself and those involved with him. For him as for all Sicilians, even the simplest project, as Luigi Barzini has written, becomes an enterprise of heroic proportions.

He shot *Rip van Winkle* in a furious five days at a studio in Los Angeles, after rehearsals that had started on November 26, 1984. But he caused ructions by bringing in his video experts and trying to improve a system and a technique of production that had not changed from one show to another. Harry Dean Stanton, long a stalwart of the Zoetrope team, played Rip, the dim-witted farmer of Washington Irving's classic novel. Coppola cast two members of his family, his daughter Sofia, and his sister Talia Shire as Rip's peevish wife. He loved the idea of doing all the opticals in the camera, as on *One from the Heart*. Unfortunately, the flair and spectacle were lacking on *Rip van Winkle*. Ishioka's outré sets reflect a palette far removed from the conventional image of the Catskills during American colonial days. "I was able to realize a lot of my ideas, using equipment I was interested in experimenting with, playing with illusions," he said when taping had ended. But the film was a prisoner of its artifice, a perfunctory scribble in the margins of Coppola's career.

Just before this, during the autumn of 1984, succour had appeared in the form of Ray Stark, veteran Hollywood producer and president of Rastar, the company responsible for some of the most august money-winners of recent decades, including *Funny Girl* and *The Goodbye Girl*, as well as various films directed by John Huston, among them the brilliant *Fat City*. Stark had cofounded Seven Arts, although he resigned to become an independent producer in 1966, one year before Seven Arts acquired

Warner Bros. He remembered Francis's working on the screenplay for *Reflections in a Golden Eye*, which he had produced in 1967. Now he offered to sign a deal with him in his hour of need, to direct *Peggy Sue Got Married*.

The project seemed as jinxed as *The Cotton Club*. The star from the outset, Debra Winger, had already seen two directors leave the movie. Jonathan Demme quit on account of what the studio euphemistically term "creative differences," and Penny Marshall was fired when she argued too persistently with screenwriters Jerry Leichting and Arlene Sarner. Then, after Coppola had been signed to take over, Debra Winger entered the hospital with a severe back ailment. Shooting, scheduled to begin in early March, was postponed. The star's health forced her to withdraw.

Kathleen Turner, who had revealed her talents as a comedienne in *Romancing the Stone*, was approached. "I decided I wanted to do it the minute Francis and I took a drive in Los Angeles and started to sing songs from that era. We had a lot of fun. Francis is a damned good singer." But Turner would not be available until she had completed shooting on *The Jewel of the Nile*. Coppola waited.

He spent the interval planning the future, exhuming his pet project—a film on auto designer Preston Tucker—and at a lavish party in Los Angeles in July 1985, he launched the 1979 vintage of his Niebaum-Coppola Rubicon wine. "I'm not giving up movies for wine," he said. "It's just a nice sideline." This plummy red came from the old Gustav Niebaum vineyards at Rutherford, which Coppola had purchased in 1977.

Zoetrope's debts remained astronomical by mortal standards, yet Coppola kept his head down and charged ahead, demanding—and getting—$2.5 million a picture, and resolved to retain his independence. He paused for a somewhat less lucrative assignment from the Disney Company. Michael Eisner, head of Disney, had discussed with George Lucas the idea of a spectacular new site for Disneyland and Disney World. Lucas agreed to plan the operation if Michael Jackson, then at the peak of his popularity, was involved. A movie of some kind looked the likeliest bet, but it had to be dramatically different from anything available in regular theaters. Walt Disney Engineering collaborated with Eastman Kodak in developing a complex double camera which could photograph scenes from two different angles simultaneously in 65mm, creating a sense of spatial depth. Thus *Captain Eo* was born—a fifteen-minute giant-screen presentation starring Jackson as a space marshal battling the forces of a She-Devil Supreme on a colorless planet beyond the solar system. With the help of music, dance, and lasers, Eo and his warriors convert this mono-chrome regime into a playground of joy and color. The more engaging characters conceived by Lucasfilm include a green baby elephant who uses his trunk as a flute, Major Domo, who can change his plated physique into drums, and Minor Domo, whose body serves as a synthesizer.

Michael Jackson wrote the songs for the film, and *Captain Eo* became the costliest short in screen history, with a budget of over $20 million. Lucas brought Coppola into the production as director, and Vittorio Storaro and Walter Murch joined the team as cinematographer and editor respectively. The result, viewed through so-called "3-U" glasses, is the ultimate music video, with the screen emitting a constant barrage of spacecraft and laser beams, and a quintuphonic soundtrack blasting the eardrums. To accommodate the film, Disney constructed 700-seat theaters in their parks in Florida and southern California, but have so far resisted any temptation to release *Eo* in any other form.

For Coppola, it was the first encounter with a SF project since 1962 when he had worked for *Battle Beyond the Sun* for Corman on a budget probably a thousand times cheaper.

By the time the cameras rolled on *Peggy Sue*, in late August 1985, Coppola was eager to work with a female star again. Since *The Rain People*, and his less than harmonious relationship with Shirley Knight, he had—by chance rather than intention—worked with male actors in the lead roles. There is even a tenuous link between *Peggy Sue* and *The Rain People*, for in both films a woman is released from her regular life, to search for the root and meaning of her existence.

Anyone approaching *Peggy Sue Got Married* with their preconceptions of a Coppola movie firmly in place will be disappointed by the film. At its best, it evokes the musical comedies of Vincente Minnelli and those homespun slices of Americana trademarked Frank Capra. At its worst, it is banal and sentimental, even maudlin. It is easy to assume that a director of Coppola's celebrity will work only on projects to which he is com-mitted. But ever since the debacle of *One from the Heart*, Coppola had been forced to take whatever came his way, in the tradition of the Hol-lywood directors of the 1930s and 1940s. At a press conference at the Havana Film Festival in December 1986, he admitted that his heart had not really been in any of his recent films. Paul R. Gurian, who produced *Peggy Sue* for Ray Stark, confirms that Coppola did not want the credits to proclaim it as "A Francis Coppola Film." Instead, he says, "I felt this film was the chance for Francis to make a small, intimate film with a simple story, and the critics would say, 'Hey, Francis, it's good, you made a nice little simple story. It's not a brilliant Francis Coppola film,' and frankly it isn't, and anyone who says it is, is crazy."

Still, Coppola has never been so cynical as to direct a movie at arm's length, and the unexpected popularity of *Peggy Sue* at the box-office does credit to the man's versatility and to his judgment of public mood. The idea of someone's voyaging back into the past is scarcely original, and the enormous success of Steven Spielberg's production of *Back to the Future* in late 1985 may even have persuaded Tri-Star to delay release of the Coppola picture, so alike are the two films.

*   *   *

American Graffiti revived the pleasures of youth in 1962. *Peggy Sue* returns its heroine to 1960. It has the same Californian small-town atmosphere (Santa Rosa as opposed to Modesto), but its basis in the music of the period is less pronounced (Lucas included no fewer than forty-one rock numbers in his film). Granted, Buddy Holly's hit single gives the film its name, and relives behind the credits. But Coppola gives us far more subtle pointers to the tastes of 1960. "Stranger in Paradise" plays in the background while Peggy Sue stays with her parents, and her boyfriend Charlie persuades a customer in his father's music shop to try some Shostakovich—a composer who was just then coming into vogue in the West, as fine recordings emerged from the studios.

Peggy Sue Kelcher has separated from her husband, Charlie Bodell. They have two children, Scott and Beth, and Peggy Sue runs her own bakery business. During a high school reunion. Peggy Sue faints and wakes up at the age of seventeen. She is forced to rerun her courtship with Charlie, enjoys a night of love with the class's scholar-athlete, Michael Fitzsimmons, seizes the chance of meeting her beloved grandparents, and eventually returns to the present, primed and ready to accept a contrite Charlie's commitment to a new relationship with her.

The intellectual at Buchanan High during Peggy Sue's time there is Richard Norvik. As she tries to convince him that she really has traveled back from the future, he compares time to a burrito, a Mexican pancake that folds over, with its edges almost touching. Coppola's triumph in *Peggy Sue* lies in his unobtrusive way of demonstrating this point. A silverfoil balloon floats past in the corridor of the hospital where Peggy Sue "wakes up" in 1960, seeming to have followed her from the reunion ball. The book that Charlie gives her in the closing scene is by Michael Fitzsimmons, and dedicated to her. The memory of her night with Michael gains in poignancy for Peggy Sue now that she has "lived" it and appreciated it with all the hindsight of adulthood.

The film opens on a bad note. Peggy Sue is prettifying herself in readiness for a reunion, while her daughter revels in her father's dire performance in a TV commercial. But the exposition sounds clumsy, and the set-ups look self-conscious. Peggy Sue is risking her all this night, squeezing into a tight-waisted, glittery ball-gown that provokes admiring words from Beth. But if Peggy Sue does indeed appear like "a blast from the past" or "a hip chick," then she seems embarrassingly overdressed at the reunion party. There she meets her two closest chums of yesteryear, Maddie and Carol. Maddie married right after leaving school and has four children. Orthodox and unadventurous, she has settled down while Carol, who still sports a spontaneous sexy charm, boasts no family and cheerfully sniffs some coke in an upstairs room at the party. Peggy has to run the gauntlet of questions about herself and Charlie. "We just married too young, I guess," she responds, "and ended up blaming each other for all the things we missed." She shares a table with Norvik, who has the relaxed air of someone who has been very successful in life without exerting himself. In one of the first of the movie's many little ironies, Richard receives congratulations from a large, overbearing man from Merrill Lynch who turns out to have been his chief tormentor at high school.

Then the whole tone of the film is enhanced by a single shot. A balloon drifts up to a doorway faraway at the back of the hall, and into a stream of moted light steps Charlie, like some extraterrestrial in his white suit, like some latterday James Dean in his forced nonchalance. It is as though he had entered the Las Vegas of *One from the Heart*, as he takes his seat and throws Peggy Sue a glance of withering sexual arrogance.

From now on, the lighting of *Peggy Sue* plays a key part in dictating the mood. Peggy Sue faints as a huge celebration cake is wheeled towards her. Light shafts down on the cake and its candles, the shrill music and the crowd's tribal clapping mount in intensity, and Peggy Sue collapses. When she regains consciousness, the lighting is more discreet, even somber. She comes to on a bed in the school gym. A banner on the wall reads, "Blood Drive 1960," and Peggy Sue is well and truly back in Buchanan High.

The entire central section of the film, the return to 1960, is photographed in subdued pastel colours, as though this were a valentine card in praise of the past. When Peggy Sue enters her old home, and meets her mother in the living room, the lighting has a reflected quality, as though we were inside not a time capsule so much as a gigantic conch. As Peggy Sue takes a call from her grandmother, whom she knows is dead, Coppola films her in silhouette; moments of grief he has always dealt with in shadow or darkness.

Flashes of whimsy enliven the atmosphere. Peggy Sue, for example, shocks her father by downing several fingers of Scotch, and declaring, "I'm an adult. I wanna have fun. I'm goin' to Liverpool to discover the Beatles!" This remark is one of many in the film that capitalize on Peggy Sue's knowledge of the future, and baffles those around her. Her parents are equally dumbfounded by her fit of laughter when she catches sight of the new car her father has driven up to the house so proudly. "You bought an Edsel!" she exclaims, referring to a model that was a joke almost from the day it appeared, with its vulgar grilles and superfluous chrome. As Vincent Canby has observed, "The 'past,' to anyone born after World War II, is rather like an Edsel—sort of quaint but, in its essentials, not very different from the present."

Back in high school, Peggy Sue startles her classmates by belting out the national anthem with a fervor that seems to satirize the Reagan era. The film is indeed politically alert. Peggy Sue's mother admits to being a closet Democrat. Her father, on the other hand, behaves like a relic of the Eisenhower period, with his bow tie, his perennial pipe-smoking, and the grotesque moose-head mounted on the wall of his parlor. The high school youths sound as conservative as their counterparts of the late 1980s. Michael Fitzsimmons stands alone in his championship of Jack Kerouac at the expense of Hemingway, and is scorned as a "commie beatnik" by another guy in his class.

The year 1960 marked a watershed in American social and political attitudes. It was the tail end of the Eisenhower presidency, and the New Frontier rhetoric of John F. Kennedy would inspire the young generation and win him the race for the White House. Michael in *Peggy Sue* fulfils a kind of Kennedy role, while the Richard Norvik character represents the brilliant scientific minds that would land an American on the moon and keep IBM as number one electronics company.

The coziest aspect of Peggy Sue's odyssey is the recognition at every step that the everyday life of adolescence possesses a charm and security we fail to acknowledge until middle age. When Peggy Sue bursts out, "Oh Mom, I forgot you were ever this young!" the remark conveys a genuine charge of nostalgia. And there's creamed chip beef on toast for supper.

It is significant that Peggy Sue finds the most understanding reception at her grandparents'. The previous generation seems to have attained a wisdom and a tranquility denied to their children. "You're browsing through time," says grandma to Peggy Sue in a tone of comfort and tolerance after hearing her story. Grandpa is reading a book about a woman in Colorado who remembers being alive 150 years ago in Ireland.

Peggy Sue has brought to this revised version of youth a tolerance of her own, acquired during the tough years of maturity and marriage. She urges her mother to sit down at breakfast instead of fussing round catering for everyone else. In Barbara Harris's understated response, asking if Peggy Sue really means just that, there is an extraordinary poignancy.

The film's central contrast matches the expectation of youth against the experience of age. Richard and Michael stand for science and the arts respectively. Peggy Sue is able to inform Richard that a man landed on the moon in 1969. "That's six years ahead of schedule," mutters Richard, his analytical complacency disturbed. She startles the budding scientist by telling him that he will invent a machine for the blind to read by, inspired by an urge to aid his blind grandfather. For Michael, she predicts a future as a novelist, and gives him the idea of writing a book about their stolen hours of romance together. And Charlie's fragile sophistication is blown away when Peggy Sue comes on to him in the car one night with the routine sexual aggression of a 1980s woman. Charlie is aghast as she fingers his fly, and from this scene onwards Peggy Sue has to acknowledge that Charlie's blow-dried, fast-car charm conceals a thoroughly trembling conservative. It makes her all the more ready to fling herself without protest into the escapade with Michael in the hills outside town, smoking pot and making love to the sound of Yeats's "When You Are Old": "But one man loved the pilgrim soul in you/And loved the sorrows of your changing face." Michael's remark that his parents are interested only in money, and mother in her status at the country club, strikes a chord in Peggy Sue, who realizes that some things simply do not change. Michael may be a Mormon who urges her to raise chickens with him and his other girlfriend in Utah, but his sloe-eyed intensity belongs to the cusp of the 1960s, and Peggy Sue regrets its passing.

The whole film betrays an undertow of disappointment. The ideals and eagerness of youth have evaporated, and at the Buchanan High reunion Michael can be seen only in a photograph on the wall, like a frozen memory. Everyone else has settled for the material comforts and traditional values of Reagan's America. Horizons have retreated, and Peggy Sue's view of the future is diminished rather than improved by her visit to the past.

By degrees Charlie develops into the most tragic character in the movie. During her spell back in 1960, Peggy Sue swoons and squeals with her gang as he sings "I Wonder Why" in a gold-lamé coat. But she knows that Charlie will never succeed as a singer, and only she realizes how much that means to him, and how vulnerable he is to failure. Still able to enter the reunion like an obnoxious god descending to meet his captive subjects, Charlie has been relegated to making TV spots and is neither the Fabian nor Beatle he doubtless dreamed of becoming.

Nicolas Cage's performance is more nuanced than it has been given credit for. His entire youth comes across as an act. His hair, his clothes, his car—all are carefully selected to mask his gauche, defensive personality. He adopts a voice so fake in its sleepy, laid-back huskiness that during a visit with Peggy Sue's father he almost strangles on his responses. His character contains none of the savvy required for triumph in latterday America. Charlie is too soft for his own good, too naïve by half. Peggy Sue tells him she's had a whole lifetime of experiences, and he nods and says gravely, "Girls mature faster than guys . . ." When at last he does react to the prospect of losing Peggy Sue, he follows the most melodramatic course available—stealing into her house at night, ready to smother her with a pillow after he has heard of her one-night stand with Michael.

Peggy Sue, however, finds this clumsiness intriguing. The decisive moment arrives when Charlie "rescues" her from the Masonic Lodge where, in a ceremony compounded of goodwill and mumbo jumbo, her grandpa and his fellow Masons try to project Peggy Sue back to the future. "Well, the girl's gone—let's play cards," says one old-timer blithely, but Peggy Sue is actually being dragged away into the bushes by Charlie. He has a gift for her—a locket. As she opens it, she knows it contains photos of her children. After all, she flashed it proudly at the reunion. But now Charlie assures her that the portraits are of her and him, and that her mother has given it to him. In a much more artful transition than the first one, Peggy Sue gives herself in an embrace to Charlie and surfaces in a hospital bed. A yearning for her kids, and the almost mystical transformation of the pictures in her locket, gives Peggy Sue the psychological motive to regain her own time.

From one standpoint, fate is cruel to Peggy Sue. She is never allowed to forget the future, and her knowledge of what will happen to people and things mars much of her excitement. It may be fun to find out that a lingerie store in 1960 has never heard of pantyhose but for much of the time she feels stifled, powerless to persuade those around her that, in her words to Richard, she's "a walking anachronism." Richard asks her to change her destiny and marry him, and the proposal bears the seeds of a terrible regret. Richard is earmarked for fame and success. He has been selected, she knows, as King to her Queen at the school reunion. At moments like this, Peggy Sue must wish that her voyage back in time had blacked out the future.

* * *

Peggy Sue Got Married does not belong among Coppola's most searching films. There are ragged edges and dangling participles that nag at us after the movie has ended. How, for example, can Peggy Sue land in high school at the age of—presumably—forty-two without appearing grotesque to her fellow teenagers? Is it just poetic licence? The romantic comedy form accommodates such contradictions, of course. In the grandiose realism of *The Godfather*, it would have been implausible for Brando to have played the young Don Vito. The difficulty lies not in the quality of the performance (even if Kathleen Turner has a limited range of expressions) so much as our eagerness to test the structure of this impudent story.

The screenplay affects much more interest in the past than the present. The dialogue at the reunion sounds artificial, from Beth's hard-boiled sophistication to the inane questions inside the hall, all of which seem to end with the question, "How's Charlie?" as though women were still mere appendices of the men they live with. Coppola might have sharpened the distinctions between the eras by modernizing the lines at the ball.

But when all is said and done, the film wears the strengths and frailties of an operetta, and Coppola has approached *Peggy Sue* without a trace of condescension. The visual texture of the movie gazes back on youth in the same golden-hued light as *The Outsiders*. Unlike most directors, Coppola genuinely believes in the wonder of childhood and of that undefined spell between adolescence and adult life.

Peggy Sue Got Married had its world premiere on the closing night of the New York Film Festival, October 5, 1986. A couple of weeks earlier, *Variety* predicted the reception with its headline, "Smashing return to form by Francis Coppola." Comparing it with *Back to the Future*, the trade paper observed that the jokes were not so much derivative of pop culture, as they were in Robert Zemeckis's movie, but were to be found "in the learned wisdom of a middle-aged woman reacting to her own teenage dilemmas." Vincent Canby, in the *New York Times*, remained his usual disenchanted self where Coppola's work is concerned. He accused the picture of being "either underdeveloped or simply not thought through." He also criticized the lack of rapport between Turner and Cage. Canby's terse dismissal of *Peggy Sue* as "a small, amiable, sort of sloppy comedy-fantasy," was softened the following weekend when he succumbed to the film's evocation of the past and wrote much more sympathetically about it.

Some reviewers burdened the movie with unjustifiable superlatives. Carrie Rickey, in *New Woman*, hailed it as "a masterpiece that is the movie of the year." Rex Reed, that arbiter of kitsch, declared that *Peggy Sue* was Coppola's "best film since *The Godfather*," and Gene Siskel and Roger Ebert, in their highly regarded TV program, described it as "a classic," accurately forecasting the Oscar nomination for Kathleen Turner. In the *San Francisco Chronicle*, Peter Stack welcomed *Peggy Sue* as "a wonderful, wistful, touching drama."

Audiences in the United States supported *Peggy Sue* to an extent that soon made the film Coppola's biggest hit of the 1980s. After just twenty-four days in release, *Peggy Sue* had attracted a cumulative box-office of $21,741,232. In its opening week alone it had grossed over $1 million from sixty-three theaters in the New York area.

European critics and audiences were less ecstatic, accepting the film more, perhaps, on its own terms and in the spirit in which it was made. David Robinson, in the London *Times*, called *Peggy Sue* "an endearing little fable," and praised Coppola's "kindly sentimentality" in the scenes with the parents and grandparents, as Peggy Sue "discovers the love and appreciation we rarely recognize while we still have the chance to show it."

CHAPTER TWELVE

Tragedy and Revival

In the spring of 1985, Coppola received a lunch invitation from Victor Kaufman, boss of Tri-Star Pictures. *Peggy Sue* was nearing completion, and Kaufman had liked what he had seen. Now he suggested that Coppola should direct a screen version of *Gardens of Stone*, a book about the Old Guard burying the dead in Arlington National Cemetery in Washington.

Nicholas Proffitt, author of *Gardens of Stone*, had served as a correspondent for *Newsweek*, and couched his novel in grave, reflective tones that set it apart from the spate of post-Vietnam literature. The blood and violence of the battlefield have been drained off; the book stares back with muted anger at the late 1960s and portrays the regular army and its NCOs in sympathetic terms. As the *New York Times* noted when *Gardens of Stone* was published in 1983, this was 'an evocation of a time when a soldier's ideal of service to his country elicited more respect than contempt from his fellow countrymen."

Coppola warmed to the idea of making a personal film about the ritual that had fascinated him ever since he had attended military academy in his teens. He felt he could bring out the individual personality of the soldiers involved. In all too many war movies the soldier emerged as a cliché, a grunt who killed and screamed obscenities and thrived on drugs. *Gardens of Stone* describes the unusual if undramatic lives of the men of the Old Guard. A young soldier yearns to serve in Vietnam and an older sergeant cautions him against leaping into combat.

Ronald Bass had already written the screenplay for Michael Levy at Tri-Star, and the prospects of Francis's being able to stamp his personality

205

on the film did not look bright. His directing fee, however, would reduce still further the debt at Zoetrope, but for the first time in more than a dozen years Francis waived the banner credit line, "A Francis Coppola Film."

Fate ensured that *Gardens of Stone* would embody a terrible poignance for Francis, his family, and his colleagues.

In the early months of 1986, he enjoyed his life and his work. On March 22, he received a carte blanche to do whatever he wished on NBC's "Saturday Night Live" TV show in New York. One of the skits brought back memories of *Apocalypse Now*, with Coppola yelling at his men in the jungles of Southeast Asia. In rehearsals the previous evening he gave careful instructions to the dancers, laughed at himself as he fluffed his lines, and ate Chinese takeout with his son Gio while the set was being dressed.

Meanwhile, Fred Roos and Tom Luddy at Zoetrope had started work on two productions for Cannon, Norman Mailer's *Tough Guys Don't Dance* and Barbet Schroeder's *Barfly*. True, Zoetrope could no longer contribute lavish studio facilities, let alone finance, but Coppola's logo still carried the glitter of excitement and prestige.

Preproduction work on *Gardens of Stone* consumed the weeks of spring. Once the army had approved the screenplay, some critical locations became available for the crew: Arlington National Cemetery, Fort Myer, and Fort Belvoir. Hundreds of soldiers and military personnel were provided, some even qualifying for minor speaking roles in the picture. The army guessed right again: just as *Apocalypse Now* had shown the military in a lurid light, so *Gardens of Stone* would do the opposite, serving as welcome propaganda for army traditions and discipline.

Dean Tavoularis revelled in the hunt for Washington locations. "These cities are rich with Greek and Roman architecture which we use to give the film an eternal look and feel. The architecture helps complement the story which, itself, is timeless," said Coppola's loyal production designer.

The familiar rhythm asserted itself. There were two weeks of thorough rehearsals for cast and crew alike. James Caan and James Earl Jones, playing Sergeant Clell Hazard and Sgt. Major Goody Nelson respectively, devoted many hours to perfecting their military drill and bearing. "One of the things that touched me when I read the script," remarked Coppola, "was the drill and ritual that give the Old Guard its splendor. There is a certain beauty and honor in being part of an exercise where hundreds of other people are performing the exact same drill in absolutely perfect harmony."

Coppola videotaped these two weeks of rehearsal, creating a "live" storyboard for the production. James Earl Jones likened this spell to "an affair with the script. Since during rehearsals it was constantly changing and nothing was set in stone, it had the excitement and spontaneity of a wonderful affair."

Francis's elder son Gio supervised the electronic cinema staff on *Gardens of Stone*. Not long after shooting had commenced, Gio spent the Memorial Day weekend with his girlfriend Jacqueline de la Fontaine and Griffin O'Neal, son of the actor Ryan O'Neal. On Monday, May 26, they hired a fourteen-foot McKee speedboat, and took it out on the South River near Annapolis. After a preliminary sortie, Jacqueline was left ashore. O'Neal was at the wheel when the craft struck a taut tow-rope linking two other boats on the estuary. Gio sustained terrible head injuries, and was pronounced dead on arrival at Anne Arundel County General Hospital. First reports declared that the young Coppola had been piloting the boat, on the strength of a statement to police by Griffin O'Neal. But during the days that followed, eyewitnesses came forward, claiming that a blond-haired man had been at the wheel at the time of the fatal accident. Less than a month later, a grand jury embarked on an investigation. Before summer's end, an indictment had been returned, charging O'Neal with "boat manslaughter," and accusing him of "gross negligence." The testimony of six witnesses indicated unequivocally that O'Neal must have been driving the craft. Jacqueline de la Fontaine entered evidence on videotape, stating that when she was out with the men in the speedboat a mere fifteen minutes prior to the crash, O'Neal "was driving really crazy. I was scared that we were all going to be killed. He was going wild."

Just before Christmas 1986, Griffin O'Neal heard himself acquitted of manslaughter but convicted of "reckless endangerment" over the death of Gian-Carlo Coppola. After a three-day trial without a jury, Judge Martin Wolff determined that O'Neal had been "operating the boat in a manner that endangered the person and property of others." Not long afterwards, the culprit suffered a derisory fine ($200) and was placed on eighteen months' probation.

Francis, who had groomed his elder son to become a film director in his own right, reacted with despair and disbelief to Gio's loss. Instinctively, he decided to press on with the shooting of *Gardens of Stone*. Gary Lucchesi, a production executive, commented: "I remember [Francis] saying the last place he'd want to be after Gio's death was home. To see Gio's room, to confront him there, he wanted time." Filming seemed like the only therapy at hand. "Work has that quality," reflected Coppola in 1987, "of being something you can do, as opposed to sitting around and weeping."

A week after the tragedy, Griffin O'Neal requested—through his manager—that he should be released from the picture. He had been known and liked for some time in Zoetrope circles, and had played the young magician in Caleb Deschanel's 1982 release for the studio, *The Escape Artist*.

Gio's talent had manifested itself in various ways. At the age of just seventeen he had acted as a video editor on *One from the Heart*. He served as associate producer on both *The Outsiders* and *Rumble Fish*. The following year his father entrusted him with the direction of several montage sequences in *The Cotton Club*, and when Francis made *Captain Eo* for Disney, Gio was second-unit director. He would have fulfilled the same role on Penny Marshall's production of *Jumpin' Jack Flash*, starring Whoopi Goldberg. Steven Spielberg liked his gifts, too, and suggested to Francis that Gio might tackle an episode in his portmanteau movie, *Amazing Stories*.

For more than a year, Francis could not bear to talk about the death of his son. Little by little he began to see it in a larger context:

I've always had the feeling that whatever movie I worked on, my own life would be a part of it, like a twilight zone. So many things that happened on *Apocalypse* reflected the story and the characters, and then to do a movie about the burying of young boys, a continuous ceremony of that, and then to find out that my own young boy would die right in the midst of it, and the ceremony would be in the same chapel where we shot a similar scene in *Gardens of Stone* . . .

But I must say that Nature does protect us, and I guess it's a form of shock but somehow it didn't get to me for a long time. I just was walking around with some crazy idea that there was still hope. I still have a little bit . . .

I don't think many fathers are with their little fourteen-year-old son every day and take him out of school and decide to educate him so that he can be the heir of the place. Gio didn't go to high school. I took him out of there, and he came with me when I was working at Zoetrope, and he was Telemachus, my helper, and he was the president of Zoetrope.

He'd written me a letter, in his terrible handwriting and with his little misspellings, and it said essentially, "I don't want to go to school. I want to be with you, I want to learn everything there is to learn about films and entertainment. I want to study them and I want to be a director." After getting a letter like that, I took him right out of school.

I've had this other joy which involves Roman, my other son. After a year or so of not knowing whether or not he would want to do something in the organization, Roman says that he wants to run Zoetrope. He's twenty-two. Gio was twenty-two when he died. Roman went to NYU; he had one more year to go, but he's leaving to take over the company. So it's almost like one of those romantic novels where you lose one son who was the prince, and now the next one comes to replace him. I was five years younger than my brother; Roman's only one year younger than Gio. They were wonderful collaborators. They would use that little bungalow across from my writing cottage in Napa. They even wrote a script together. I'd go in there and find Coke bottles on the floor, beer cans, posters everywhere . . .

In the early phase of *Apocalypse Now*, Coppola deploys red and orange smoke to tell the viewer that the film is a screen opera. So the first sequence of *Gardens of Stone* dictates the mood and tone of a requiem. To audiences unaware of Gio's death in the midst of production, this film looked and sounded puzzling in its restraint, its gentleness, tolerance, and elegiac tone. August Coppola maintains that his brother's work is not so much autobiographical as "bio-imaged," and the phrase suits *Gardens of Stone*. The army corresponds to the family, with what one British reviewer termed "the python coils of loyalty." Fort Myer may be a peaceful barracks close to Washington, but its name, and the bluff camaraderie that sustains it, evoke the western forts of John Ford's cinema, the focus of sanity beyond whose walls lurk the enemy and the infidel. The army forms a closed community, with its own uniform, routine, and even lingua franca—Sgt. Hazard asks Samantha to dinner at 19:30, before laughing apologetically and converting it to 7:30. Coppola lingers on the minutiae of rank and accomplishment: insignia, cap badges, medals, buttons, lanyards, boots. Like the precisely folded flags, each emblem must be shined or cleaned to excess. These well-laundered, close-cropped NCOs can afford to symbolize army honor. Yet each of the older men harbors the memory of battle in Southeast Asia, whether it be Korea or Vietnam. They have grown to become the fathers of the family. When young Jackie Willow joins the Old Guard, Sgt. Hazard treats him like a son, a surrogate for his own boy, who is separated from him as a result of divorce. When Hazard meets his neighbor, Samantha Huff, a reporter on the *Washington Post*, he tries without a moment's hesitation to draw her too into the warm embrace of army life—its coded slang, its outmoded gentility, its espousal of duty.

When Samantha asks what Hazard and his buddy, Sgt. Nelson, do on their army post at Fort Myer, Goody Nelson pouts with mock pride, and declares: "We are the nation's toy soldiers . . . We are the Kabuki theater of the profession of arms." The film reinforces this image during one sequence where the soldiers parade on green lawns before a laundered crowd of relatives and friends, and an offscreen emcee intones a potted history of the United States infantry. (After the film had opened, the U.S. Army presented Coppola with a "Certificate of Appreciation for Patriotic Civilian Service," praising his capture on film of essential soldierly values—a devotion to duty, a caring attitude, and strong leadership.)

A note of lament for a lost cause meanders through the film. "We are the middle management of America," asserts Nelson during a scene with his captain (Dean Stockwell). All the time, *Gardens of Stone* reminds us that most men join the army for decent, even honorable reasons. The NCO is the unsung hero of Proffitt's book and Coppola's film alike. Only two heavies bring a blemish to the proceedings. One is a grotesque, almost caricatured intellectual lawyer, Brubaker, who taunts Hazard at a garden party about the Army's conduct in Vietnam; the other sneers from within the profession of arms—the colonel who becomes a reluctant father-in-law to Jackie Willow, and whose only comment on Vietnam is "This war's a boon to R & D." Both men are outsiders, for the heros of *Gardens of Stone* remain the NCOs, the "lifers" who exercise a modicum of authority but never aspire to the nonchalant swagger of the officer corps.

First Nicholas Proffitt and then screenwriter Ronald Bass sought to redress the balance of public opinion in favor of the NCO. Both Sgt. Hazard and his friend Sgt. Nelson have applied themselves to culture in a most unmilitary fashion. Hazard admits to a passion for Persian rugs, and explains the different types to Samantha; he even takes her to a dealer in Washington and buys her one. The music we hear played in his apartment toward the end of the film is a Schubert piano trio. Up on the mantel, spine facing towards the camera, lies a red Michelin Guide to France. Goody Nelson gleams with learning in the original novel, reciting chunks of *Othello* at the dinner table, and matching Hazard and Willow name for name in a run-through of history's greatest military thinkers. In the movie, Coppola has encouraged James Earl Jones to give Nelson an aura of relaxed, worldly wise discernment. He joins Hazard in serving as godfather to young Willow, saving his hide in a barroom brawl, persuading the captain to get Willow his lieutenant's bars, and saluting his grave in the final shot of the picture.

Some critics have contended that Coppola (and, by extension, Proffitt) misrepresents the state of America during the late 1960s. Protest marches sound conspicuous by their absence from *Gardens of Stone*. The spirit of Jane Fonda seems as remote as Hanoi to these soldiers. But the age of

Hazard and Nelson provides the answer to that puzzle. Both men are veterans, not just of the tail end of World War II, but more vividly of Korea, where intervention had been endorsed by the United Nations, and where task forces from countries as disparate as Australia, Britain, and Ethiopia had landed on that distant Asian peninsula in "the struggle against communism." Through all these years of service, the NCOs of the Old Guard have become inured to issues of morality and ethics.

Anjelica Huston, playing Samantha, praises the fact that *"Gardens of Stone* took no sides; it was really quite original in that respect. It may have shown the soldier in a somewhat glorified light, but it also showed the absurdity of the whole process." On paper, Coppola may have intended to preserve just such an equal balance, but the sudden death of his son tipped the tone of the film toward retrenchment, and respect for the values of hearth and home. The screenplay provides plenty of scope for conflict of opinion: Samantha's antiwar attitudes contrast with Willow's gung-ho scorn for the primitivism of the NVA; the youthful petulance of Rachel, Willow's girlfriend and then wife, are set against the condescension of her father, the colonel who snores on a sofa while the TV drones out its nightly chronicles from Vietnam.

Coppola, though, plays down all such confrontations save the explosive fight between Hazard and the sneering attorney Brubaker at the garden party. Even the book's most torrid passage, describing Hazard and Samantha's first night of sex together, does not appear in the movie. Discretion, Coppola seems to be saying, is the better part of valor. The barrack-room invective lacks bite and conviction, especially in a year when Kubrick's *Full Metal Jacket* made the theater ring with the bark and scream of the NCO in full cry. Sgt. Nelson, despite the authority of James Earl Jones's performance, looks and sounds like a genial bear.

The screenplay errs most gravely in its presentation of Samantha, who as a *Post* reporter should be the voice of dissent. Anjelica Huston appears too old for the part (even if Proffitt describes Sam as being around the forty mark); her responses are those of a much younger woman, and her acceptance of the military ethos altogether too glib. Hazard "sees this war as a screw-up," she tells Willow; "I see it as genocide." But when news of Willow's death arrives toward the end of the movie, she is content to accept Hazard's unspoken wish to ship out to Vietnam for a third tour of duty: "You've got your job to do—and I've got mine," she laments with a stoicism that, one must admit, suffuses the entire film. Anjelica Huston perceived Samantha as "a good girl, sweet and strong and full of heart. And I wanted to be able to say those things about war that she says—that it's genocide." But the screenplay does not allow her to do that to any developed degree. In a concluding scene that must be one of the worst ever directed by Coppola, she meekly accommodates the notion of Hazard's shipping out to Southeast Asia while she remains behind, the loyal army widow-in-waiting. The overriding impression is not so much lachrymose as contrived.

Other flaws diminish *Gardens of Stone*. The screenplay paints Brubaker as a crass and repellent intellectual. The only voice raised in fury against the war, Brubaker's is unlikely to gain many points even with a liberal audience. His patronizing diatribe against Hazard assures the sergeant of our sympathy. Besides, we have been appeased by Captain Thomas's description of Clell Hazard as his "peacenik platoon sergeant."

Jack Willow's role was reduced considerably in comparison with the novel, where his character develops through long scenes in adolescence and, later, under fire in Vietnam. Proffitt charts his voyage towards disillusion by interleaving the Fort Myer sequences with italicized extracts from a board of inquiry hearing in Vietnam, where Willow gives evidence about a hideous incident in Quang Tin province. These and subsequent passages betray the extent of Willow's bitterness. In one scene he even disconnects the tubes sustaining an officer in hospital; later he admits to considering going AWOL in Canada or Sweden. In the film, however, Willow remains a one-dimensional hero, a symbol of bright young manhood and no more.

While the blurred configurations of the screenplay often serve to irritate in *Gardens of Stone*, its tone does work to Coppola's advantage in treating the war in remote terms. The fighting is felt at one remove—seen on TV in comfortable livingrooms, the sounds of conflict forming part of the background hum of everyday life, like the commercial jets moaning high above the tranquil ceremonies in Arlington Cemetery.

Philip French, reviewing the film in the *Observer*, called to mind Keats's line, "I have been half in love with easeful death," and there's no denying that *Gardens of Stone* exudes a private melancholy commensurate with Francis's feelings at the time. Jordan Cronenweth's lighting emphasizes autumnal tints and dark, wood-grained interiors. Grief occasionally threatens to overwhelm the characters, for example when Willow hears the news of his father's fatal cardiac arrest and sobs in helpless anguish, or at the end, when news of Willow's own death comes through. Even the last supper, where Hazard reads aloud Jackie's latest (and of course last) letter from the war zone, is cut to a dirgelike rhythm. And throughout the movie, Hazard's face assumes the monolithic, immobile features of a gravestone itself, as though the emotion had calcified. This acceptance of things as they are—what the Japanese call *mono no aware*—marks the short, poignant scene when Hazard sends a greetings card and some money to his son.

Coppola's more familiar zest for life emerges in set-pieces like the first dinner in Hazard's apartment, and the wedding breakfast with its echoes of *The Godfather*. Here is palpable evidence that the army does indeed approximate to a family, an entity that transcends patriotic sentiment. As Hazard says when under pressure from his colleagues, "I care about the United States Army—that's my family," almost as though he were Sonny Corleone reincarnate.

Probably few were surprised when *Gardens of Stone* flopped at the box-office. Geoff Brown, in the London *Times*, described the film as "thoughtful and technically impeccable; but it desperately lacks that thrust of excitement guaranteed to put bottoms on seats." *Variety* took a sterner stance. "As storytelling, it is a seriously flawed film. As a political tract, it is shamelessly incomplete. And as filmmaking, it is a major disappointment." After eighteen days on release in the United States, *Gardens of Stone* had accumulated $4,358,779 in gross rentals. When the film reached Europe, audiences failed to respond to the picture at all. Most critics chastised Coppola for the morbid tone of the film, and his seeming inability to come to grips with the legacy of Vietnam.

Such quick condemners should reflect that for numerous Americans, the trauma of Vietnam belonged to the private conscience: and that for many others, parents who lost their sons in action, the ceremonies in Arlington were all the more tolerable for being dignified. Coppola, recalling his time in military academy, said just after editing the production: "I've always been fascinated by the role of ritual in the military, particularly the code of honor." *Gardens of Stone* cannot be viewed in isolation. Sgt. Hazard has much in common with Clint Eastwood's Highway in *Heartbreak Ridge*, and Samantha Huff shares something of the same experience as Jane Fonda's Sally Hyde in *Coming Home*. The fact that its gush of sentiment reminds us of John Ford may be explained (if not, from an audience standpoint, excused) by the bereavement Francis Coppola himself suffered during the shooting of the film. In all other respects he served as Tri-Star's hired hand.

C H A P T E R   T H I R T E E N

Tucker—
The Dream Triumphant

While much of Coppola's work has mirrored the grain and pattern of his personal life, no film until *Tucker* has lit on such a perfect blend of popular entertainment and private conviction. On paper, the project looked dubious, even arcane. Who would be interested in the career of an automobile designer of the 1940s, whose name—Preston Tucker— meant nothing to anybody under middle age, and whose plant had turned out a mere fifty cars before being closed down by the might of Detroit and the authorities in Washington? Ed McBain once commented that sex and violence are the only two things to write about in America, and in his classics like *The Godfather* diptych and *Apocalypse Now* Coppola had confirmed this dictum. But in the tale of Preston Tucker the violence is confined to the courtroom and the sex sublimated into a strong and passionate domestic life.

Tucker—subtitled *The Man and His Dream*—had germinated in Francis's imagination over more than a decade. In the heady days of 1976, the film was announced as being in preproduction, and in his famous private memorandum to his staff in April 1977, Coppola declared with some optimism: "The sums spent on *Tucker* two years ago will finally reach the cashbox in two years from now." There was talk of Brando playing the eccentric, rebellious inventor, and at one point the picture was announced as *The 1948 Tucker*. Then Francis tried another tack. Composer-conductor Leonard Bernstein flew out to Napa for two weeks to develop the idea of *Tucker* as a musical comedy. For Francis, it could have been "a slice of Americana" like *On the Town*—"a dark kind of piece

215

. . . a sort of Brechtian musical in which Tucker would be the main story, but it would also involve Edison and Henry Ford and Firestone and Carnegie." The plan was abandoned as impractical.

Then, in late 1986, George Lucas guaranteed the budget for *Tucker* and urged Francis to do this project instead of making a succession of movies holding no challenge for him. He would enjoy the benefit of Lucasfilm's state-of-the-art technology in San Rafael and Nicasio, just north of San Francisco. It would be like *American Graffiti* in reverse, with George supervising the production and Francis directing the show. "I just felt it was very dramatic," Lucas reflected later. "I only knew about it from Francis, who'd sit telling me all these stories about Tucker over the dinner table: 'Let's do that movie, do that movie' for ten to fifteen years. . . . It's about creativity and the problems of surviving in a system that doesn't encourage that—which I don't think *any* system does."

The offer could not have come at a better juncture. Overwhelmed by the loss of Gio (to whom *Tucker* would be dedicated), and still checking the final cut and mix on *Gardens of Stone*, Francis needed both freedom and a subject that could excite his enthusiasm for movies and technology.

The budget ran to a generous $25 million. For the screenplay, Coppola had turned to Arnold Schulman, a writer who, he recalled, had once come up to him on a plane and offered his services for free as a token of his admiration for Francis's work as a director. Early treatments did not please the Tucker family, who bristled at the concept of Preston as "a simpleton." The script, they felt, "assumed because [Tucker] was from a small town in northern Michigan that he wasn't as worldly or as sophisticated as he was. He wasn't a supereducated man and sometimes used words incorrectly—exhilaration for acceleration—but he was self-taught."

The subtle changes that rendered the final screenplay so appealing to Tucker's relatives stemmed, one feels, from a gradual merging of identity between Preston Tucker and Francis Coppola. Throughout the movie, the resemblance between the two men—and their dreams—is unmistakable. Tucker tried to produce cars in Chicago instead of the hallowed Detroit; Coppola broke away from Hollywood in the 1960s and sought to make San Francisco a viable base for his independent studio. The small, loyal, zealous team assembled by Tucker reminds one of Coppola's tight-knit group at Zoetrope. When Tucker unveils his car to an audience of stockholders and supporters, he presents all his family at the same time —something Francis did at his press conference after acquiring the Hollywood General Studios. Tucker's young son tells him he wants to quit school in order to learn his father's profession; Gio said virtually the same thing to Francis. Even the Victorian country manor where the Tuckers live looks similar to the Coppolas' house in Rutherford, with its sense of family life proceeding alongside a creative working existence. In short, the bass line of *Tucker, The Man and His Dream* is solidarity in the face of crisis, whether in the home or in the business arena. A line from Eddie, one of Tucker's engineers, shows how conscious Coppola is of his own shortcomings: "However much he makes he always ends up spending twice as much."

The passion and commitment that drive this film along so triumphantly have their origin far back in Francis's youth. His father was one of the original investors in Tucker stock—and of course lost every cent. But Francis, who was more attracted to the pages of *Popular Mechanics* than to the classics great artists are supposed to have read in childhood, recalls being fascinated by the Tucker saga. "Yes, it was that beautiful, gleaming car that caught my imagination, but it was also something else: the whole notion of what our country was going to be like in twenty or thirty years, based on our new position in the world . . . our technological inventiveness." Already during his days at Hofstra University, he wrote a "somber" play about Preston Tucker. He was not alone in his fondness for the inventor. Carroll Ballard's father used to sell Tuckers: "My father raced this guy on a beach in Florida to prove that a Tucker would go faster than a Dynaflow, which had just come out." Not that Coppola idealized the man beyond reason. "I like him," he said during the 1970s, "because he feels human, the lovable American con man, the used-car salesman with his heart in the right place. In his way he was a charlatan. He wore those brown and white pointy shoes, and he was handsome and good with the ladies. He talked fast. He was a little stinky."

The Tucker car, like all revolutionary concepts, was regarded as subversive, even dangerous, by the established auto manufacturers. First of all, it was clear that once he was up and running, Tucker could build his car for a fraction of the money devoted to new models by the giants of Detroit. Next, the extra facilities incorporated in the vehicle were likely to have mass appeal: disc brakes, seat belts, a fuel-injected engine in the rear, a padded dashboard, an additional central headlight that swiveled in whichever direction the front wheels were turned, and a windshield ready to pop out in a severe collision. "Newer than the A-Bomb. See the revolutionary rear-end motor," proclaimed placards sent to dealers. In Coppola's words, "It was a safe car, a revolutionary car in terms of engineering, and it was a beautiful car. In every way, it was a much better machine than the stuff the major companies were offering." Tucker's inventiveness seemed boundless and when the financial going grew rough he aimed to sell "futures" in the form of accessory packages such as seat covers, a built-in radio, and custom-fitted luggage.

Only forty-six of the fifty vehicles built by Tucker still exist and Coppola owns two of them. He managed to round up twenty-one of the surviving cars to appear in the movie, which ends with a cavalcade of Tuckers circling a square in Chicago. One owner explained that while the screenplay wanted the cars to be only about eighteen inches apart in this grand finale, several of the Tuckers were no longer in running order. "They had to be chained together—one that ran hooked to one that didn't. It was pretty hairy trying to keep them from running into the car in front especially when the brakes on both started to heat up and fade." In other scenes, for example in the assembly plant, technicians built replicas of the Tucker in various colors.

The film began principal photography on Monday, April 13, 1987. Much of it was shot on location in and around the Bay Area—in Richmond, Martinez, Oakland, and San Pablo. A Victorian manor in Sonoma offered a convincing impression of the Tucker home in Ypsilanti, Michigan, in the mid-1940s. Most of the climatic courtroom scenes were shot in a converted ballroom in a senior citizens' hotel in Oakland, and a vast enclosed building (formerly used by the Ford Motor Company) on Harbor Way in Richmond served as the original Tucker plant—although that was even bigger, and at the time was the world's largest plant under one roof, at seventy-three acres.

A Directors' Guild strike looked imminent during the summer, and Coppola and his crew worked at considerable speed. The stoppage never occurred, however, and the main shoot ended on July 10. One of the final sessions took place in the great hangar housing Howard Hughes's massive aircraft, the "Spruce Goose," in Long Beach.

Coppola had from the start availed himself of the superb equipment owned by George Lucas in San Rafael. After the customary reading of the script by the entire cast on a sound stage, the actors ran through the film scene by scene. This was committed to video, and used as a live-action storyboard for the production.

The struggle to make *Tucker* into a major entertainment movie occupied Coppola for months after the completion of shooting. George Lucas took a personal interest in the picture, and succeeded in giving it all the slickness and pace of an *Indiana Jones* adventure. In Eleanor Coppola's words:

I think that it's a remarkable collaboration. Francis has suffered from not having a producer he can believe in. Usually he's been at odds with the production side of things; they haven't understood him, and haven't given him money in the areas where he needed it. On *Tucker*, he felt relieved to turn over some of the responsibility to George, who's a fellow filmmaker. Both men have become established in their own realm, and now they are reunited as equals. Francis listened to George's opinions and ideas with respect.

In October, the crew reassembled to film what the industry calls "pickups"—short scenes providing links in a storyline that may have seemed unclear in the first rough assembly of the picture. Not until mid-April 1988 was Francis satisfied with the final mix of sound and image. Richard Beggs, the sound designer, continued even beyond this date to fine-tune the technical aspects of the film, prior to its release by Paramount in August.

*   *   *

No Coppola film opens with such fizz and confidence as *Tucker*. A brash title sequence tells the audience that the film has been "Produced for the Public Relations Department of the Tucker Corporation." As Coppola himself points out, "It's like a promo film of the 1940s, the sort of thing that Detroit manufacturers used to show their dealers." Gradually this high-spirited introduction folds into the authentic, narrative re-creation of Tucker's career. Recognizing that few young people—or foreigners—will have heard of Preston Tucker, Coppola and Lucas use an off-screen narrator to tell the story of his early life and exploits. It is a device that Orson Welles would have liked and there is much in *Tucker* reminiscent of *The Magnificent Ambersons*, both in the nostalgia for vanished times and the notion of an auto inventor being spurned. The influence of Lucas emerges in the sheer clarity of the story. The characters are boldly cast and drawn. Jeff Bridges is Tucker, Joan Allen his loyal and spunky wife, and Martin Landau the city slicker, Abe Karatz, who joins Tucker to promote his dream and get it accepted by the money-men. There are plenty of bright figures in the background, too: Frederic Forrest as Eddie, the devoted engineer who overcomes his early scepticism to believe in the greatness of Tucker's vision; Elias Koteas as Alex, the ex–Air Force guy who develops and perfects Tucker's initial designs; and Mako as Jimmy, the Japanese auto-worker employed by Tucker even throughout the war.

The villains relish their roles. Lloyd Bridges appears in a significant if uncredited part as the senator acting in cahoots with the major-league car manufacturers to drag Tucker into court. Dean Goodman, too, brings a smooth, vicious tenacity to Bennington, who is appointed chairman of the board by Tucker and proceeds to sabotage the inventor at every opportunity.

Coppola has made a film that portrays a period as much as a personality. In the first years after the war, prosperity crept back into the American home. Advertising took hold. Every family craved a new car, or a prefab house. New products poured from the factory floor. It was a time of optimism and enterprise. *Tucker* with its splendid Technicolor, Technovision photography by Vittorio Storaro, and its Dolby stereo soundtrack, is every inch a film of the 1980s, but its *look* recaptures the postwar fashion: warm, earthy colors in the costumes and decor, glowing interiors, and natty gents' suiting for the attorneys and press agents.

During World War II, Tucker designed a combat car but the U.S. military turned it down as being too fast. He kept the prototype, however, and in the film's opening sequence (set in 1945) announces to his stunned family that he has traded their Packard for a pack of twelve Dalmatian dogs, then promptly takes them on a wild nocturnal ride through the country roads in his armored car—all to buy some ice cream! Determined to press ahead with his inventions, he joins with Abe Karatz to seek both funding and plant facilities. At a presentation to the War Assets Administration in Washington, he shocks members of the committee with his apocalyptic account of the rising death toll on America's roads but they like his emphasis on safety features for the new car and vote to give him a disused plant in Chicago, providing he can raise $15 million. Abe sets to work, chipping in with $6,000 from his own meager resources and then foolishly compromises Tucker by acquiescing in the appointment of Bennington, a retired Detroit executive, as chairman of the board.

Preston Tucker, though, remains rash and irrepressibly optimistic. Joined by his son, who rejects an invitation to go to Notre Dame University in order to work on the prototype car, he blithely ignores the economic woes piling up around him. He is a born salesman and a master of that vital medium of the period, the radio commercial. He can improvise, too. Oil leaks delay the appearance of the first Tucker at a gathering of investors and well-wishers. So Preston brings on the dancing girls. When they pall, he introduces his entire family while a last-minute oil leak is fixed. Coppola films and cuts this sequence with glorious panache, giving it the showbiz glamor of a premiere.

His car at last assembled and acclaimed. Tucker embarks on a hectic promotion tour around the States, flying with one of the cars in a chartered plane. But Bennington is bent on undermining Tucker's control over the project. Tucker's wife marches into a board meeting and argues skillfully and wittily for Preston's cause, but that does not prevent Bennington from trying to charge the public $2,000 per vehicle, compared with Tucker's own stated price of just $1,000. By degrees, the original vision of the car diminishes: the board wants to eliminate some of its most innovative features such as disc brakes, seat belts, and even the rear engine. In such moments, *Tucker* approaches the cinema of Frank Capra, whose small-town heroes took on the Establishment and fought for the fix of ordinary people. ("The Big Three [auto manufacturers] don't care a damn about people—they just care about profits," bellows Tucker to an investors' committee.) Coppola avoids the whimsy and folksiness that make much of Capra's work unpalatable today. There's a hard edge to *Tucker* born of recent years, when American industrial muscle and innovation have slackened. It is as though Coppola were indicting the 1980s, during which even the Italians have outscored the mighty U.S. in terms of design and creativity.

In the film's one awkward sequence, Tucker is summoned to meet tycoon Howard Hughes, played by Dean Stockwell, in the hangar where the "Spruce Goose" stands grounded. He urges Tucker to persist in his fight with Washington and the big car companies, and claims that the same senator has been trying to balk his aircraft program also. The "Spruce Goose," with its awesome array of engines and immense wingspan, is too predominant in this weird scene, reducing the impact of Hughes's own personality, and it seems unlikely that Tucker would meet him in such a place in quite this manner, even if in real life he had.

Something valuable does come from the Howard Hughes encounter. Hughes tells Tucker about an ailing helicopter firm in Syracuse, New York, with plenty of steel to sell. And steel is vital to Tucker's plant if he is to meet production targets and justify the faith of his stockholders. Soon the car itself is fitted with a modified version of a helicopter engine and although a Tucker crashes during its proving trials, the family remains optimistic—besides, the windshield flips out in the crash and the motor still runs without apparent difficulty.

Then, disaster. Tucker finds himself isolated and betrayed. FBI agents have wired the entire plant and boardroom. Abe Karatz tenders his resignation. "Captains go down with their ships," he tells Tucker, "not businessmen." It emerges that Abe has a criminal record, having served a jail term for bank fraud ten years earlier. In a poignant scene with Tucker outside the plant one evening, he utters one of the film's most memorable lines: "If you get too close to people, you catch their dreams." So Tucker loses his right-hand man just when he needs him, as a congressional probe into the company's finances is announced. Tucker comes home to find the cops waiting to arrest him and leads them on a frenetic and amusing chase through the neighborhood, demonstrating the pace and ingenuity of his car in the process.

Called by the Securities and Exchange Commission to answer charges before a grand jury in Chicago ("the same courtroom where Al Capone was tried and convicted"), Tucker seems destined for a prison sentence for fraud. At first he observes the charade with cynicism and resignation. "This whole trial's been bought and paid for and wrapped up like a Christmas present," he says. But he decides to speak in his own defense and delivers a stinging Capra-esque harangue that echoes many of Coppola's own convictions.

He talks of a world in which dreams are squashed and the little guy with a new idea put down, despite the effort of the war and everything America stood for in that conflict. He speculates on a future in which "we'll be buying radios and cars from our former enemies. I don't believe it, I can't believe it," he concludes while we, with our Japanese VCRs and Walkman headsets, can accept the irony of the situation.

Acquitted by the jury, Tucker musters all fifty of the cars already built and takes everyone on a joyous parade around the square outside the court. Fifty cars or fifty million, he tells Abe Karatz, "It's the idea that counts, and the dream." Coppola leaves Tucker on a buoyant note, gleefully devising a mini-refrigerator for people in poorer countries . . .

An end-title announces that Preston Tucker died six years after the trial, not mentioning that he continued to the last to raise more investment money for his work. During his final year of life he made three trips to Brazil seeking finance, before succumbing to cancer in the early 1950s.

Tucker vindicates its hero and wisely leaves aside the embarrassing questions. Contemporary press reports claimed that the Tucker Corporation had put members of the family on the payroll and had charged yacht and plane rentals to the company as well as photo fees incurred at Marilyn Tucker's wedding. What happened to the $26 million raised by Tucker is more difficult to explain. Could it really have been swallowed up in design development and the construction of those first fifty vehicles? Perhaps so, but $26 million in the late 1940s must equate to more than $50 million today—enough for two *Tucker* movies! John DeLorean's much-maligned DMC-12 sportscar project in Northern Ireland absorbed less investment capital than that. Tucker may have been both more of a designer and less of a business animal than DeLorean.

"We did show, perhaps, a certain vanity in him, and that he was a phenomenon of the early days of advertising—he who lives by the ad shall die by the ad. So there *were* flaws in him, but we didn't do the film as a psychodrama, with all the angst we see so often now, with Tucker breaking down and that stuff."

Coppola has never been a director to focus on the literal details of a life or a topic. *Tucker, The Man and His Dream* reflects a mood and an era in mythic terms. Its message reaches the audience in strong, entertaining terms, untainted by didacticism. Coppola reminds Americans that unless they acknowledge and nurture creative talent, the future looks bleak. If Tucker were alive today, he says, "he'd be hired by one of the major car companies and his inventions would be shelved or filtered out to the public as the company deemed economically prudent. Not to benefit the public but the company and only the company."

Jeff Bridges, who has never played a screen role with such evident zest as Tucker, calls the film "a story about a fellow who really bucks the system. He's got a better idea and knows it, and the system sort of beats him. But it doesn't completely crush his spirit. The spirit lives on." As does the spirit of Zoetrope, and Bridges is not alone when he muses, "Maybe Francis is the Tucker of our day!"

Although *Tucker* rentals reached only $8.9 million in the United States and Canada, Lucas could expect to recoup his costs thanks to a lively welcome for the film in overseas territories like France and Japan, where the name Coppola really counts for something. The American reviews sympathized with the emotional charge of *Tucker*, and *Variety* wrote that it "represents the sunniest imaginable telling of an at least partly tragic episode in recent history. . . . [Its] rousing approach to Tucker's life here takes the view that it was the man's dreams, and his inspiring attempt to make them come true, that remain important, not the fact that he lost when the final buzzer sounded. This may make the picture more accessible to the general public than it might have been otherwise, but it also flattens out the ironies, complexities, and richness inherent in the story itself." In Britain, David Robinson in *The Times* described the film as "ebullient, defiant, vivid. Tucker is played by Jeff Bridges as charming, manic, irrepressible, facing every new obstacle with laughter, flair, and steely obstinacy." Derek Malcolm in *The Guardian* felt that "*Tucker* is a Hollywood rarity—a populist tub-thumper which manages to be highly personal both in the way it harangues its audience and in what it leaves out for fear of boring us."

* * *

As 1988 began, Francis seemed more at ease with himself than he had been for many years. Zoetrope, while not prosperous, could at least function without regular threats of bankruptcy looming overhead. Symbolizing this was an accord with United Artists that wiped out the final debts incurred on *Apocalypse Now*. Zoetrope had owed UA some $7 million, due for payment by January 15, 1981. As further revenues from the movies came in, that sum declined to some $4 million and when Zoetrope agreed to give U.S. TV rights to United Artists, the debt finally disappeared.

In February 1988, Francis and Eleanor celebrated their silver wedding by flying to Hawaii for the first time and enjoying a vacation away from the business. Eleanor had fought throughout those twenty-five years for a family existence. The Coppolas never relished the Hollywood dream of a mansion in Beverly Hills and shopping on Rodeo Drive; indeed they have lived in Los Angeles for only eight of their years together. Eleanor concedes that she

> was never the perfect wife, because at no time could I get into this "Italian" mode, and the fact that I retained other interests, and did other things (against all odds), may be part of the dynamic that has kept us together. People who have been together for a really long time are equally as strong or weak as each other, and I think that Francis and I are strong in different ways—but there is some kind of balance between us. At the bottom line, Francis is very conservative. He is a family man with old-fashioned Italian values, such as maintaining your wife, your family, and your children. I believe that underlying theme is something he himself cannot escape from. He is radical and innovative in his work, but not in his family life.

* * *

Coppola's interest in wine-making, which began as a hobby and a diversion, has developed into a successful enterprise in recent years, and has the advantage of being created and managed only a few steps away from his house in the Napa Valley.

His desire to own an active vineyard goes back to the early 1970s. He acquired the Niebaum Estate in 1975. Nestling in the lee of Mount St.

George on the western side of the valley in Rutherford, this 1,700-acre property had been cultivated during the late nineteenth century by Gustav Niebaum, a colorful Finnish sea captain, who also founded the neighboring Inglenook Vineyard (Robert Mondavi rears his vines not far down the road). In 1867, when the United States purchased the territory of Alaska from the Russians, there was a transition period of some months during which Niebaum bought and sold his seal pelts with uncanny timing, amassing vast profits. His wife persuaded him to settle down in Napa. Niebaum loved the vines he had brought from Europe but could not resist pursuing his rapacious career and is reputed to have sold his wares to the Indians and then ridden into the reservations with his henchmen and seized the seal pelts so he could resell them to other victims.

Francis remarks with a grin that he draws almost more money from his wine than he does from movies. But wine-making is a capital-intensive business. For years before the Coppolas purchased the estate, Niebaum grapes had been sold for use by other wineries. Francis resolved to establish his own operation. He placed Rafael Rodriguez in charge of the vineyard in 1976. Russell Turner (at the outset) and C. Stephen Beresini have served as resident wine-makers, and since 1983 Coppola has benefited from the viticultural wisdom of Andre Tchelistcheff, for thirty-five years winemaster at Beaulieu Vineyards. When he first considered how the Niebaum-Coppola wine would be achieved, Francis "conceived of it as a claret blend of Cabernet Sauvignon, Cabernet Franc, and Merlot, and asked that it be a full, rich wine that would live one hundred years." The 1980 Rubicon matured in 1,200-gallon French oak casks for fifteen months. It was then transferred to sixty-gallon French oak barrels for a further eighteen months and finally bottled in 1983. This and subsequent vintages have been released in strictly limited quantities—between 3,000 and 5,000 cases—and retail for around $35 a bottle.

Coppola introduced his wine in flamboyant, cheerful fashion in 1985. Alice Waters, whose Chez Panisse restaurant is rated one of the best in the state, prepared a dinner at Coppola's home in Rutherford and journalists, dealers, and cognoscenti sampled the 1978, 1979, and 1980 vintages as accompaniment to grilled pigeon and potato pancakes. Reaction proved favorable among wine experts and commentators. "Dark and thick in color, rich and ripe in fruit, warm and vigorous," wrote Barbara Ensrud in the New York *Daily News*. Robert N. Parker the guru of the American wine world, described the 1979 Rubicon as possessing "a rich bouquet of tarry, black cherry fruit and oak. It is very concentrated, fullbodied and, while drinkable now, will keep 8–10 years." And the *Underground*

Newsletter exclaimed, "Perfumed nose. Dusty, cassis-like. Some vanilla. Rich. Lots of cassis-like fruit. Some chocolate. Tannic. A powerhouse. Outstanding potential." When the 1982 Rubicon was released in September 1989, Frank J. Prial in the *New York Times* hailed it as "an exceptional wine, intense, concentrated and beautifully textured."

Sometimes Francis's commitment to wine and movies results in some bizarre conjunctions. In 1987, Zoetrope discussed a possible barter of Latvian wine barrels for the distribution rights to certain Zoetrope films in the Soviet Union. It is the kind of deal that would have appealed to Preston Tucker.

Back to the Future

The spirit of Zoetrope has survived the dream of Zoetrope. As Francis Coppola works in the quietness and sobriety of his library at Napa, he sits surrounded by mementos of the past: praxinoscopes, zoetropes, and other toys presented to him by Mogens Skot-Hansen of Laterna Film in Denmark, posters used in various films, miniature models deployed in others. "Zoetrope is an idea that kept being reborn," he reflects.

It was born in San Francisco in the early 1970s and then reborn in a Hollywood studio. I always tried to do the same thing, but in another way. Zoetrope was nothing more than an attempt to do in the grown-up world what I had done at Hofstra University, where I had galvanized all the young people there and got them working together doing productions, and creating a lot of fun and excitement for ourselves.

I never really had the money to do it. I'd sell my house, or I earned some money from *The Godfather* to do it, but I never actually went to five guys in suits and said, "I need $300 million." If you open a restaurant, you must run it for a couple of years, even though you're not making money; you have to be able to catch on—the same with a magazine. On the one hand, Zoetrope failed because I never was realistic about the finances. I never wanted to give up any control to the money types who would come in and tell me, "Well, you can't do *Napoléon*, you can't do *Koyaanisqatsi*, you can't do George Lucas's film."

I think that the other area concerns my own psychology—at my age I would be much more content, having gone through all these years, to work with just a few people, and not have to divert my attention to paying 300 employees' salaries. I think I could do it again, and maybe succeed from what I've learned, but I'm very frightened at being involved with lots of people. Perhaps I'll do it again in a miniature sense, but perhaps in the future a miniature sense is a more appropriate sense.

In his heart of hearts, says Francis, the favorite films of his career are *The Conversation* and *Rumble Fish*. Both were created along "miniature" lines. Neither attracted a wide public. But *The Conversation* won the top prize at the world's top movie festival, Cannes, and *Rumble Fish* remains a cult film throughout Europe.

The spirit of getting away from it all, of independence in a fundamental sense, will always inspire Coppola. "Even now, if I'm on a trip with my wife in the car," he laughs, "and we're up in Eureka, California, and we see a pretty building, I say—'Ah, we could have Eureka Zoetrope, and we could be up here and everyone would leave us alone.' There's just an urge I have to be in some cute little place, away from all the corruption and bullying that go on whenever the big guys take over."

As his films confirm, Coppola's personality and philosophy share much in common with those of the late Orson Welles. Both artists adhered to the tradition of Méliès, rather than Lumière—the fantasy approach rather than the realistic, documentary approach. As Coppola explains:

Coming from the theater, I had a love for the theatrical tradition, illusion, lighting, sets, gauze . . . I saw *Citizen Kane* like everyone else at that time, when I was fifteen or sixteen, and was just bowled over by it, because it *was* theatrical. And even though Eisenstein invented something so totally cinematic, even he is very theatrical in his use of images. I always loved the magic when suddenly he or Welles was able to use the elements at their disposal and just hypnotize you with them.

I would give anything to have a life like Orson Welles. But some of the negative things were repeated in my career as well, because just as Welles proceeded forward while neglecting his Hollywood base, his base of support, so in a familiar way I did that by leaving Hollywood in my time of triumph with *The Godfather* films. Instead of really insinuating myself with the giants of Hollywood, I let their feelings for me slip, just as Welles did.

Could it be that, whereas Orson Welles ended up in Europe eating in Spain and stuff, the fiber of *my* life, being a married man, meant I couldn't really do what he did? Maybe having the same wife, and being a family man, saved me from certain things—the whole wine, women, and song syndrome, failed American directors getting a few final years in Europe, etc.

I not only always admired Orson Welles, I always was drawn to the kinds of things he seemed to have been interested in—the theater, magic, cinema, as having powerful illusion-creating abilities. And just innovation in general, to be able to use the tools of theater or radio in a new way, that's a most wonderful thing.

When we were shooting *Peggy Sue*, Welles died, and I remember I had sent away for a record on which he sings, called "I Know What It Is To Be Young, But You Don't Know What It Is To Be Old"—and I made the crew stop, and I played it for everyone.

Talk of Europe brings him to another director he admires, Francesco Rosi.

He's really an advanced director, in a lot of ways. His adaptation of the Salvatore Giuliano story was so unusual—you hardly ever see Giuliano! It must be so satisfying, to be able to work in a form, and have a vision, and do it. I suppose they must have a million problems in Europe also, but it just seems like the baggage of working in American films and being part of the American system, which is the studios, the unions (which have never done anything good for me, always drove me crazy), the press—which is as much a part of this wheel—and the distributors. It's as though you're entering into some kind of life-support system of little fishes and big fishes, and I think of Francesco Rosi as working like a real artist, expressing himself.

He laments the changing face of the movie business.

When I first started, right after Hofstra, people weren't all that interested in cinema and reviews and grosses. It seemed like we went to the movies to enjoy the movie, to see a good show. At Hofstra I tried to start a cinema workshop, and we put a big announcement up about a meeting at 3 o'clock—and three people came, one was me, one was my friend, and one was my girlfriend. Today, *everyone* is interested in cinema. There are cinema T-shirts, and in the *San Francisco Chronicle* you get the grosses of the top ten pictures—what place does that have in the pages of the newspapers? Maybe in *Variety*. The implication is that you should go see those pictures with the high numbers, and not go see those that don't have the high numbers, or not on those lists. I almost hate to see the cinema scooped up and made part of all that. I liked it better when everyone wasn't so interested in movies. I felt it was something that belonged to *me* a little bit.

Now I even wonder if I'm part of it.

Coppola continues to be torn between the two extremes of filmmaking, between the massive, epic form, and the small, intimate picture. As late as November 1987 he dismissed any thought of returning to Paramount to do a *Godfather Part III*, "because I know that if I had to do it, I would just take the story and tell it again, which is what they do on these sequels. I'm not really interested in gangsters anymore."

In June 1988 he made a small-scale movie called *Life without Zoe*, which formed one of the three segments of *New York Stories* (Martin Scorsese and Woody Allen contributed the other episodes).

> It's a story of a little girl about twelve years old who lives in Manhattan. It's about these little girls who have credit cards and eat at the Russian Tea Room, and live in hotels and apartments in New York. It's sort of like Pippi Long-stocking, except that she's twelve. It's about the daughter-father relationship, and about the loyalty of the daughter to the father—like the old Athena-Zeus story. There's something really interesting in the relationship between a daughter and a father. That was *meant* to be the relationship with a man that makes it possible for the daughter to go off and have a husband.

Francis's seventeen-year-old daughter Sofia assumed much of the creative responsibility on this sketch. She collaborated on the dialogue with her father, designed the costumes, and did the graphics on the main titles. "The costumes play a really big part in this piece," said Sofia. "The movie is very visual . . . it's like a painting. And it doesn't look like modern-day New York; no one on the street is wearing sweat pants. *Life without Zoe* should remind people of those '40s films in which everyone is polished and dressed; all of the uniforms worn by the staff of the Sherry-Netherland Hotel are perfect. It's a distinctly romantic version of reality." Tavoularis, the production designer, referred to the setting as "a kind of Noël Coward–like world for children."

Although *Life without Zoe* emerges as a creative mess, it carries a certain charm and poignancy. Zoe's father is a famous flautist, forever traveling to far-flung destinations like India or Greece. Zoe, like Sofia Coppola in real life, must cope with the confusing burden of wealth as well as a celebrated father. She lives alone in the hushed opulence of the Sherry-Netherland Hotel on Fifth Avenue, cosseted by Hector the butler and surrounded at school by other poor little rich girls. A meeting with another twelve-year-old, Hasid, opens the way to an Arabian Nights fantasy for Zoe. She embarks with her schoolfriends on a luxurious romp through Manhattan, and eventually flies her mother to Athens to watch papa performing at the Acropolis.

Life without Zoe may not be an auspicious debut for Sofia Coppola as a screenwriter, but the film shows that she is already alert to the dangers and potential of having a famous artist for a father. Instead of rejecting the charmed circle of her parents, she embraced it with relish, and already in her teens had worked at the Chanel Studio in Paris for two seasons, assisting Karl Lagerfeld. Sofia also became the youngest member of the

United Scenic Artists union. She cannot be blamed if *Life without Zoe* looks like a children's caprice alongside the more adult segments of *New York Stories*. The basic device of having kids behave like adults needs to be maneuvered with greater skill than Coppola *père* bothered to bring to bear, at a time when he was trying to take a sabbatical from the movies.

In company with most filmmakers, Coppola does not often see his pictures after the mixing stage. Now he wants to review all his work, to build up his confidence as he tackles this time of transition ahead of him. He acknowledges that contemporaries like Roman Polanski and Carroll Ballard are blessed with "a pure, kind of god-given talent" that eludes him. His prowess stems from his theatrical ability, his limitless energy, and what he himself terms "a distorted idea of everything." Ballard once told him, "You have a million ideas a day, and most of them are god-awful, but a few of them are really great." Persistence has been a factor also: "I'm the kind of person who always does what he says he's going to do—it may take ten more years, but I try always to check off everything, or at least turn it into something better." The gestation of *Tucker* exemplifies this reluctance to abandon a project; this was a film in active development during the mid-1970s and went before the cameras some ten years later.

Coppola differs from others of his generation in his lack of political motivation. He wants to write about the emotional and psychological make-up of his characters. He believes that man is governed by the pattern of his emotions. It is not surprising that he adores the work of Bernardo Bertolucci, who like himself draws upon operatic idioms in his films.

When his son Gio died, Francis began, in the face of the tragedy, to examine his priorities.

> I figured, well, it doesn't seem like I'm going to be able to undo this one. Maybe if I die I'm going to run into my kid again, because who knows what's there. I no longer think about things in the same way. I just want to be part of everything, rather than to put my imprint on it so much. When I write now, I come up with some pretty interesting observations about things in life, which I'd like to incorporate into any future work I do, rather than trying to do, say, the story of Sacco and Vanzetti, and tackling an adaptation, making a period picture, casting around for $42 million. That doesn't interest me any more. But the idea of being able to scratch around and come up with some thoughts about things and then figure out how to put *that* into a movie—a more amateurish movie, a simpler movie—*that* interests me.

The same applies to his behavior. "I have a temper," he admits, "and when I was younger I knew less about it, so it would just kind of rage up on me. Then I began to realize that every time I lost my temper or shouted at someone, whether justified or not, I was sick and limp and depressed for a week afterward. So as I got older, I learned that you pay the price for that behavior, and that it's better to avoid losing your temper, because it's easier on you."

Coppola's restless search for new means of electronic expression may always conflict with his yearning for intimacy at every level of the film-making process. He once told his brother August how, having the screen rights to *Peter Pan*, he wanted to do the picture in such a way as to reflect the incredible loneliness of J. M. Barrie and his difficult relations with children. Subsequently, the rights passed to Paramount.

Setbacks have never blunted his insatiable curiosity about all matters technical. In childhood, he played with gadgets of every kind, much as Bergman reveled in his magic lantern. On *The Rain People*, editor Barry Malkin remembers how he and Francis installed a Steenbeck editing table in a Dodge mobile home, and how they rigged up some primitive but efficient equipment to serve them on the long trek across the country. When Richard Beggs was first involved with Zoetrope, as an outside jobber on *The Godfather Part II*, "Francis had this idea of developing the soundtrack the way they make records—a multitrack technique. At the time, in movies it was unheard of. There was no technology available to buy, so through a bailing wire and spit operation we locked the twenty-four-track to a video of the film—it's actually what they call sweetening in TV."

Dean Tavoularis shares Coppola's obsession, and prior to principal photography on *The Conversation* subscribed to dozens of electronics magazines in the name of Harry Caul at his apartment. Kathy Phair, who used to run the Spring Street restaurant in Napa, recalls how Francis was always taking videotapes back to his children, stimulating their interest long before video was all the rage.

The screenwriting and postproduction phases appeal to him more than the actual shooting of a movie. He loves tapping away at his portable Olivetti, which he carries everywhere. He types one draft of every scene or screenplay himself before it goes to his secretary for fair typing. "I don't enjoy anything so much as writing," he confirms. "It's the greatest pleasure for me, and a marvelous way to spend the day." If the dreams are implanted in the screenplay, then the editing stage permits the authentic operatic nature of the film to emerge. George Lucas and Francis used to paraphrase the Jackson Pollock quip about the emotion being in the paint itself by saying, "The emotion is the emulsion."

The visitor to Coppola's home in Napa may be shown his collection of tools, located in the workroom just a few feet from his typewriter. It is like some conjunction of art and science Technology sets the fancy free. Coppola deplores the marketing philosophy that regulates and exploits contemporary culture, putting a leash on the new technology initiated by TV after the war. "I'm waiting for that technology to snap the leash," he says excitedly.

I feel that it's a good inclination when something new is invented. Men and women start doing creative things with it, and it's only when the Harvard Business School gets ahold of it that they beat it down and control it. I believe essentially that there is a way of working with something that resembles live TV, except it's of extremely high quality; that's like theater in its traditional methods of gathering people together in actor-director-stage company relationships; like cinema, with its extraordinary ability of montage and cinematic principles; and like the novel!

Somehow, out of all these things we can create almost a new medium, and that's basically what I want to do with my life. Although there are always many reasons for saying that television does not have good enough quality, I'm behaving now like a car speeding at ninety m.p.h., going my way, knowing that by the time I reach the junction, the bridge will be built. The bridge is not there right now, the new technology can't do the things that I imagined it could do, but I'm still committing myself in those directions knowing that in 1990, or 1992, it's going to be possible to do certain things.

If I'm right, I'll be the only one who has the project to do on it. I'm like someone who believed that one day the phonograph record would come along, and got my songs ready, because when that day does arrive, I'll have the songs.

Coppola pauses in midflight, then commits himself: "I am basically interested in a form of super television."

*   *   *

On November 27, 1989, Coppola embarked on the shooting of a third episode in the *Godfather* saga. In *Part III*, Michael Corleone, white-haired and ailing, seeks to legitimize his mighty Family fortunes. Inspired by the fiscal and political scandals of recent years, and especially those involving the Vatican and the Banco Ambrosiano, Coppola and coscreenwriter Mario Puzo measure the shrewd manipulation of the Corleone empire against the formidable challenge of a Europe ever more conscious of its own power.

Until the summer of 1989, Coppola had expressed a repugnance toward any further *Godfather* movies. When Paramount offered him complete freedom to develop a *Part III*, on his terms, and not attached to the futile screenplays already drafted for the studio, he responded positively.

"I told Paramount that for $40,000, we at Zoetrope could prepare a feasibility study. At the end of a couple of months, they would get the proposed budget, the schedule, who would appear in the movie, the essential themes, and so on." Coppola reminded Paramount chairman Frank Mancuso that his concept differed from that of the studio. If he were to do another *Godfather* episode, he wanted it to concentrate on the character of Michael Corleone (played by Al Pacino), "because that's where the tragedy lies," while in Paramount's other drafts Michael had always been relegated to minor status.

Ever since the completion of *Tucker, The Man and His Dream*, Francis had immersed himself in *Megalopolis*, an epic venture that would blend the characters of republican Rome at the time of the Catiline Conspiracy with the dynamics and corruption of contemporary New York. He rented space at Cinecittà Studios in Rome, where Dean Tavoularis and his design team constructed offices in a gracious, classical idiom, and an art studio where draftsmen prepared a meticulous storyboard for the movie.

While the focus of Coppola's own attention shifted to Italy and the projects he was developing there, Zoetrope slowly began to recover its earlier momentum. During 1989, Fred Fuchs was appointed head of Zoetrope "3" (the group's production arm), and supervised the making of a pilot and seven episodes of *The Outsiders* for televison, as well as an "American Dream" anthology for HBO. Curtis Hanson's *Brotherhood of the Grape*, from a novel by the modish John Fante, was almost ready to roll, and Tom Luddy negotiated with various producers in the Far East concerning a slate of four or five films to be made with China and Hong Kong.

When Paramount urged him to return to *The Godfather*, Coppola realized that the hiatus might be fruitful in more than merely monetary terms. "I think that's a very good technique for someone with a big project—you work on it for a few years and then you make something else. Now [December 1989] I can see that I wrote it on so much bigger a scale than I should have done. I ought to narrow in on certain aspects of the subject, and you can only achieve that perspective over a period of time, or by throwing yourself into another project."

Zoetrope prepared the feasibility study for Paramount for $40,000. The report detailed Coppola's concept of *The Godfather Part III*, his suggestions for casting, the shooting schedule, and the cost of the production. Once this was accepted by the studio, Coppola and Mario Puzo began work on a new screenplay; the budget was eventually settled at $44 million, with location work in Sicily and New York City, as well as in Rome.

Rumors about controversial material in the new film began to percolate through the pages of the tabloid press. Actors' agents were copying pages from earlier drafts of the screenplay, and so, in an effort to stanch these leaks, Coppola circulated the final shooting script only to those who needed to know its contents. The final twelve pages remained out of bounds for even the Zoetrope team (save for Dean Tavoularis and one or two others who had to know details of each scene for construction purposes).

The screenplay deals with the themes of redemption and reconciliation close to Coppola's heart, and once again revolves around the Corleone Family. Michael sells off his casinos and becomes embroiled in a complex scheme to "launder" the Family's fortunes through the one state in the world that seems above reproach—the Vatican. The tragedy of the film is that his motives are foiled by a combination of ill health, treachery, impetuous relatives, and the subtle scheming of the Europeans from whom, ironically, the American Corleone Family sprang.

> There is a lot of hope in this new screenplay, which I believe is stronger than what Mario and I wrote for the other two. Much of what made *those* films so good emerged from the alliance of those particular actors, that material, that photographer, that art director, and my being the ringleader. Of course it is a lot easier to write a script of this sort when you have freedom from the studio rather than having to write a custom job. The script went through twelve drafts between April and November, with both Mario and I working hard every day.
>
> *The Godfather Part III* deals with this kind of American family that functions almost like royalty. This Family is famous from the other two pictures and there are many generations within it. Sometimes the younger members are more into the past than the future, and sometimes the older folk are concerned more with the future than the past. When you talk about money in some stories it may be the microfilm that the Russians want to buy, or some thriller involving twenty pounds of heroin. I was more curious about pure wealth, pure power, on a much grander scale. That's why I was turned off by *Godfather* scripts that had been written involving the world cocaine trade. So I concentrated on what *I* found to be interesting. Michael Corleone's instincts were always to be legitimate, so it would be odd now, when he's almost in the King Lear period of his life, if his prime aim and purpose were not indeed to become legitimate. The result is a very classical piece; in the tradition of a Shakespeare

play, one of the characters [Vincent Mancini, played by Andy Garcia] is the illegitimate son of Sonny Corleone. Before I began writing I read a lot of Shakespeare, looking for inspiration to Edmund in *King Lear*, Lear himself, Titus Andronicus, even Romeo and Juliet.

To me, the term Mafia doesn't refer to membership of the Italian Club, but to the highest level of power operating on their own clandestine terms. What would happen, I asked myself, if the Corleones, as they grew bigger and more legitimate, ran into the *real* Mafia, whether that be in the White House, or the Quirinale, or wherever? We found ourselves involved in some extremely rich research into the history of the past ten or twelve years, and then we fictionalized our existing characters into that material.

The one member of the original cast whom Coppola dearly wanted to participate was Robert Duvall. But during the intervening years Duvall had himself become a leading star, and felt reluctant to join *The Godfather* again as a mere family lawyer. He requested a fee of $3.5 million, which could not be found in the budget. Francis rewrote his part so that it could be filmed in two or three weeks, but still Duvall demurred. Gordon Willis, who had not worked with Coppola since *The Godfather Part II*, was persuaded to join the team. Perhaps the boldest piece of casting involved George Hamilton, whose image as a playboy has masked his acting abilities since he made his breakthrough in the late 1950s and early 1960s. Andy Garcia, star of Ridley Scott's *Black Rain*, plays a kind of James Caan redux figure, hot-headed, violent, and fiercely loyal to the Corleone family.

Frank Sinatra, who had reacted so angrily to the alleged portrayal of his personality in the Johnny Fontane character of the original *Godfather*, was keen to appear in *Part III* as Altobello, a revered friend of the Corleone Family from the 1930s and 1940s. But he would have been required on set in Rome for up to two months, and could not juggle his engagements to accommodate such a long stint abroad. Madonna, too, might have featured in a major part, and she performed a screen test opposite Robert De Niro that impressed Coppola enormously. When it was decided that a younger man should take the role of Vincent, however, both De Niro and Madonna faded from the picture.

Coppola reveled in the opportunity to make a major motion picture with the technological tools that he and his colleagues had been experimenting with at Zoetrope throughout the 1980s. Even in the midst of shooting *Part III* he found time to write a ten-page letter to Akio Morita, chairman of Sony Corporation, reporting on his experiences with the latest equipment. "The movies have always been impacted by technology," says Coppola. "They were born because of technology. At Zoetrope, we experimented with a lot of small low-budget pictures but now we can use those same implements on a big film. Preproduction, production, and postproduction are rapidly turning into a single, very powerful phase instead of being separate entities."

He is also hopeful that audiences will flock to *The Godfather Part III* in larger numbers than they did to *Tucker*. "Whenever you make something unusual, it doesn't succeed unless it really is the greatest work of its kind. People do not want unusual films, and I like to make unusual films! I think *Tucker* would have been more popular had it not been so offbeat. It did not attempt to be a deep, angst-ridden movie, pointing fingers and so on. It was meant to be more like a promo-film. This new *Godfather* is in an altogether different style, much deeper, more tragic. It is bigger in scale than its two predecessors. This is the cathedral of the *Godfather* movies."

Coppola sits in his tasteful office in Cinecittà. Behind him is a huge bulletin board on which are pinned a photograph of his idol Akira Kurosawa and a chart of every pontiff in the history of the Roman Catholic church. Looking leaner and more at ease than at any time in the past two years, he reflects on his films and his dreams:

> Unfortunately the low-budget movie industry around the world is dying right now. At Zoetrope we were putting together little genre films, westerns, horror films, and that kind of stuff. But it was good because we used that period to assemble our technological know-how and to give a lot of young people some experience. But I do not think that dream of mine is ever going to be given me—that dream of having a company along studio lines that is full of creative opportunities and develops talent. I think it would be very appropriate to these times. A company like Sony could make a dream studio from the old MGM lot. Maybe I'll get to enjoy it by their inviting us to do some projects. . . . My dream of being in a studio like that is not *owning* it all. It's just that I want to be able to tell the police at the gate that they are not police but rather belong to the show-business tradition. I would like to set the tone and style of a studio, but I don't think I'm always going to get what I want in life!
>
> I was attracted to Cinecittà because it's beautiful and reminds me of my old studio in Los Angeles. Of course Rome has now become as expensive as America and so, as in Tokyo, the labor and artists you use need to earn as much as they would in the States. The cost-saving factor which attracted George Lucas to England to do his *Star Wars* and *Indiana Jones* productions, and me to Rome to do *Megalopolis*, is rapidly evaporating. Cinecittà is now very full, and we have helped to stimulate a mini-renaissance here. Nowhere is life perfect where moviemaking is concerned. Every place has different ad-

vantages and disadvantages. You might find the dry cleaning terrible but the mozzarella just great, so you tend to avoid doing much dry cleaning and you eat a lot of mozzarella!

The Godfather Part III will give us a great shot in the arm to subsidize our operation, and when it is finished we will return to *Megalopolis*. Each movie is an experiment for the one that follows after.

Although I'd like to have a subsidiary company over here in Rome, and buy a small apartment and come to visit, I would never leave my home. I love San Francisco, I love Napa.

* * *

As the months passed, however, it became evident that a combination of corporate greed and maladroit casting might prevent *The Godfather Part III* from scaling the heights of its predecessors. Paramount insisted that the film be ready for the lucrative Christmas season, which meant that Coppola had to shoot and edit his epic in just twelve months. In December 1989 the first gasket blew. Winona Ryder, cast as Mary, Michael Corleone's daughter, arrived in Rome with her boyfriend Johnny Depp. Given less than a day to acclimatize before plunging into an arduous schedule, she collapsed from the strain on her nerves and failed to show for her first scene. After a flurry of meetings and consultations, it was agreed that she would be replaced. The parting was amicable, but massively inconvenient. With some eight weeks of shooting behind him, Coppola was thus confronted with the loss of a star in a crucial role.

Against all advice, he selected his eighteen-year-old daughter Sofia to replace Ryder. Sofia possessed scarcely any formal acting experience. Visiting Rome to be with her parents at Christmas, she plucked up courage and began learning Mary's lines. Coppola vigorously defended himself against charges of nepotism. "If I were Michael [Corleone], and I had this nice daughter, she'd be sort of like Sofia. She'd be cute, she'd be beautiful but she wouldn't be like-a-movie-star beautiful. She'd be Italian, so in her face you could see Sicily."

Coppola also wanted to maintain the momentum of production. To have shut down the film for two weeks or more might have proved disastrous from both a creative and a financial standpoint. Even so, rumors began circulating that *The Godfather Part III* was already exceeding its budget and falling behind schedule. As if these problems were not enough, Al Pacino and Diane Keaton, who had been living together for some years, decided to end their romantic attachment while on location in Rome.

Somehow, the film lumbered on, shooting in Caprarola, in Sicily, and then in New York City (The Waldorf-Astoria Hotel, Little Italy, the Red Zone nightclub) and on Long Island.

By now, Paramount's prospects for opening the picture at Thanksgiving 1990 looked bleak. The studio had requested a final cut of 2 hours 20 minutes maximum; Coppola wanted it to run longer, in tune with the grandeur and pace of the first two parts. As late as September, he was in New York shooting additional snippets of film with Al Pacino. The tension mounted as *The Godfather Part III* entered the final throes of post-production. Supervising editor Barry Malkin and his team worked 16 to 18 hours a day on assembling the negative. Even during the first week of November, Pacino was looping his lines in Los Angeles, while Carmine Coppola recorded his score for the production.

By December 10, the first answer prints were ready for screening to hundreds of impatient critics and journalists in New York and Los Angeles. Paramount, in a jittery mood, did not arrange these sessions in the most congenial of circumstances. The screening at Loew's Astor Plaza in Manhattan on December 12, for example, was overcrowded and poorly air-conditioned. Reviews had to be written within hours, not days, as editors strived to make their deadlines before Christmas. Millions of dollars were at stake; if the film opened over the holiday period it would not only qualify for the Academy Awards the following spring, but would also reach its maximum potential audience at the peak movie-going time of the year.

The trade response to the film left Paramount with the hope that its gamble had succeeded. Todd McCarthy wrote in *Variety* that, "faced with the extraordinary task of recapturing magic he created 16 and 18 years ago, Francis Ford Coppola has come very close to completely succeeding with *The Godfather Part III*." The review waxed ecstatic over the climax of the picture: "The best is still to come. In one of the most masterful examples of sustained intercutting in cinema, Anthony's performance in *Cavalleria Rusticana* serves as the back-drop for several murderous missions." Duane Byrge, in *The Hollywood Reporter*, called Al Pacino's acting "brilliant". "A complex depiction of Michael Corleone's dying-days attempt to cement the family in the 'legitimate' business world and attain spiritual redemption, this third installment of the Corleone Family chronicle is a full-bodied, albeit somber dramatic orchestration."

In the consumer publications, however, reviewers adopted a more cynical attitude to the film. Weaned on tales of woe from the set earlier in the year, they denounced Sofia Coppola for her amateurish appearance as Mary Corleone. Even the sympathetic Todd McCarthy had gauged the general feeling: "ungainly, afflicted with a Valley Girl accent and not an actress who can hold her own in this august company, the director's daughter simply doesn't cut it." The critics discovered other flaws, too. Hugo Davenport, writing in London's *Daily Telegraph*, protested against being asked to accept Michael Corleone as a tragic figure after seeing him commit fratricide in *Part II*.

Many reviewers wanted to like the film and yet found themselves compelled to qualify their praise. Philip French, in the British *Observer*, conceded that "this engrossing movie is conceived and executed on a grand scale [...] But, oddly enough, Michael seems to shrink in stature as the picture proceeds and the *Lear*-like tragedy at which Coppola aims is not realized." Notices in Europe were more respectful than those in the U.S., especially when the film unspooled at the Berlin Festival in February 1991. But the word-of-mouth on *The Godfather Part III* expressed disappointment and militated against long runs in theaters that had guaranteed handsome sums to Paramount and its international distributor, U.I.P., for the privilege of screening the picture. "Every theater in Japan wants to show [it]," declared a jubilant Hy Smith, Senior Vice-President at U.I.P.

When the film opened in America on December 25, the lines were immense; in the first three days receipts exceeded $15 million at 1,820 screens. Word soon leaked out that Coppola had trimmed a couple of minutes from the version shown to critics. Some prints were rushed to theaters barely twelve hours prior to screening time. Quality control faltered, leaving one copy entirely out of focus and another without dialogue recording on certain reels. Ironically, Coppola would add to the length of the film before allowing Paramount to release it on video. The version on cassette and laser-disc includes several minutes of footage not seen on the large screen, most of it featuring Sofia Coppola, as if the director were determined to convince his critics that they had been wrong to scorn her performance.

The Godfather Part III cost $55 million and earned some $67 million at the U.S. box-office. Its international release attracted a further $60 million so that, taking account of television, video, and ancillary revenues, the studio more than broke even on one of its most sorely-tested productions of recent times. Yet the abrupt departure of Frank Mancuso from the presidency of Paramount in the spring of 1991 in no small way reflected the sense of commercial dejection that enveloped *The Godfather Part III*. Nor did the Academy Awards yield any consolation. Nominated for seven statuettes, the film won none.

* * *

One of Vito Corleone's old cronies, Don Altobello, confides to Michael in an early scene of *The Godfather Part III* that he has lost the "venom and juices" of youth. Although sporadic outbursts of violence and passion mark the film, this is essentially a winter's tale: a prolonged sigh of agony from a Mafia boss yearning to achieve respectability, craving forgiveness from the Church for his manifold sins, and striving to reconcile his children. It is also more closely bound than its predecessors to the visual grandeur of Italian opera. To take but one example of Coppola's intermarriage of stage and street, as it were: The shrouded figures who bear aloft an effigy of Christ during the feast-day procession in Manhattan's Little Italy when Joey Zasa is murdered, reappear identically during the performance of *Cavalleria Rusticana* in Palermo.

Like the two earlier *Godfather* films, *Part III* swings from the New World to the Old, from Atlantic City to the Vatican and from Manhattan to Palermo. The money drained and torn from the pockets of gullible Americans is sent back to Sicily in the form of a $100 million check donated by the "Vito Corleone Foundation," an ill-disguised exchange for the Papal honor bestowed on Michael in the opening sequence of the film. Yet within hours, Michael and his financial adviser are persuading the Archbishop to conspire with them to take control of Immobilare, a billion-dollar corporation decisively influenced by the Vatican's 25% share. Michael Corleone intends not so much to relinquish his ill-gotten gains but rather to launder them. As the Archbishop declares with a wry smile, "It seems in today's world that the power to absolve debt is greater than the power of forgiveness."

So the central thrust of the film involves the collision between business and idealism, the venal and the spiritual. Coppola and Puzo express this struggle in terms of age versus youth, experience against immaturity, the restraint of Michael Corleone confronting the bloody impetuosity of his illegitimate son Vincent, who, in his own words, wants "the power to preserve the family." These divided loyalties give the character of the Archbishop a particular fascination: Chain-smoking, hand-wringing, lamenting his involvement in the Church's financial affairs, he finds himself tempted by Michael's offer of $600 million in cash to save the Vatican bank, and yet lacks the courage to withstand the guile and pressure of Lucchesi, the suave, master villain who describes politics as "knowing when to pull the trigger."

So the film more than just touches upon the multinational business warfare and scandals of recent times. The Vatican bank (Banco Ambrosiano) really *did* lurch into a mire of difficulties in the late 1970's; "God's banker" (Roberto Calvi) really *was* found hanging from a bridge (Blackfriars in London, rather than in Rome); and Pope John Paul I really *did* "die in his sleep" in suspicious circumstances after reigning just 33 days in 1978. In the United States, the Mafia shifted the focus of its activities to drugs and then to casinos.

Family values at once dominate and undermine Michael's final months. The relatives gather to celebrate his Papal honor, and the singing and dancing and cake-cutting recall the lyrical, sunlit overture to the original *Godfather* film. But now there are dark memories that well up to torment the conscience of a Corleone. Even as he hears the Archbishop intoning the "Hail Mary" at his award ceremony, Michael harks back to the murder of Fredo at Lake Tahoe. Later, his son Anthony's singing of a Sicilian melody triggers a memory for Michael of his first wedding, to Apollonia. And at the climax of the film the abrupt loss of his daughter Mary (one of the best inventions of the screenplay) resounds with a fearful irony, making a mockery of those offscreen words spoken by Michael Corleone at the very outset: "The only wealth in this world is children, more than all the money and power on earth." The anguish seems especially personal to Coppola, in the wake of his son Gio's death in a boating accident only three years earlier. Coppola finds at once the starkest and most forceful of images to communicate that pain—Michael's mouth gaping wide in a silent scream of anger and agony as he slumps on the steps of the opera house.

Michael's physical fragility (notably his diabetes) illustrates what Cardinal Lamberto mutters during the confession scene: "The mind suffers—and the body cries out." In the aftermath of his stroke, he is tended by his sister Connie. But she, who throughout the saga has interceded in family disputes, now assumes a more sinister role, becoming a barrier between Michael and his expiation. Treachery always strikes from within the Corleone entourage and while Connie never betrays her brother in the way that Don Altobello or Joey Zasa does, she tries to legitimize the past. Even after Michael has confessed to the murder of Fredo, in one of the most poignant scenes ever filmed by Coppola, Connie assures him that the crime was "God's will—a terrible accident." She substitutes for Michael in giving permission for Zasa to be eliminated, and in offering Altobello the poisoned pastry at the opera house. In caring for her ailing brother, she perpetuates his life as a sinner.

The development of a personality like Connie underlines the basic strength of *The Godfather* saga. These films hinge on character, not action. Some—Connie, Michael, Kay, even the bodyguard Al Neri—figure in all three parts of the trilogy. Most characters, however, dominate a particular episode before dying or slipping out of the narrative. Just as the Corleone family renews itself from generation to generation, so Coppola and Puzo have resuscitated the appeal of the *Godfather* story by inventing fresh individuals like Vincent, Altobello, and Joey Zasa. The audience identifies readily with them as they did with Brando's Don, De Niro's young Vito Corleone, Duvall's Tom Hagen, or Strasberg's Hyman Roth.

While the flaws of the film tend to dim nisn with each passing year, and are submerged into the persuasive fabric of the Corleone story, it is undeniable that the love strands running through *Part III* (Vincent and Mary, Michael and Kay) fail to stir the emotions. There is little chemistry at work between Andy Garcia and Sofia Coppola, while Diane Keaton looks more than ever like a visitor to the set, unable to grasp Michael's need for atonement.

*   *   *

In accentuating the metaphors and lineaments of opera, Coppola lays the film open to criticism in small but unexpected ways. For example, Al Pacino's wry reactions to certain dramatic, often horrifying developments may be faithful to Verdi or Mascagni, but strikes a jarring chord in the mind of an audience accustomed to believing in the narrative drama of *The Godfather* films. Eli Wallach's ham-fisted performance as Don Altobello belongs to the stage, not the screen. Again, the context—a modern gangster film with palpable links to real-life events of the late 1970's—will not tolerate such stylized playing. In *Bram Stoker's Dracula*, however, Anthony Hopkins can render Van Helsing in camp terms without undermining the film.

True to the traditions of grand opera, the closing sequence reprises musical moments from all three parts of *The Godfather* story— Michael's dancing with Apollonia in Sicily *(Part I)*, with Kay at Lake Tahoe *(Part II)*, and with Mary in New York (an early scene from *Part III)*. These reminiscences are dovetailed both rhythmically and sentimentally and become a fusion of bliss in the wandering mind of the dying Michael—a forlorn alternative to the redemption that has eluded him. There is a close-up of his withered face and white hair, as he dons the dark glasses to shut out the memories and the horrors of life alike; then a long shot of him alone in the garden. His dog approaches and as he reaches idly to fondle it, Michael Corleone crumples to the ground in silence as an orange—that fruit so closely associated with imminent death throughout the film—rolls from his hand. So one of the most eloquent and stirring tales in the history of the American cinema concludes not with a bang but a whimper.

* * *

In the midst of the last-minute frenzy of completing the Corleone saga, Coppola decided to join Creative Artists Agency. For the previous several years, he had relied on his own attorneys to vet his contracts, but John Peters had departed Zoetrope and Coppola knew that he would be working more frequently with the Hollywood studios and thus needed the services of a major agency. His move was timely, for Columbia Pictures had been eager to resume its partnership with Coppola both as producer and director, and before *The Godfather Part III* had opened, both sides had agreed to make a new screen version of *Dracula,* based on a screenplay by James V. Hart. Other Zoetrope productions took shape, including Carroll Ballard's *Wind,* a drama involving sailing's Americas Cup, and in February 1992 it was announced that American Zoetrope would join forces with Jim Henson's company to make an "animatronic" film of *Pinocchio.*

Financial hurdles remained, however, and it was with some relief that in San Francisco on June 30, 1992 Coppola and his wife, along with Zoetrope Corporation, filed for bankruptcy protection under Chapter 11. Liabilities were listed as \$98 million and assets at \$52 million. The largest creditor was Coppola's long-time friend and co-producer, Fred Roos, whose company Hot Weather Pony Boy Films was owed $71 million and would receive 25% of the stock of Zoetrope Corp., the parent company of Zoetrope Productions. In addition, Roos would be given 15% of the shares in Zoetrope Productions itself. "This bankruptcy filing closes the book on a complicated decade-long series of financial and legal problems stemming from *One from the Heart*," declared Coppola in a statement quoted in *Daily Variety*. "It will finally let us resolve all remaining debts and obligations stemming from this film and enable me to focus my attention on current projects."

Winona Ryder, anxious to make amends for her unfortunate withdrawal in Rome, brought Francis some ideas, among them the script by Hart. Within four months she had been cast as Mina in what would be called *Bram Stoker's Dracula*, and Hart and Coppola were hard at work on a strategic approach to the aesthetics of the project. The director found himself seduced by the extreme fidelity of the script to Stoker's novel, while recognizing with Hart that the narrative would require a compelling theme to engage audiences in the 1990s, and to convince them to see what would be at least the eighth screen version of the book since the Bela Lugosi *Dracula* of 1931, not forgetting innumerable sequels and variations on its vampire theme. So he and Hart developed the abiding passion that sustains Prince Vlad Tepes through the centuries as he searches for his beloved—the wife who had committed suicide at their castle in 1462 and who appears reincarnated as Mina more than four hundred years later.

"Originally, as a kid," said Coppola. "I always thought Dracula was the scariest of all monsters. I was more scared of Dracula than of Frankenstein—mainly because kids were comforted with the thought that they could probably outrun Frankenstein. But Dracula was weird—he wanted to suck your blood, and he could change into things. Dracula is more in your subconscious and has to do with your hidden desires."

Most of Coppola's finest sequences have been filmed on location. Yet he remains fascinated by the challenge and potential of controlling every shot under studio conditions. Like *One from the Heart*, this new film would be made exclusively on the Sony sound stages in Hollywood, apart from just one "location" scene—when Mina encounters the prince in a London street—which was photographed on the

Universal backlot. The cutting and sound-editing were, essentially, computerized, with videotape replacing film so that rushes could be seen and managed more easily.

So much depended on the skills of the technicians involved. Peter Ramsey and his team drew and painted storyboards for around 1,000 shots. Stitched into this animated version of the production were clips from Cocteau's *Beauty and the Beast*, as well as reproductions of paintings by Gustav Klimt, Caspar David Friedrich, and other artists to point the production designers and other technicians in the right direction. "Give me something that either comes from the research or that comes from your own nightmares," Coppola told his team. "I gave them paintings, and I gave them drawings, and I talked to them about how I thought the imagery could work."

Tom Sanders joined the team as production designer, eventually building 58 sets on six stages. Alison Savetch supervised the special visual effects, aided and abetted by an enthusiastic Roman Coppola. Eiko Ishioka, who had designed the costumes for Paul Schrader's *Mishima*, was given a sweeping brief to create a mood for the film through the clothes worn by the characters—scarlet, white, black, and gold for Dracula himself, green for the inexperienced Mina, and so on. The costumes proved to be a dramatic blend of the exotic and the sensual, the Oriental and the symbolist imagery associated with the late 19th century.

Just as he had invited the actors in *The Godfather* to eat spaghetti together, so Coppola summoned the cast of *Dracula* to his estate in Rutherford, and encouraged a mood of banter and relaxation amid exercises that included a two-day read-through of the original Stoker novel. "I don't really like rehearsing that much," says Anthony Hopkins, "but I'm glad we did on [*Dracula*] because it helped to find something for myself."

Dracula began principal photography on October 14, 1991. Freed of the enormous burden of expectation that had attended *The Godfather Part III*, Coppola could proceed purposefully and in comparative privacy. Gary Oldman, playing Dracula, suffered the most taxing moments during the production, on one occasion slipping in a pool of blood and striking his head hard on the floor of the set, and on several days finding that his costumes provoked an allergic reaction, not to mention claustrophobia. His makeup often required up to five hours of application.

The film opened on November 13, 1992, although shooting continued into early September. Francis's uncle, Anton Coppola, conducted the score with a 100-piece orchestra in September. As late as August, Anthony Hopkins returned to Hollywood for a new scene, and to narrate the picture. Francis himself flew to Venice to receive a Golden Lion in recognition of his career achievement, and then rushed back to complete the mix, and to mull the results of sneak previews in San Rafael and Seattle. "I never had such good screenings," he told *Daily Variety*'s Army Archerd. "I was in my toughest time a month ago. The turning point was three weeks back. I'm always under the gun. But I'm still a big believer that if you put a one of a kind [movie] out there, there's some reward." A later preview in Denver, after Coppola had made significant changes to the composition of the picture (Van Helsing would now act as a narrator, linking past and present), pleased its audience more.

Columbia's campaign to launch the film began in September with the one-sheet poster showing a threatening gargoyle above the title with the teaser phrase "Love Never Dies" engraved above. Merchandizing gathered pace, although alliances with the American Red Cross's blood drive, and with toy companies or fast-food chains, withered in the face of the film's erotic and AIDS-oriented theme. No fewer than eight books appeared in connection with *Dracula*, the most lavish among them a coffee-table volume celebrating the costumes for the film, designed by Eiko Ishioka. A video game version had been in development at Sony Electronic Publishing (part of the group that includes Columbia Pictures) from the earliest stages of *Dracula*'s pre-production.

*   *   *

Despite the R rating, which excluded a large portion of the moviegoing public in America, *Bram Stoker's Dracula* stunned Hollywood with the strength of its opening five days—a remarkable $35,035,556, the highest initial gross of any picture in Columbia's history. Francis was on vacation in Guatemala and did not hear the figures until some days later. Although the film fell away in ensuing weeks, to end up with around $82 million at the U.S. box-office, its popularity around the world was such that the global gross exceeded $200 million. Coppola's participation deal meant that he could pay off all his debts at Zoetrope and start with a clean slate yet again. The Academy Awards also turned up trumps, with Oscars for best make-up, sound-effects editing, and Eiko Ishioka's extraordinary costumes. Reviewers, though, sought refuge in condescension and the *Variety* notice exemplified the misunderstanding of Coppola's aims: "Both the most extravagant screen telling of the oft-filmed story and the one most faithful to its literary source, this rendition sets grand romantic goals for itself that aren't fulfilled emotionally, and it is gory without being at all scary."

*　　*　　*

All credit to Columbia for giving Coppola such creative freedom on *Dracula*. The dominant themes of the film are those that have obsessed him for many years—the quest *(The Conversation, Apocalypse Now)*, the elision of the Old and New Worlds *(The Godfather)*, the legitimacy of the fairy-tale and the supernatural *(Peggy Sue Got Married)*, and the constant hounding of the non-conformist by a crass society *(Tucker)*.

If green was the assertive color of *Apocalypse Now*—the green of the jungle, the green of fatigues—then scarlet transfigures *Dracula* as surely as it does Bergman's *Cries and Whispers*. The lurid battle sequence at the beginning looks as though its silhouetted figures were bathed in gore. When the Prince goes berserk in his private chapel, the altar is drenched in blood. In the Transylvanian castle scenes, Dracula's cloak glides after him like a distended puddle of blood, ready to envelop, perhaps infect, those about him. When, in Harker's presence, the Count seals the contract to buy Carfax Abbey, the wax settles like a huge droplet of blood on the parchment. As Lucy awaits the coming of her vampire mate, the screen fills with microscopic close-ups of red corpuscles, swirling and commingling. Red appears unique to Dracula himself save when Mina wears a vermilion gown during the "absinthe" seduction scene, and when Lucy dons a flame-orange dress as she enters the garden to be ravished by the vampire.

Coppola and Hart use this imagery to make metaphorical comment on the AIDS epidemic and its association of sex with mortality—"a disease of the blood unknown" in Van Helsing's words. Lucy and then Mina are condemned when they exchange "precious bodily fluids" with the vampire. Van Helsing talks to his students about "the diseases of Venus [...] involved in that sex problem about which the ideals and ethics of Christian civilization are concerned." And perhaps the most jolting moment of the film occurs when Van Helsing asks Harker: "During your infidelity with those creatures, those demonic women, did you for one instant taste of their blood?" Blood may be "the life" for Dracula, but its invasion may mean death for ordinary mortals, and perhaps James V. Hart is right when he comments that "in a sense, vampirism is the Victorian equivalent of AIDS."

Against this, and soaring beyond its risks, is the passion that links Prince Vlad and Mina across the centuries. They are, according to Coppola, "souls reaching out through a universe of horror and pathos." Poor susceptible Jonathan Harker almost thanks Dracula for noting the portrait of Mina on his table in the castle. "You found Mina—I thought she was lost," he says, as the Count gazes mesmerized at the tiny picture, aware that he has found a reincarnation of his beloved Elisabetta. The single-mindedness of this ardor makes the discreet courtship of Mina on the one hand, and of Lucy and Dr. Seward on the other, seem anemic and ineffectual. In a skillful montage sequence, Coppola contrasts the formal wedding between Jonathan and Mina in Romania with the savage, bloody coupling of Lucy and Dracula. During the climax of the film, just before plunging his sword through the heart of her beloved, Mina says, "Our love is stronger than death." Indeed the lovers do survive, frozen in flight across the sky in a painted cupola high above the carnage.

Coppola raids tradition to trigger responses in our collective cinematic memory. The chapel and marriage scenes, replete with icons and gold costumes, evoke *Ivan the Terrible;* the opening battle pays conscious homage to both Kurosawa *(Kagemusha)* and Welles *(Chimes at Midnight)*. Miniatures in any other film of the 1990s might provoke ridicule, but in *Dracula* they form part of the aesthetic language. So too does the notion of technology percolating into late 19th century society: Mina's typewriter, Dr. Seward's phonograph cylinder, and the cinematograph screenings on display in London when the Prince courts Mina. This notion of science encroaching on a world where faith and mysticism have held sway was explored in similar tongue-in-cheek manner by Bergman in *The Magician*. The nervous laughter among the audience watching *Bram Stoker's Dracula* also belongs to the genre, and indeed the very word "camp" was first used in *The Listener* magazine, during the 1930s, in describing Bela Lugosi's performance in Tod Browning's original *Dracula*. Coppola kindles that laughter with unmistakable delight, as when he cuts from a shot of Lucy's severed head floating in darkness to a close-up of a bloody baron of beef being delivered to the restaurant table.

The Conversation and *The Godfather* films dealt in no small measure with the power of religion to influence lives. Prince Vlad, pledged to defend the Church against all enemies of Christ, renounces his God when his wife commits suicide, and ever after must—like Lucifer and Mephistopheles—face the Cross as a mortal adversary. Jonathan is given a miniature cross when he alights from his carriage before meeting the Count (who dismisses it as a "trinket of deceit"), and Van Helsing brandishes a silver crucifix in front of the "undead" Lucy in her tomb, provoking a belch of blood worthy of *The Exorcist*. The image of the Cross frustrates the vampire, despite the irony of his uttering precisely Christ's own words in the final sequence.

On various occasions throughout the film, fire too will thwart Dracula and keep him at bay. Torches and candles are lit to counter the darkness in which he lurks, and at the climax outside the castle, Van Helsing ignites a circle of flame to ward off the marauding spirits of the vampire's three brides.

The appeal of *Dracula* lies in the unashamed aestheticism of Coppola's approach to this tale of *amour fou*. He eschews the "naturalism" of such contemporary horror films as *The Silence of the Lambs* in favor of a stylized, enchanted world already familiar to lovers of *Peggy Sue Got Married* and *Tucker, The Man and His Dream*.

*   *   *

Basking in the success of the film, Francis took his mother and his family to Monaco for the Formula One Grand Prix in May 1993. But by August he was all set to produce *Mary Shelley's Frankenstein*—in association with John Veitch and *Dracula* screenwriter James V. Hart for Columbia Pictures, with Kenneth Branagh as director, Robert De Niro as the creature, John Cleese, Branagh himself as Victor Frankenstein, Aidan Quinn, and Helena Bonham-Carter. Principal photography began at Britain's Shepperton Studios on October 21. Yet another, related project was *Van Helsing's Chronicles*, starring Anthony Hopkins in a kind of sequel to his *Dracula* role, contending with malevolent forces around the world.

And, enjoying the rest from directing motion pictures, Coppola told Army Archerd in September 1993 that he was preparing to open his Blancaneaux Lodge in Belize. The resort, close to some distinguished Mayan ruins, would have its own waterfall and hydro-electric plant, and could even be the site of a future communications and cultural oasis for the Central Americas. The success of *Dracula* meant that Francis could revive his dream of making *Megalopolis* in Rome, and also progress on another project, *Cure*, about the search for an antidote to AIDS. The international box-office for Agnieszka Holland's *The Secret Garden*, a Zoetrope production for Paramount, also delighted Coppola and his team. In January 1994 Arthur Penn signed with American Zoetrope to direct *Californios*, an historical drama set during the Gold Rush, and produced by Tom Luddy and novelist Thomas Sanchez.

In December 1993, his old pal Frank Mancuso, now chairman/CEO of the revived Metro-Goldwyn-Mayer Inc., invited Coppola to join the board of directors. A dozen years earlier, such an idea would have provoked hoots of laughter in the Hollywood commissaries.

*   *   *

"I think the main difficulty with any movie or anything related to art is: Can you make something with its own heartbeat? If you're successful with that, then a lot of the other problems fall by the wayside." This was Coppola talking about *Bram Stoker's Dracula*. Now in his mid-fifties, he has reconciled the humanitarian side of his nature with the restive, reckless passion of the technophile, and has survived as a bankable director after so many observers had written him off. As he said in 1992, "You're stepping off a cliff when you start to make a film."

Like some neo-renaissance man, Coppola has dazzled his contemporaries. He knows Italian culture and society intimately, he is devoted to Japanese life and art, he based his original Zoetrope studio on a Danish model, and he found one of his major influences, Sergei Eisenstein, in Russia. On a more frivolous level he can sing and dance with more abandon than most amateurs, fly a helicopter, fake-play a double bass to soothing effect, and be at home with a tuba. He revels in cooking a superb meal, and in producing his fine Californian Rubicon wine. Yet he remains a child of the American empire, responsive to its efficiency and ever-mutating technology, but aware of its high regard for power.

Filmography

Note: FFC refers to Francis [Ford] Coppola as director.

AS PRODUCER:

THX 1138 (1971)
American Graffiti (1973)

AS SCREENWRITER:

This Property Is Condemned (1966)
Is Paris Burning? (1966)
Reflections in a Golden Eye [first version] (1967)
Patton (1970)
The Great Gatsby (1974)

AS ASSISTANT DIRECTOR:

The Premature Burial (1962)

AS DIALOGUE DIRECTOR:

The Tower of London (1962)

AS ASSOCIATE PRODUCER/SECOND UNIT
DIRECTOR:

The Terror (1962)

AS SECOND UNIT DIRECTOR/SOUND RECORDIST:

The Young Racers (1963)

Coppola also supervised the dubbed version of the Soviet film *Nebo zowet,*
which was released as *Battle Beyond the Sun* (1963).

1961 TONIGHT FOR SURE

Screenplay: Jerry Shaffer, Francis Ford Coppola. Direction: FFC. Photography (black-and-white): Jack Hill. Editing: Ronald Waller. Music: Carmine Coppola. Art direction: Al Locatelli. Produced by Francis Ford Coppola. Circa 75 mins.
(*Note*: this film is an expanded version of FFC's own medium-length nudie, *The Peeper*.)

1963 DEMENTIA 13
(UK: THE HAUNTED AND THE HUNTED)

Screenplay and direction: FFC. Photography: Charles Hannawalt (black-and-white). Editing: Stewart O'Brien. Music: Ronald Stein. Art direction: Albert Locatelli. Produced by FFC for Roger Corman Productions. 97 mins. Premiere: September 25, 1963.

Cast: William Campbell (*Richard Haloran*), Luana Anders (*Louise Haloran*), Bart Patton (*Billy Haloran*), Mary Mitchell (*Kane*), Patrick Magee (*Justin Caleb*), Eithne Dunn (*Lady Haloran*), Peter Reed (*John Haloran*), Karl Schanzer (*Simon*), Ron Perry (*Arthur*), Derry O'Donovan (*Lillian*), Barbara Dowling (*Kathleen*).

1967 YOU'RE A BIG BOY NOW

Screenplay: FFC, from the novel by David Benedictus. Direction: FFC. Photography (Eastmancolor): Andy Laszlo. Editing: Aram Avakian. Music: Bob Prince. Songs: John Sebastian (performed by the Lovin' Spoonful). Art direction: Vassele Fotopoulos. Costumes: Theoni V. Aldredge. Choreography: Robert Tucker. Produced by Phil Feldman for Seven Arts, released through Warner Bros. 97 mins. Premiere: March 20, 1967

Cast: Peter Kastner (*Bernard Chanticleer*), Elizabeth Hartman (*Barbara Darling*), Geraldine Page (*Margery Chanticleer*), Julie Harris (*Miss Thing*), Rip Torn (*I. H. Chanticleer*), Tony Bill (*Raef*), Karen Black (*Amy*), Michael Dunn (*Richard Mudd*), Dolph Sweet (*Policeman Francis Graf*), Michael O'Sullivan (*Kurt Doughty*).

1968 FINIAN'S RAINBOW

Screenplay: E. Y. Harburg and Fred Saidy, based on the Broadway play (book by E. Y. Harburg and Fred Saidy, lyrics by E. Y. Harburg, music by Burton Lane). Direction: FFC. Photography (Technicolor, Panavision, 70mm): Philip Lathrop. Editing: Melvin Shapiro. Music direction: Ray Heindorf. Associate music supervisor: Ken Darby. Production design: Hilyard M. Brown. Choreography: Hermes Pan. Sound: M. A. Merrick, Dan Wallin. Costumes: Dorothy Jeakins. Associate producer: Joel Freeman. Produced by Joseph Landon for Warner Bros.–Seven Arts. 144 mins. Premiere: October 9, 1968.

Cast: Fred Astaire (*Finian McLonergan*), Petula Clark (*Sharon Mc-Lonergan*), Tommy Steele (*Og*), Don Francks (*Woody*), Barbara Hancock (*Susan the Silent*), Keenan Wynn (*Senator Billboard Rawkins*), Al Freeman, Jr. (*Howard*), Ronald Colby (*Buzz Collins*), Dolph Sweet (*Sheriff*), Wright King (*District Attorney*), Louil Silas (*Henry*), Brenda Arnau (*Sharecropper*), Avon Long, Roy Glen, Jerster Hairston (*Passion Pilgrim Gospellers*).

1969 THE RAIN PEOPLE

Screenplay and direction: FFC. Photography (Technicolor): Wilmer Butler. Editing: Blackie Malkin. Music: Ronald Stein. Art direction: Leon Ericksen. Sound: Nathan Boxer. Sound montage: Walter Murch. Production associates: George Lucas, Mona Skager. An American Zoetrope production, produced by Bart Patton and Ronald Colby for Warner Bros.–Seven Arts. 101 mins. Premiere: August 27, 1969.

Cast: James Caan (*Kilgannon*), Shirley Knight (*Natalie*), Robert Duvall (*Gordon*), Marya Zimmet (*Rosalie*), Tom Aldredge (*Mr. Alfred*), Laurie Crews (*Ellen*), Andrew Duncan (*Artie*), Margaret Fairchild (*Marion*), Sally Gracie (*Beth*), Alan Manson (*Lou*), Robert Modica (*Vinny*).

1972 THE GODFATHER

Screenplay: Mario Puzo, FFC, based on the novel by Puzo. Direction: FFC. Photography (Technicolor): Gordon Willis. Editing: William Reynolds, Peter Zinner. Production designer: Dean Tavoularis. Art direction: Warren Clymer. Music: Nino Rota (additional music by Carmine Coppola). Costumes: Anna Hill Johnstone. Sound recording: Christopher Newman. Associate producer: Gray Frederickson. Produced by Albert S. Ruddy (Alfran Productions) for Paramount. 175 mins. Premiere: March 11, 1972.

Cast: Marlon Brando (*Don Vito Corleone*), Al Pacino (*Michael Corleone*), James Caan (*Sonny Corleone*), Richard Castellano (*Clemenza*), Robert Duvall (*Tom Hagen*), Sterling Hayden (*McCluskey*), John Marley (*Jack Woltz*), Richard Conte (*Barzini*), Al Lettieri (*Sollozzo*), Diane Keaton (*Kay Adams*), Abe Vigoda (*Tessio*), Talia Shire (*Connie*), Gianni Russo (*Carlo Rizzi*), John Cazale (*Fredo Corleone*), Rudy Bond (*Cuneo*), Al Martino (*Johnny Fontane*), Morgana King (*Mama Corleone*), Lenny Montanna (*Luca Brasi*), John Martino (*Paulie Gatto*), Salvatore Corsitto (*Bonasera*), Richard Bright (*Neri*), Alex Rocco (*Moe Greene*), Tony Giorgio (*Bruno Tattaglia*), Vito Scotti (*Nazorine*), Tere Livrano (*Theresa Hagen*), Victor Rendina (*Philip Tattaglia*), Jeannie Linero (*Lucy Mancini*), Julie Gregg (*Sandra Corleone*), Ardel Sheidan (*Mrs. Clemenza*), Simonetta Stefanelli (*Apollonia*), Angelo Infanti (*Fabrizio*), Corrado Gaipa (*Don Tommasino*), Franco Citti (*Calo*), Saro Urz (*Vitelli*).

1974 THE CONVERSATION

Screenplay and direction: FFC. Photography (Technicolor): Bill Butler. Supervising editor, sound montage, and rerecording: Walter Murch. Editing:

Richard Chew. Production design: Dean Tavoularis. Set decoration: Doug Von Koss. Music: David Shire. Costumes: Aggie Guerard Rodgers. Technical advisers: Hal Lipset, Leo Jones, Jim Bloom. Produced by FFC and Fred Roos (Coppola Company) for The Directors Company, released through Paramount. 113 mins. Premiere: April 7, 1974.

Cast: Gene Hackman (*Harry Caul*), John Cazale (*Stan*), Allen Garfield (*Bernie Moran*), Frederic Forrest (*Mark*), Cindy Williams (*Ann*), Michael Higgins (*Paul*), Elizabeth MacRae (*Meredith*), Harrison Ford (*Martin Stett, assistant to the Director*), Robert Duvall (*the Director*), Mark Wheeler (*Receptionist*), Teri Garr (*Amy*), Robert Shields (*Mime in Union Square*), Phoebe Alexander (*Lurleen*).

THE GODFATHER PART II

Screenplay: Francis Ford Coppola, Mario Puzo, from the novel by Puzo. Direction: FFC. Photography (Technicolor): Gordon Willis. Editing: Peter Zinner, Barry Malkin, Richard Marks. Production design: Dean Tavoularis. Art direction: Angelo Graham. Music: Nino Rota (conducted by Carmine Coppola). Costumes: Theadora van Runkle. Sound montage and rerecording: Walter Murch. Associate producer: Mona Skager. Coproducers: Gray Frederickson, Fred Roos. Produced by FFC for The Coppola Company/Paramount. 200 mins. Premiere: December 12, 1974.

Cast: Al Pacino (*Michael Corleone*), Robert Duvall (*Tom Hagen*), Diane Keaton (*Kay Adams*), Robert De Niro (*Vito Corleone*), John Cazale (*Fredo Corleone*), Talia Shire (*Connie Corleone*), Lee Strasberg (*Hyman Roth*), Michael V. Gazzo (*Frankie Pentangeli*), G. D. Spradlin (*Senator Pat Geary*), Richard Bright (*Al Neri*), Gaston Moschin (*Fanucci*), Tom Rosqui (*Rocco Lampone*), B. Kirby Jr (*Young Clemenza*), Frank Sivero (*Genco*), Francesca De Sapio (*Young Mama Corleone*), Morgana King (*Mama Corleone*), Mariana Hill (*Deanna Corleone*), Leopoldo Trieste (*Signor Roberto*), Dominic Chianese (*Johnny Ola*), Amerigo Tot (*Michael's bodyguard*), Troy Donahue (*Merle Johnson*), John Aprea (*Young Tessio*), Joe Spinell (*Willi Cicci*), Abe Vigoda, Tere Livrano, Gianni Russo, Maria Carra, Oreste Baldini, Giuseppe Sillato, Mario Cotone, James Gounaris, Fay Spain, Harry Dean Stanton, David Baker, Carmine Caridi, Danny Aiello, Carmine Foresta, Nick Discenza, Father Joseph Medeglia, William Bowers, Joe della Sorte, Carmen Argenziano, Joe Lo Grippo, Ezio Flagello, Livio Giorgi, Kathy Beller, Saveria Mazzola, Tito Alba, Johnny Naranjo, Elda Maida, Salvatore Po, Ingnazio Pappalardo, Andrea Maugeri, Peter LaCorte, Vincent Coppola, Peter Donat, Tom Dahlgren, Paul B. Brown, Phil Feldman, Roger Corman, Yvone Coll, J. D. Nicols, Edward Van Sickle, Gabria Belloni, Richard Watson, Venancia Grangerard, Erica Yohn, Theresa Tirelli, James Caan.

1979   APOCALYPSE NOW

Screenplay: John Milius, Francis Coppola, based on the novel *Heart of Darkness* by Joseph Conrad. Direction: FFC. Photography (Technicolor, Technivision): Vittorio Storaro. Editing: Walter Murch, Gerald B. Greenberg, Lisa Fruchtman. Production design: Dean Tavoularis. Art direction: Angelo Graham. Music: Carmine Coppola, Francis Coppola; extract from Wagner's *Die Walküre*, and various songs of the 1960s. Sound montage/design: Walter Murch. Supervisory sound editing: Richard Cirincione. Costume supervision: Charles E. James. Creative consultant: Dennis Jakob. Offscreen commentary: Michael Herr. Second-unit photography: Stephen H. Burum. Insert photography: Caleb Deschanel. Associate producer: Mona Skager. Coproducers: Fred Roos, Gray Frederickson, Tom Sternberg. Produced by Francis Coppola for Omni-Zoetrope. 153 mins (35mm version with end title sequence), 141 mins (70mm). Premiere: August 15, 1979 ["Work in Progress" copy screened at Cannes Film Festival on May 19, 1979].

Cast: Marlon Brando (*Colonel Walter E. Kurtz*), Robert Duvall (*Lt. Col. Bill Kilgore*), Martin Sheen (*Captain Benjamin L. Willard*), Frederic Forrest ("*Chef*" *Hicks*), Albert Hall (*Chief Phillips*), Sam Bottoms (*Lance B. Johnson*), Larry Fishburne ("*Clean*"), Dennis Hopper (*Photojournalist*), G. D. Spradlin (*General Corman*), Harrison Ford (*Colonel Lucas*), Jerry Ziesmer (*Civilian*), Scott Glenn (*Captain Richard Colby*), Bo Byers, James Keane, Kerry Rossall, Ron McQueen, Tom Mason, Cynthia Wood, Colleen Camp, Linda Carpenter, Jack Thibeau, Glenn Walken, George Cantero, Damien Leake, Herb Rice, William Upton, Larry Carney, Marc Coppola, Daniel Kiewit, Father Elias, Bill Graham, Hatti James, Jerry Ross, Dick White, Francis Coppola.

1982 ONE FROM THE HEART

Screenplay: Armyan Bernstein and FFC, from the original screenplay by Armyan Bernstein. Direction: FFC. Photography (Technicolor): Vittorio Storaro. Editing: Anne Goursaud, with Rudi Fehr and Randy Roberts. Songs and music: Tom Waits, sung by Crystal Gayle and Tom Waits. Production design: Dean Tavoularis. Costumes: Ruth Morey. Sound design: Richard Beggs. Art direction: Angelo Graham. Special visual effects: Robert Swarthe. Choreography: Kenny Ortega. Electronic cinema: Thomas Brown, Murdo Laird, Anthony St. John, Michael Lehmann, in cooperation with the Sony Corporation. Associate producer: Mona Skager. Executive producer: Bernard Gersten. Coproducer: Armyan Bernstein. Produced by Gray Frederickson and Fred Roos for Zoetrope Studios. 103 mins. Premiere: January 15, 1982 (Radio City Music Hall).

Cast: Frederic Forrest (*Hank*), Teri Garr (*Frannie*), Raul Julia (*Ray*), Nastassia Kinski (*Leila*), Lainie Kazan (*Maggie*), Harry Dean Stanton (*Moe*), Allen Goorwitz [Garfield] (*Restaurant Owner*), Jeff Hamlin (*Airline Ticket Agent*), Italia Coppola, Carmine Coppola (*Couple in Elevator*), Edward Blackoff, James Dean, Rebecca de Mornay, Javier Grajeda, Cynthia Kania, Monica Scattini.

1983 THE OUTSIDERS

Screenplay: Kathleen Knutsen Rowell, from the novel by S. E. Hinton. Direction: FFC. Photography (Technicolor, Panavision): Stephen H. Burum.

Editing: Anne Goursaud. Production design: Dean Tavoularis. Special visual effects: Robert Swarthe. Music: Carmine Coppola. Sound design: Richard Beggs. Costumes: Marge Bowers. Associate producer: Gian-Carlo Coppola. Produced by Fred Roos and Gray Frederickson for Zoetrope Studios/Ponyboy Productions. 91 mins. Premiere: March 25, 1983.

Cast: Matt Dillon (*Dallas Winston*), Ralph Macchio (*Johnny Cade*), C. Thomas Howell (*Ponyboy Curtis*), Patrick Swayze (*Darrel Curtis*), Rob Lowe (*Sodapop Curtis*), Emilio Estevez (*Two-Bit Matthews*), Tom Cruise (*Steve Randle*), Glenn Withrow (*Tim Shephard*), Diane Lane (*Cherry Valance*), Leif Garret (*Bob Sheldon*), Darren Dalton (*Randy Anderson*), Michelle Meyrink (*Marcia*), Gailard Sartain (*Jerry*), Tom Waits (*Buck Merrill*), William Smith (*Store Clerk*), Tony Hillman, Hugh Walkinshaw, Domino, Teresa Wilkerson Hunt, Linda Nystedt, S. E. Hinton, Brent Beesley, John C. Meier, Ed Jackson, Dan Suhart, Steve M. Davison, Reid Rondell, Scott Wilder.

RUMBLE FISH

Screenplay: S. E. Hinton and FFC, based on the novel by S. E. Hinton. Direction: FFC. Photography (black-and-white): Stephen H. Burum. Editing: Barry Malkin. Music: Stewart Copeland. Production design: Dean Tavoularis. Sound design: Richard Beggs. Costumes: Marge Bowers. Executive producer: FFC. Associate producers: Gian-Carlo Coppola and Roman Coppola. Produced by Fred Roos and Doug Claybourne for Zoetrope Studios, released through Universal. 94 mins. Premiere: October 7, 1983 (New York Film Festival).

Cast: Matt Dillon (*Rusty-James*), Mickey Rourke (*The Motorcycle Boy*), Diane Lane (*Patty*), Dennis Hopper (*Father*), Diana Scarwid (*Cassandra*), Vincent Spano (*Steve*), Nicolas Cage (*Smokey*), Christopher Penn (*B. J. Jackson*), Larry Fishburne (*Midget*), William Smith (*Patterson, the Cop*), Michael Higgins (*Mr Harrigan*), Glenn Withrow (*Biff Wilcox*), Tom Waits (*Benny*), Herb Rice (*Black Pool-player*), Maybelle Wallace (*Late Pass Clerk*), Nona Manning (*Patty's Mom*), Domino (*Patty's Sister*), Gio (*Cousin James*), S. E. Hinton (*Hooker on Strip*), Emett Brown, Tracey Walter, Lance Guecia, Bob Maras, J. T. Turner, Keeva Clayton, Kirsten Hayden, Karen Parker, Sussannah Darcy, Kristi Somers, Buddy Joe Hooker, Bill Hooker, Tim Davison, Fred Hice, Dick Ziker.

1984 THE COTTON CLUB

Screenplay: William Kennedy, Francis Coppola from a story by William Kennedy, Francis Coppola, and Mario Puzo. Direction: FFC. Photography (Technicolor): Stephen Goldblatt. Editing: Barry Malkin, Robet Q. Lovett. Production design: Richard Sylbert. Art direction: David Chapman, Gregory Bolton. Music: John Barry, Bob Wilber. Sound editing: Edward Beyer. Principal choreographer: Michael Smuin. Tap choreographer: Henry Le Tang. Montage and second unit director: Gian-Carlo Coppola. Costumes: Milena Canonero. Producer consultant: Milton Forman. Coproducers: Silvio Tabet,

Fred Roos. Executive producer: Dyson Lovell. Line producers: Barrie M. Osborne, Joseph Cusumano. Produced by Robert Evans. 128 mins. Premiere: December 14, 1984.

Cast: Richard Gere (*Dixie Dwyer*), Gregory Hines (*Sandman Williams*), Diane Lane (*Vera Cicero*), Lonette McKee (*Lila Rose Oliver*), Bob Hoskins (*Owney Maden*), James Remar (*Dutch Schultz*), Nicolas Cage (*Vincent Dwyer*), Allen Garfield (*Abbadabba Berman*), Fred Gwynne (*Frenchy*), Gwen Verdon (*Tish Dwyer*), Lisa Jane Persky (*Frances Flegenheimer*), Maurice Hines (*Clay Williams*), Julian Beck (*Sol Weinstein*), Novella Nelson (*Madame St. Claire*), Larry Fishbourne (*Bumpy Rhodes*), John Ryan (*Joe Flynn*), Tom Waits (*Irving Stark*), Ron Karabatsos, Glenn Withrow, Jennifer Grey, Wynonna Smith, Thelma Carpenter, Charles "Honi" Coles, Larry Marshall, Joe Dallesandro, Ed O'Ross, Frederick Downs Jr, Diane Venora, Tucker Smallwood, Woody Strode, Bill Graham, Dayton Allen, Kim Chan, Ed Rowan, Leonard Termo, George Cantero, Brian Tarantina, Bruce MacVittie, James Russo, Giancarlo Esposito, Bruce Hubbard, Rony Clanton, Damien Leake, Bill Cobbs, Joe Lynn, Oscar Barnes, Edward Zang, Sandra Beall, Zane Mark, Tom Signorelli, Paul Herman, Randle Mell, Steve Vignari, Susan Meschner, Gregory Rozakis, Marc Coppola, Norma Jean Darden, Robert Earl Jones, Vincent Jerosa, Rosalind Harris.

1985 RIP VAN WINKLE

Direction: FFC, from the story by Washington Irving. Lighting director: George Riesenberger. Produced for HBO's "Faerie Tale Theatre" series. Circa 50 mins. Premiere: March 23, 1987.

Cast: Harry Dean Stanton (*Rip van Winkle* , Talia Shire (*Rip's Wife*), Sofia Coppola, Hunter Carson.

1986 CAPTAIN EO

Direction: FFC. Photography (70mm, 3-D): Vittorio Storaro. Second unit director: Gian-Carlo Coppola. Editing: Walter Murch. Music: Michael Jackson. Choreography: Jeffrey Hornaday. Produced by Lucasfilm Ltd. for Disney. 17 mins. Screened only at Disneyland and Disney World. Premiere: September 19, 1986.

Cast: Michael Jackson (*Captain Eo*), Anjelica Huston (*She-Devil Supreme*).

PEGGY SUE GOT MARRIED

Screenplay: Jerry Leichting, Arlene Sarner. Direction: FFC. Photography (DeLuxe): Jordan Cronenweth. Editing: Barry Malkin. Production design; Dean Tavoularis. Art direction: Alex Tavoularis. Music: John Barry. Supervisory sound editing: Michael Kirchberger. Costumes: Theadora Van Runkle. Electronic cinema: Murdo Laird, Ted Mackland, Ron Mooreland. Executive producer: Barrie M. Osborne. Produced by Paul R. Gurian for Tri-Star—

Delphi IV and V. For Rastar. A Paul R. Gurian/Zoetrope Studios Production. 103 mins. Premiere: October 5, 1986 (New York Film Festival).

Cast: Kathleen Turner (*Peggy Sue Kelcher [Bodell]*), Nicolas Cage (*Charlie Bodell*), Barry Miller (*Richard Norvik*), Catherine Hicks (*Carol Heath*), Joan Allen (*Maddie Nagle*), Kevin J. O'Conor (*Michael Fitzsimmons*), Jim Carrey (*Walter Getz*), Lisa Jane Persky (*Delores Dodge*), Lucinda Jenney (*Rosalie Testa*), Wil Shriner (*Arthur Nagle*), Barbara Harris (*Evelyn Kelcher*), Don Murray (*Jack Kelcher*), Sofia Coppola (*Nancy Kelcher*), Maureen O'Sullivan (*Elizabeth Alvorg*), Leon Ames (*Barney Alvorg*), Randy Bourne, Helen Hunt, Don Stark, Marshall Crenshaw, Chris Donato, Robert Crenshaw, Tom Teeley, Graham Maby, Ken Grantham, Ginger Taylor, Sigrid Wurschmidt, Glenn Withrow, Harry Basil, John Carradine, Sachi Parke, Vivien Straus, Morgan Upton, Dr. Lewis Leibovich, Bill Bonham, Joe Lerer, Barbara Oliver, Martin Scott, Marcus Scott, Carl Lockett, Tony Saunders, Vincent Lars, Larry E. Vann, Lawrence Menkin, Dan Suhart, Leslie Hilsinger, Al Nalbandian, Dan Leegant, Ron Cook, Mary Leichting.

1987 GARDENS OF STONE

Screenplay: Ronald Bass, based on the novel by Nicholas Proffitt. Direction: FFC. Photography (De Luxe): Jordan Cronenweth. Editing: Barry Malkin. Music: Carmine Coppola. Production design: Dean Tavoularis. Art direction: Alex Tavoularis. Costumes: Willa Kim, Judianna Makovsky. Sound designer: Richard Beggs. Executive producers: Stan Weston, Jay Emmett, and Fred Roos. Coexecutive producer: David Valdes. Produced by Michael I. Levy and Francis Coppola for Tri-Star–ML Delphi Premier Productions. 112 mins. Premiere: May 8, 1987.

Cast: James Caan (*Clell Hazard*), Anjelica Huston (*Samantha Davis*), James Earl Jones (*Goody Nelson*), D. B. Sweeney (*Jackie Willow*), Dean Stockwell (*Homer Thomas*), Mary Stuart Masterson (*Rachel Feld*), Dick Anthony Williams (*Slasher Williams*), Lonette McKee (*Betty Rae*), Sam Bottoms (*Lt. Webber*), Elias Koteas (*Pete Deveber*), Larry Fishburne (*Flanagan*), Casey Siemaszko (*Wildman*), Peter Masterson (*Colonel Feld*), Carlin Glynn (*Mrs. Feld*), Erik Holland (*Colonel Godwin*), Bill Graham (*Don Brubaker*), Terrence Currier, Terry Hinz, Lisa-Marie Felter, William Wiliamson, Joseph A. Ross Jr, Matthew Litchfield, Nick Mathwick, Robert Frerichs, Grant Lee Douglass, Mark Frazer, Terry Foster, Marshall Sizemore, Steve Barcanic, Hajna O. Moss, Arthur V. Gorman Jr., Louis Rangel.

1988 TUCKER, THE MAN AND HIS DREAM

Screenplay: Arnold Schulman and David Seidler. Direction: FFC. Photography (Technicolor, Technovision): Vittorio Storaro. Editing: Priscilla Ned. Music: Joe Jackson. Production design: Dean Tavoularis. Art direction: Alex Tavoularis. Costumes: Milena Canonero. Sound designer: Richard Beggs. Executive producer: George Lucas. Associate producer: Teri Fettis. Produced by Fred Roos and Fred Fuchs for Lucasfilm Ltd.. released through Paramount. 111 mins. Premiere: August 12, 1988.

Cast: Jeff Bridges (*Preston Tucker*), Joan Allen (*Vera*), Martin Landau (*Abe Karatz*), Frederic Forrest (*Eddie*), Mako (*Jimmy*), Elias Koteas (*Alex*), Christian Slater (*Junior*), Nina Siemaszko (*Marilyn Lee*), Anders Johnson (*Johnny*), Corky Nemec (*Noble*), Marshall Bell (*Frank*), Jay O. Saunders (*Kirby*), Peter Donat (*Kirby*), [Lloyd Bridges (*Senator Ferguson*)—uncredited], Dean Goodman (*Bennington*), John X. Heart (*Ferguson's Aide*), Don Novello (*Stan*), Patti Austin (*Millie*), Sandy Bull (*Stan's Assistant*), Joseph Miksak (*Judge*), Scott Beach (*Floyd Cerf*), Roland Scrivner (*Oscar Beesley*), Howard Hughes (*Dean Stockwell*), Bob Safford (*Narrator*), Larry Menkin (*Doc*), Ron Close (*Fritz*), Joe Flood (*Dutch*), Leonard Gardner, Bill Bonham, Abigail Van Alyn, Taylor Gilbert, David Booth, Jessie Nelson, Al Hart, Cab Covay, James Cranna, Bill Reddick, Ed Loerke, Jay Jacobus, Anne Lawder, Jeanette Lana Sartain, Mary Buffett, Annie Stocking, Michael McShane, Dean Goodman, Hope Alexander-Willis, Taylor Young, Jim Giovanni, Joe Lerer, Morgan Upton, Ken Grantham, Mark Anger, Al Nalbandian, Gary McLarty, Jimmy Nickerson, Tim Davison, Steve Davison, Dick Ziker.

1989 LIFE WITHOUT ZOE (episode in NEW YORK STORIES)

Screenplay: FFC, Sofia Coppola. Direction: FFC. Photography (Technicolor): Vittorio Storaro. Editing: Barry Malkin. Production design: Dean Tavoularis. Art direction: Speed Hopkins. Music: Carmine Coppola, Kid Creole and the Coconuts. Costumes: Sofia Coppola. Sound recording: Frank Graziadei. Segment producers: Fred Roos and Fred Fuchs for Touchstone Pictures. 34 mins. Premiere: February 26, 1989.

Cast: Heather McComb (*Zoe*), Talia Shire (*Charlotte*), Gia Coppola (*Baby Zoe*), Giancarlo Giannini (*Claudio*), Paul Herman (*Clifford, the Doorman*), James Keane (*Jimmy*), Don Novello (*Hector*), Bill Moor (*Mr. Lilly*), Tom Mardirosian (*Hasid*), Jenny Bichols (*Landy*), Gina Scianni (*Devo*), Diane Lin Cosman (*Margit*), Selim Tlili (*Abu*), Robin Wood-Chapelle (*Gel*), Celia Nestell (*Hillry*), Alexdra Becker (*Andrea*), Adrien Brody (*Mel*), Michael Higgins, Chris Elliott (*Robbers*), Thelma Carpenter (*Maid*), Carmine Coppola (*Street Musician*), Carole Bouquet (*Princess Soroya*), Jo Jo Starbuck (*Ice Skater*).

1990 THE GODFATHER PART III

Screenplay: Mario Puzo and FFC. Director: FFC. Photography (Technicolor): Gordon Willis. Editing: Barry Malkin. Production design: Dean Tavoularis. Art direction: Alex Tavoularis. Music: Carmine Coppola. Costumes: Milena Canonero. Special effects coordinator: Larry Cavanagh. Production supervisor: Alessandro von Normann. Associate producer: Marina Gefter. Executive producers: Fred Fuchs, Nicholas Gage. Co-producers: Fred Roos, Gray Frederickson, Charles Mulvehill. Produced by Francis Ford Coppola for Zoetrope Studios/Paramount. 163 mins. Premiere: December 25, 1990.

Cast: Al Pacino (*Michael Corleone*), Talia Shire (*Connie Corleone*), Diane Keaton (*Kay*), Andy Garcia (*Vincent*), Franc D' Ambrosio (*Anthony Corleone*), Sofia Coppola (*Mary*), John Savage (*Andrew Hagen*), Eli Wallach (*Altobello*), Donal Donnelly (*Archbishop*), Richard Bright (*Al Neri*), Al Martino (*Johnny Fontane*), Joe Mantegna (*Joey Zasa*), George Hamilton (*B.J. Harrison*), Robert Cicchini (*Lou Penino*), Terri Liverano Baker (*Theresa Hagen*), Bridget Fonda (*Grace*), Raf Vallone (*Lamberto*), Mario Donatone (*Mosca*), Vittorio Duse (*Don Tommasino*), Rogerio and Carlos Miranda (*Best Twins*), Jeanne Savarino (*Francesa Corleone*), Janet Savarino Smith (*Kathryn Corleone*) Helmut Berger (*Keinszig*), Carmine Caridi (*Old Don*), Don Castello (*Parisi*), Al Ruscio (*Volpe*), Vito Antuofermo ("*The Ant*"), Rick Aviles (*Masked Man #1*), Michael Bowen (*Masked Man #2*), Jeannie Linero (*Lucy Mancini*), Mickey Knox (*Frank Romano*), Julie Gregg (*Sandra*), James Chan Leong, Kellog Smith, John Abineri, Brian Freilino (*Stockholders*), Don Novello (*Dom*), Peter Schweitzer (*Vatican Journalist*), Morgan Upton (*TV Newscaster*), Franco Citti (*Calo*).

1992 BRAM STOKER'S DRACULA
Screenplay: James V. Hart. Direction: FFC. Photography (Technicolor): Michael Ballhaus. Editing: Nicholas C. Smith, Glen Scantlebury, Anne Goursaud. Production design: Thomas Sanders. Art direction: Andrew Precht. Set design: Joseph Hodges. Music: Wojciech Kilar. Costumes: Eiko Ishioka. Visual effects: Roman Coppola. Visual effects supervisor: Alison Savetch. Make-up design: Michele Burke. Sound design: Leslie Schatz. Associate producer: Susie Landau. Executive Producers: Michael Apted, Robert O'Connor. Produced by FFC, Fred Fuchs, and Charles Mulvehill for American Zoetrope/Osiris Films for Columbia Pictures. 127 mins. Premiere: November 13, 1992.

Cast: Gary Oldman (*Dracula*), Winona Ryder (*Mina Murray/Elisabeta*), Anthony Hopkins (*Professor Abraham van Helsing*), Keanu Reeves (*Jonathan Harker*), Richard E. Grant (*Dr. Jack Seward*), Cary Elwes (*Lord Arthur Holmwood*), Bill Campbell (*Quincey P. Morris*), Sadie Frost (*Lucy Westenra*), Tom Waits (*Renfield*), Monica Bellucci, Michaela Bercu, Florina Kendrick (*Dracula's Brides*), Jay Robinson (*Mr. Hawkins*), L.M. Hobson (*Hobbs*), Laurie Franks (*Lucy's Maid*), Maud Winchester (*Downstairs Maid*), Octavian Cadia (*Deacon*), Robert Getz (*Priest*), Dagmar Stanec (*Sister Agatha*), Eniko Oss (*Sister Sylva*), Nancy Linehan Charles (*Older woman*), Tatiana von Furstenberg (*Younger woman*), Jules Sylvester, Hubert Wells (*Zoo-keepers*), Danirel Newman (*News hawker*), Honey Lauren, Judi Diamond (*Peep-show girls*), Robert Buckingham (*Husband*), Cully Fredicksen (*Van Helsing's assistant*)

1994 MARY SHELLEY'S FRANKENSTEIN
FFC served as co-producer (with James V. Hart and John Veitch) on *Mary Shelley's Frankenstein*, directed by Kenneth Branagh for American Zoetrope and distribution through Columbia TriStar.

Notes

By far the greatest number of quotations come from interviews I have conducted with Francis Coppola, his wife, Eleanor, and various colleagues.

Introduction

p. 3 "I began asking" is from author's interview with FC in Napa on November 17, 1987.
"I'm embarrassed by my duality": ibid

p. 4 "Everything had to be remembered" is from author's interview with August Coppola in San Francisco on December 10, 1985.
"Francis has a wonderful" is from author's phone conversation with John Milius on November 18, 1986.
"make a better telephone" is from "The Greek Key in the Design of Coppola's Production," by Judy Stone in *San Francisco Chronicle*, October 9, 1983.
"While mired in the turmoil" is inspired by "The Making of *The Cotton Club*, A True Tale of Hollywood," by Michael Daly in *New York Magazine*, May 7, 1984.
"If we were stuck in a blazing building" is from author's conversation with Michael Powell aboard a London–San Francisco plane in December 1985.

p. 5 "I always operate as if I'll be rich" is quoted in *Skywalking*, by Dale Pollock (Harmony Books, New York, 1983).
"Francis is very likeable" is from author's interview with Dean Tavoularis in Helsinki on November 29, 1987.

p. 6 "I think that it comes" is from author's interview with FC.
"Coppola *is* the Godfather" is from *Final Cut* by Steven Bach (New American Library, New York, 1985).
Harry Chotiner quote comes from "Two Who Made a Revolution," by David Osborne in *San Francisco Magazine*, March 1982
"Something that is destructive" is from the author's interview with Walter Murch in San Rafael on December 12, 1985.
"Francis is an individual" is quoted in *American Film*, Washington, October 1981.

p. 7 "When I was first married" is from author's interview with FC.

263

p. 8 "In our family life" is from author's interview with August Coppola.
"We travel together" is quoted in "Some Figures on a Fantasy," by Lillian Ross in the *New Yorker*, November 8, 1982.
"What brings me the greatest joy" is quoted in *Playboy* interview with FC, dated [?] 1975.
"I'm always trying to have a party" is from author's interview with FC.
"Incredible scenes at [his] place" is from author's interview with Carroll Ballard in Berkeley on December 10, 1985.

p. 9 "Coppola puts spontaneous trust in his friends" is inspired by author's phone conversation with Mona Skager on December 12, 1985.

p. 10 "My worst fear" is from author's interview with FC.
"When Walter Murch ran into difficulties" is quoted in *American Film*, Washington, May 1985
"I'm no tough cookie" is quoted in "Coppola the Artist: 'I Think I'm a Threat,' " by Dale Pollock in *Los Angeles Times*, December 23, 1984.
"He lets you respond" is quoted in *Show*, April 1972.
"Francis's films invent themselves" is from author's interview with Walter Murch.

1 The Italian Connection

p. 13 "Carmine had shown" Most of this paragraph inspired by "Dynasty, Italian Style," by Stephen Farber and Marc Green in *California Magazine*, April 1984.

p. 14 "There are wonderful stories" is from author's interview with FC.

p. 15 "In Detroit, Carmine" is inspired by "Dynasty, Italian Style" (see p. 13).
"The family was a living presence" is from author's interview with August Coppola.
"Francis and I attended" is from "Arts and the Man, August Coppola, Dean of Creativity," by William Rodarmor in *San Francisco Examiner Image*, November 24, 1985.
"It was very dramatic" is from author's interview with August Coppola.

p. 16 "It rained tremendously" is from author's interview with FC.
"The Coppola household" is inspired by "What's It All Really Mean?" by FC in *Video Review*, January 1985.
"His ventriloquist's dummy" is inspired by "Francis Coppola and Gay Talese," in *Esquire*, July 1981.

p. 17 "This is very significant" is from author's interview with FC.

p. 18 "Was funny-looking, not good in school" is quoted in "Dynasty, Italian Style" (see p. 13).
"As a younger man" is from the author's interview with FC.
"He edited pieces of film" is inspired by interview with FC in *The Film Director as Superstar* by Joseph Gelmis (Secker and Warburg, London, 1971).

"the original video ranger" is from *Video Review* (see p. 16).
"the way the older cadets" is from BBC-TV profile of FC shown in Britain on April 6, 1985.
"He made pocket money" is from *Hollywood Renaissance*, by Diane Jacobs (A. S. Barnes & Co., New York, and The Tantivy Press, London, 1977).

p. 19 "sleeping where I could" is from BBC-TV profile.
"My parents were concerned" is from author's interview with FC.
"According to Eleanor" is inspired by *Notes*, by Eleanor Coppola (Simon and Schuster, New York, 1979).

p. 20 "the whole tone of my regime" is quoted in *San Francisco Chronicle*, August 25, 1985.
"Hofstra was significant" is from author's interview with FC.

p. 21 "I discovered that" is from author's interview with FC.
"I didn't want the typical" is from author's interview with FC.
"I left Hofstra": ibid.

p. 22 "He admired the genius" is from *The Film Director as Superstar*.
"Once again I was like a cipher" is from author's interview with FC.
"My first impression": ibid.

p. 23 "The image I had of Francis" is from author's phone conversation with Paul Bartel on March 29, 1987.
"The whole department" is from author's interview with Carroll Ballard.
"By all accounts" is inspired by *The Spirit of Zoetrope*, companion booklet issued by the Santa Fe Film Festival to a tribute to FC's career in 1983.
"I just wanted to make a film" is from author's interview with FC.

p. 24 "I wanted to flunk my physical": ibid.

p. 25 "It was pure Tennessee Williams": ibid.
"I needed someone" is from the author's phone conversation with Roger Corman on October 9, 1986.
"I heard in school" is from author's interview with FC.
"There was one scene": ibid.
"Roger's training": ibid.

p. 26 "We had to go to Liverpool" is from author's phone conversation with Corman.

p. 27 "So I went up to him" is from author's interview with FC.
"I was told that" is from author's interview with Eleanor Coppola in Napa on April 21, 1988.
"When I reached Ireland": ibid.

p. 28 "to be an exploitation film" is quoted from *The Film Director as Superstar*.

p. 29 "I tried to impress Roger" is quoted in *A Biographical Dictionary of the Cinema*, by David Thomson (Secker and Warburg, London, 1975).

2   The Studio Grind

p. 31   "I had to return" is from author's interview with Eleanor Coppola. "I was twenty-six": ibid.

p. 32   "To this day" is quoted from *Playboy* interview with FC, [?] 1975.
"Morally this screenplay" is from *George Byron Who?*, by Tom Stempel in *Sight and Sound*, Summer 1985.
"The studio like Coppola's screenplay" is inspired by *The Film Director as Superstar*.

p. 33   "I was really frustrated": ibid.
"I feel that I'm basically a writer" is quoted in *Hollywood Renaissance*.
"Coppola bought an option" is from *The Film Director as Superstar*.
"He transposed" is quoted in radio interview with Gerald Pratley aired on CBC (Toronto) in 1967.

p. 34   "His fee was a mere $8,000" is from *The Film Director as Superstar*.
"Coppola was desperate" is from *World Journal Tribune*, February 5, 1967.
"I wanted it to be a farce" is from Gerald Pratley radio interview (see p. 33).

p. 35   "I hadn't seen *The Knack*": ibid.
"to a dramatic story" is quoted from BBC-TV profile.
"Andy Hardy gets hit" is quoted in *Glamour*, January 1967.

p. 37   "It was a point of pride" is from author's interview with FC.
"a youthful film" is from *World Journal Tribune*, March 21, 1967.

p. 38   "the fair-haired boy at Warners" is from *The Godfather Journal* by Ira Zuckerman (Manor Books, New York, 1972).

p. 39   "I made a promise" is from author's interview with FC.
"A lot of liberal people" is from *The Film Director as Superstar*.
"He can still sing" is from BBC-TV profile.

p. 40   "He phoned Carmine" is from "Dynasty, Italian Style" (see p. 13).
"a couple of guys" is from author's interview with FC.
"I was like a fish out of water" is from BBC-TV profile.
"a demonstration of the naturalness" is from *Sight and Sound*, London, Winter 1968/69.

p. 43   "I felt the leprechaun" is from *The Film Director as Superstar*.

p. 44   "They decided to make it a road show" is from *American Film Now*, by James Monaco (New York Zoetrope, New York, 1979, revised edition 1984).

3   Independence and the Dream of Zoetrope

p. 45   "People are hampered by money" is from "Francis Coppola and Gay Talese" (see p. 16).
"I lived on what I made" is from *The Film Director as Superstar*.

"If you're not willing" is from soundtrack of George Lucas's documentary, *Filmmaker*.
"Sensing that *Finian's Rainbow*" is from author's interview with Carroll Ballard.

p. 46   "At the end of several months" is from *Action*, Los Angeles, January-February 1969.
"After an argument" is from author's interview with FC.
"Then several years later" is quoted in *The Spirit of Zoetrope*.
"She was crying": ibid.

p. 47   "It's the story of a human being" is from *The Film Director as Superstar*.

p. 52   "I wanted [the film]" is quoted from BBC-TV profile.

p. 53   "The theory was that we would travel" is from *Masters of Light, Conversations with Contemporary Cinematographers*, by Dennis Schaefer and Larry Salvato (University of California Press, Berkeley, 1984).

p. 54   "He didn't know me" is from author's interview with Walter Murch.
"When we made *Rain People*" is from author's interview with FC.
"It was intended" is from author's phone conversation with Fred Roos, October 8, 1986.

p. 55   "The one big capital investment" is from author's interview with Walter Murch.
"The first took place" is from *Skywalking*.
"He inspired us both" is from author's interview with FC.
"We were standing" is from author's phone conversation with Mona Skager.
"My wife had traveled" is from author's interview with FC.

p. 56   "We exchanged ideas" is from author's interview with Carroll Ballard.
"Warners were paying" is from author's phone conversation with Mona Skager.

p. 57   "There was a silver espresso machine" is from *Show* magazine, April 1970.
"The facility comprised" is from the *San Francisco Chronicle*, December 11, 1969.
"Francis likes to buck the system" is from author's conversation with Mona Skager.
"dreamed of this group of poets" is from *Notes*.
"During the first year" is from "Dynasty, Italian Style."
"The fatal flaw" is from author's interview with FC.

p. 58   "I was an executor" is from author's phone conversation with Roger Corman.
"The apprentice program" is from "Dynasty, Italian Style."
"At no stage did Zoetrope" is from "Coppola—What His Friends Have to Say," by Judy Stone in the *San Francisco Chronicle* (1975, clipping undated).

p. 59   "After all, Lucas" is from *The Film Director as Superstar*.

4 The Godfather

p. 61   "All seven projects in development" is from *Skywalking*.
"Zoetrope was picked clean": ibid.

p. 62   "Its author, Mario Puzo" is inspired by article in *Show* magazine, April 1972.

p. 63   "Coppola was not the first director" is from *The Godfather Journal*.
"Ruddy really wanted him" is from "Dynasty, Italian Style" (see p. 13).
"He knew the way these men": ibid.
"I was at Paramount": ibid.
"After a late-night negotiating session" is from author's phone conversation with Mona Skager.

p. 64   "He rewrote one half" is from *The Godfather Papers and Other Confessions*, by Mario Puzo (G. P. Putnam's Sons, New York, 1972).
"Soon afterward, Jaffe" is from *The Godfather Journal*.
"Don't quit. Make them fire you!" is quoted in *Adventures in the Screen Trade*, by William Goldman (Warner Books, New York, 1983).

p. 65   "They'd never met before really" is from BBC-TV profile.
"Tally's too pretty" is from "Dynasty, Italian Style."
"The director's parents" is from *The Godfather Journal*.
"Francis himself lived" is from *Notes*.
"In February 1971" is from *Show* magazine, April 1972.

p. 66   "On March 20," is from *The Godfather Journal*.
"According to Mario Puzo" is from *The Godfather Papers*.
"And while Vic Damone" is from *Hollywood Renaissance*.
"a monstrous insult" is from *The Godfather Journal*.
"By the end of the fifteenth day": ibid.
"I had told [the studio]" is from "Coppola and *The Godfather*," by Stephen Farber in *Sight and Sound*, London, Autumn 1972.
"Other snags conspired" is from *Filmmaking: The Collaborative Art*, edited by Donald Chase (Little, Brown, Boston, 1975).
"So we went out": ibid.

p. 67   "It's a little resort" is from author's interview with FC.
"felt I was great" is from "*Godfather Part II*: Nothing Is a Sure Thing", interview with FC in *City* magazine, San Francisco, Vol 7, No. 54, 11–24 December 1974.
"He donned earplugs" is from *Show* magazine, April 1972.
"Special effects expert Dick Smith" is from *The Godfather Journal*.
"August Coppola feels" is from author's interview with August Coppola.

p. 68   "a deeply unhappy experience" is from interview with Nicolas Roeg in *Time Out*, London, 8–14 August 1985.
"People love to read about" is from "Dynasty, Italian Style."

p. 70   "Coppola has said in an interview" is from *Playboy* interview with FC, [?] 1975.

p. 71 "has to *start out* ambivalent" is from *Vanity Fair*, October 1989.

p. 73 "in the father" is from author's interview with FC.

p. 75 "Clemenza *fries* some sausage": ibid.
"According to undercover agents" is from "Last Shudder of the Mafia," by Trevor Fishlock in *The Times*, London, [?] December 1985.

p. 76 "I can't do this" is from Fred Roos, quoted by Judy Stone in the *San Francisco Chronicle*, August 26, 1975.

p. 77 "A sequence that required" is from *The Craft of the Screenwriter*, by John Brady (Touchstone/Simon and Schuster, New York, 1982).

p. 78 "an almost Kodachromey" is from *Masters of Light*.
"Louis Malle 'directed' " is from *Variety*, October 11, 1972.

p. 79 "In July 1974" is from *Variety*, July 31, 1974.
"A year later" is from *Variety*, July 16, 1975.
"My dream of dreams" is from *City* (see p. 67)
"I was sure people": ibid.
"He and Al Ruddy" is from *Filmmaking: The Collaborative Art*.

p. 80 "I can remember being in New York" is from author's interview with Eleanor Coppola.

5   Picking up The Conversation

p. 81 "Francis turned the set" is from "Coppola—What His Friends Have to Say" (see p. 58).
"As money flowed into Coppola's coffers" is from the *San Francisco Chronicle*, December 29, 1979.

p. 82 "I had the job in Hollywood" is from author's interview with FC.
"Following a preview" is from *Skywalking*.
"You should get down" is from author's interview with FC.
"At the box-office" is from *Positif*, Paris, Number 161.

p. 83 "It started" is from BBC-TV profile.
"Kershner then sent Coppola" is from *The Spirit of Zoetrope*.
"He had been impressed" is from author's interview with Walter Murch.

p. 84 "although its $2 million ceiling" is from *Positif*, Paris, Number 161.
"After only a week" is from the *San Francisco Chronicle*, October 9, 1983.
"It was a real location" is from author's interview with Dean Tavoularis.
"Listen, I'm going to go straight from" is from author's interview with Walter Murch.

p. 85 "This is Coppola's most complete" is from *Variety*, April 3, 1974.

6   Back to Corleone

p. 95 "sequels are usually cheap imitations" is from *City* magazine (see p. 67).

p. 96 "he didn't want Michael": ibid.
"This time, Coppola took charge" is from *Positif*, Number 161.
"Coppola had written scenes" is from interview in *Playboy*, [?] 1975.
"After his friction with Gordon Willis" is from interview with Vittorio Storaro in *Filmrutan* magazine, Sundsvall, Sweden, Number 4, 1984.
"It was somewhat dated equipment" is from *Masters of Light*.
"Francis insisted that the cars" is from author's interview with Walter Murch.

p. 97 "But Brando demanded more money" is from author's phone conversation with Fred Roos.

p. 98 "Francis is ready to delegate" is from author's phone conversation with Gray Frederickson, December 2, 1986.
"We wanted the people": ibid.
"The Coppolas were quartered" is from *Notes*.

p. 99 "The movie is meant to be like" is from "Dynasty, Italian Style."
"It's something in the direction" is from *Positif*, Number 161.

p. 102 "As August Coppola has said" is from author's interview with August Coppola.

p. 103 "To some extent I have become Michael" is from *Positif*, Number 161.

p. 113 "When you finish a movie" is from author's interview with FC.
"I was in San Francisco": ibid.

p. 114 "We had to modify" is from author's phone conversation with Barry Malkin, February 18, 1987.
"Only one part of the saga" is inspired by "La Saga du Parrain," by Michel Cieutat, in *Positif*, Paris, Number 288.

p. 115 "Francis, you can't win 'em all" is from *City* (see p. 67).
"Advisers had urged Francis" is from the *San Francisco Chronicle*, August 26, 1975.
"He wanted a headquarters" is from the *San Francisco Chronicle*, December 28, 1984.
"I thought if we had a theater" is from the *San Francisco Chronicle*, August 26, 1975.

p. 116 "Along with the Little Fox" is from *American Film*, November 1975.
"More and more people" is from author's interview with Eleanor Coppola.

p. 117 "When his accountant warned him" is from the *San Francisco Chronicle*, August 26, 1975.
"For six months" is from *American Film Now*.
"I'll be broke and back to zero": ibid.

7 Lost in the Jungle

p. 119 "There were times" is from "Francis Coppola and Gay Talese" (see p. 16).
"United Artists, who had invested" is from *Final Cut*.

p. 120   "*Apocalypse Now* started out" is from author's interview with Carroll Ballard.
"My whole career is justified" is from author's phone conversation with John
Milius.
"If it's based on *Heart of Darkness*" is from "Milius the Barbarian," by Kirk
Honeycutt, in *American Film*, Washington, May 1982.
"My writing teacher had told me" is from author's phone conversation with
John Milius.

p. 121   "I'd have done it in Cinerama" is from BBC-TV profile.
"McQueen was approached to play Willard" is from *Notes*.

p. 122   "On March 1, 1976": ibid.
"He found it difficult" is from author's interview with FC.
"When Coppola heard Hopper" is from interview with FC by Fred Robbins
in *Genesis* magazine, April 1980.
"I'd lived in New York" is from author's phone conversation with Frederic
Forrest on November 18, 1986.

p. 123   "A typhoon occurs" is from author's phone conversation with Fred Roos.
"I was trapped for days" is from author's interview with Dean Tavoularis.
"More and more" is from *Notes*.
"At home in Napa": ibid.

p. 124   "Coppola began to enumerate" is from "Coppola, After his 'Apocalypse,' "
by Judy Stone, in the *San Francisco Chronicle*, August 14, 1979.
"I went with suggestions" is from BBC-TV profile.
"Brando's part was twice as long" is from author's phone conversation with
Michael Herr on June 17, 1986.
"The Kurtz in *Heart of Darkness*" is from "Coppola, After His 'Apocalypse.' "

p. 125   "On March 5" is from *Vanity Fair*, New York, August 1987.
"The notion of the film's" is from BBC-TV profile.
"There were never *five* endings" is from author's interview with Richard
Beggs.
"I think Francis feared a coup!" is from author's phone conversation with
John Milius.
"He's on his way" is from author's interview with Richard Beggs.
"the finished movie" is from author's phone conversation with John Milius.
"I was really on the spot" is from author's interview with FC.

p. 126   "For me, it was a mind-altering" is from author's interview with Richard
· Beggs.
"It is scary" is from *Notes*.
"Everybody I knew" is from author's interview with Eleanor Coppola.
"so many people" is from *Notes*.
"The script had been narrated" is from author's interview with Walter Murch.

p. 127   "The narration written thus far" is from author's phone conversation with
Michael Herr.
"So when they came back" is from the author's interview with Richard Beggs.
"Actually it was a" is from author's interview with Walter Murch.

p. 128 "decided that it will not be possible" is from *Notes*.
"Fred Rexer turned up" is from author's conversations with Richard Beggs.
"To Jim Harvey, from Francis Coppola" is from *Final Cut*.
"Confidence had been eroded" is from *Notes*.

p. 130 "We had access to too much money" is from article by Roger Ebert in *Chicago Sun-Times*, May 1979.
"I shouldn't have spoken that way" is from author's interview with FC.
"Then, coming out of the intermission" is from author's phone conversation with Michael Herr.

p. 131 "Joseph Farrell and his National Research Group" is from *Final Cut*.

p. 132 "I don't know who it was" is from author's interview with FC.
"*Apocalypse* was always intended": ibid.
"He felt that her comments" is from author's interview with Eleanor Coppola.

p. 133 "wanted to express" is from *Masters of Light*.

p. 136 "*Apocalypse Now* mystifies the facts" is from "Apocalypse Now and Again," by Margot S. Kernan in *Washington Journalism Review*, November-December 1979.
"There had been one man" is from *Dispatches*, by Michael Herr (Alfred Knopf, New York, 1977).

p. 137 "covered the field with copies": ibid.

p. 138 "whose life only made sense" is from *Notes*.
"unspeakably attractive" is from "Milius the Barbarian" (see p. 120).
"The tiger was a real" is from author's phone conversation with Frederic Forrest.

p. 140 "knocked everyone out": ibid.
"as on a darkling plain" is from *Dover Beach*, by Matthew Arnold.

p. 141 "a kind of upgraded" is from *Dispatches*.
"In Welles's storyboard" is from *The Making of Citizen Kane*, by Robert L. Carringer (John Murray, London, 1986).

8 Blows to the Heart

p. 145 "I can see a communications revolution" is quoted in *Home Video* magazine, May 1981.
"Still, he hugged Cimino" is from *Final Cut*.
"This was an unbelievably spectacular" is from author's interview with FC.

p. 146 "I have an ability like a pied piper" is from *Skywalking*.
"Fred Roos had been filleting" is from *The Spirit of Zoetrope*.
"Once Carroll Ballard finishes" is from FC's memo to staff leaked to *Esquire* magazine, November 1977.

p. 147 "I am cavalier": ibid.
"really wanted was to be" is from *American Film Now*.
"The very qualities that attract" is from *American Film*, October 1981.
"Such a spontaneous gesture" is from *The Spirit of Zoetrope*.
"When, at Kurosawa's invitation" is from author's interview with Tom
Luddy in Berkeley, December 14, 1985.

p. 148 "Francis had a dream" is from author's phone conversation with Fred Roos.
"In June of the same year" is from author's interview with Tom Luddy.
"One day": ibid.

p. 149 "The critic Susan Sontag" is from *The Spirit of Zoetrope*.
"Zoetrope signed a deal" is from author's interview with Tom Luddy.
"So when Coppola gave him" is from *The Spirit of Zoetrope*.
"He planned, for example" is from the *New York Times*, September 15, 1975.

p. 150 "He was reported as being signed" is from the *New York Times*, April 8,
1975.
"John Levin and Dan Cassidy" is from the *San Francisco Chronicle*, December
29, 1979.
"A screen version of Jack Kerouac's" is from *The Spirit of Zoetrope*.
"I'm trying" is from "Francis Coppola and Gay Talese" (see p. 16).
"People are sick of watching actors" is from *American Film*, October 1981.

p. 151 "that the medium was about to" is from BBC-TV profile.
"I don't believe that talented people" is from *The Spirit of Zoetrope*.
"Martha Coolidge saw her Zoetrope production" is from *American Film*,
October 1981.
"David Lynch, fresh from" is from *Cinefantastique*, September 1984.

p. 152 "The four lead actors" is from *American Film*, October 1981.
"Francis is a maverick" is from author's phone conversation with Frederic
Forrest.
"A neophyte actress" is from *American Film*, October 1981.
"I told them to scrap" is from author's conversation with Michael Powell
(see p. 4).
"The first scriptwriter had been" is from *The Spirit of Zoetrope*.
"According to Wenders" is from *Passeport pour Hollywood*, by Michel Ciment
(Editions du Seuil, Paris, 1987).

p. 153 "Francis wrote an ending" is from *American Film*, October 1981.
"Orion, the company" is from author's phone conversation with Fred Roos.
"A fourth screenwriter" is from *The Spirit of Zoetrope*.
"Wenders learned that" is from *Passeport pour Hollywood*.
"Ninety pages of screenplay": ibid.

p. 154 "Warners, who had rashly committed" is from article by Judy Stone in the
San Francisco Chronicle, May 8, 1983.
"reckless and flamboyant gesture" is from *Napoléon*, by Kevin Brownlow
(Alfred Knopf, New York, 1983).

"As early as 1979" is from author's interview with Tom Luddy.
"Francis and George Lucas always used to say": ibid.
"I told myself, rather slyly" is from an interview with FC in *Positif*, Paris, Number 262.

p. 155   "I wanted to do a story" is from BBC-TV profile.
"The city is a metaphor" is quoted in *Monthly Film Bulletin*, London, June 1985.
"Kenny Ortega received" is from *American Film*, October 1981.
"had the idea to use" is from *Masters of Light*.

p. 156   "a Las Vegas of the mind" is from *American Film*, October 1981.
"In March 1980" is from *Variety*, March 26, 1980.

p. 157   "I was seeking a compromise method" is from author's interview with FC.
"This method enabled Coppola" is from *Home Video*, May 1981.
"He actually directed one scene" is from author's interview with Richard Beggs.

p. 158   "Despite the unrelenting monetary pressure" is from the *San Francisco Chronicle*, February 12, 1981.
"Actual money has come in . . .": ibid.

p. 159   "After stopping over in Europe" is from *American Film*, October 1981, and *The Spirit of Zoetrope*.
"I almost think the film" is from "Coppola has 'Heart' Trouble," by Judy Stone, in the *San Francisco Chronicle*, August 21, 1981.
"Paramount required the print" is from author's interview with FC.

p. 160   "terminated Paramount's release" is from "Some Figures on a Fantasy" (see p. 8).
"our studio couldn't survive it" is from the *Los Angeles Times*, quoted in the *San Francisco Chronicle*, March 5, 1982.
"There were forty-three people" is from "Some Figures on a Fantasy" (see p. 8).

p. 161   "In Sweden": ibid.
"The purchaser was none other" is from *Variety*, March 4, 1981.

p. 162   "Everyone knows that this kind of situation" is from interview with FC in *Positif*, Paris, Number 262.

p. 164   "The French critic Christian Viviani" is from article by Viviani in *Positif*, Paris, Number 311.

p. 165   "I never wanted the decor" is from interview with FC in *Positif*, Paris, Number 262.
"something in the style of Puccini" is from article by Jean-Loup Bourget in *Positif*, Paris, Number 262.

9   Back to Back in Tulsa

p. 167   "on behalf of the students" is from *The Spirit of Zoetrope*.

"I bet kids have a good idea" is from article by Aljean Harmetz for the *New York Times*, reprinted in the *San Francisco Chronicle*, March 28, 1983.

p. 168   "When the crisis had hit" is from BBC-TV profile.
"Chemical Bank gave Zoetrope" is from *The Spirit of Zoetrope*.
"One of the best young actors" is from interview with FC in *Positif*, Paris, Number 262.

p. 169   "wanted a stark-and-brutal look" is from "The Greek Key in the Design of Coppola's Productions" (see p. 4).
"It was ninety-nine percent" is from author's interview with Richard Beggs.
"Michael Powell believes" is from author's conversation with Powell (see p. 4).
"Movies have always been thought of" is from the *San Francisco Chronicle*, September 26, 1982.

p. 172   "When the film was screened" is from author's interview with Richard Beggs.

p. 173   "marks the closing of a phase" is from author's interview with August Coppola.

p. 176   "There's a scene in there" is from a profile of Mickey Rourke in the London *Sunday Times*, November 10, 1985.
"a character out of Tennessee Williams" is from "The Greek Key in the Design of Coppola's Productions" (see p. 4).

p. 177   "It was damage to the negative" is from author's interview with Richard Beggs.

10   Playing The Cotton Club

p. 180   "I could be worth $100 million" is from "Francis Coppola and Gay Talese" (see p. 16).

p. 181   "My approach" is from author's interview with FC.
"Michael Daly, in an exhaustive" refers to Michael Daly's article in *New York Magazine*, May 7, 1984.

p. 182   "a futile gangster story": ibid.
"Coppola glimpsed a means of" is from BBC-TV profile.
"a plantation, with black talent" is from "Francis Ford Coppola's Mood Indigo," by Carrie Rickey, in the *Boston Globe*, December 20, 1984.

p. 183   "Together, the men screened": ibid.
"Francis was constantly trying" is from 'The Man Has Legs," by David Thomson, in *Film Comment*, New York, April 1985.

p. 184   "The Tiffany concept of the production" is from "Coppola the Artist: 'I Think I'm a Threat,' " by Dale Pollock, in the *Los Angeles Times*, December 23, 1984.
"black people could be proud of" is from "Tapped for Stardom," by Barbara Graustark, in *American Film*, Washington December 1984.

"a very manipulative" is from NBC's *Today Show*, December 13, 1984.
"In this case, the director" is from author's interview with Walter Murch.
"a very open way of working" is from interview with Gregory Hines by Joan Goodman, in the London *Times*, May 2, 1985.

p. 185 "Who needs this?" is from "Coppola the Artist: 'I Think I'm a Threat' " (see p. 184).
"We would rehearse a scene" is from "Tapped for Stardom" (see p. 184).

p. 186 "In a ruling in July 1984": ibid.

p. 187 "like jazz itself " is from "It Is, Too, Good," by Richard T. Jameson, in *Film Comment*, New York, April 1985.

11 From Rip van Winkle to Peggy Sue

p. 193 "An agreement worked out" is from the *San Francisco Chronicle*, February 11, 1984.

p. 194 "He shot *Rip van Winkle*" is from *Variety*, December 26, 1984.
"I was able to realize": ibid.

p. 195 "I'm not giving up movies" is from the London *Sunday Times*, July 21, 1985.

p. 196 "Coppola was eager to work" is from "Coppola the Artist: 'I Think I'm a Threat' " (see p. 184).

p. 199 "The 'past,' to anyone" is from "Peggy Sue Visits a Changeless Past," by Vincent Canby, in the *New York Times*, November 19, 1986.

12 Tragedy and Revival

p. 206 "These cities are rich" is from Tri-Star press pack.
"One of the things that touched me": ibid.

p. 207 "an affair with the script": ibid.
"Gio sustained" is from *Variety*, May 28, 1986.
"Before summer's end" is from *People*, New York, August 11, 1986.
"was driving really crazy" is from the London *Evening Standard*, December 16, 1986.
"reckless endangerment" is from the London *Times*, December 19, 1986.
"I remember [Francis] saying" is from *People*, New York, August 11, 1986.
"Work has that quality" is from author's interview with FC.

p. 208 "A week after the tragedy" is from *People*, New York, August 11, 1986.
"I've always had the feeling" is from author's interview with FC.

p. 209 "bio-imaged" is from author's interview with August Coppola.
"the python coils of loyalty" is from review by Geoff Brown in the London *Times*, January 21, 1988.

p. 211 "*Gardens of Stone* took no sides" is from interview with Anjelica Huston in *Film Comment*, New York, September–October 1987.
"a good girl": ibid.

p. 213 "I've always been fascinated" is from interview with FC in the *New York Times*, May 3, 1987.

13 Tucker—The Dream Triumphant

p. 215 "a slice of Americana" is from article by Glenn Lovell in the *San Jose Mercury News*, July 26, 1987.
"a dark kind of piece" is from profile by Robert Lindsy in the *New York Times Magazine*, July 24, 1988.

p. 216 "assumed because [Tucker]": ibid.

p. 217 "Yes, it was that beautiful": ibid.
"My father raced this guy" is from author's interview with Carroll Ballard.
"I like him" is from profile of FC by Susan Braudy in *The Atlantic*, August 1976.
"It was a safe car" is from interview with FC in *Playboy*, [?] 1975.

p. 218 "They had to be chained together" is from undated article by Bob Hagin in the *Contra Costa Times/Valley Times*.

p. 219 "I think that it's a remarkable collaboration" is from author's interview with Eleanor Coppola.
"It's like a promo film" is from author's interview with FC.

p. 223 "We did show, perhaps . . ." is from interview with Geoff Andrew in *Time Out* (London), November 2–9, 1988.
"he'd be hired" is from interview with FC in *Playboy*, [?] 1975.
"a story about a fellow" is from article by Glenn Lovell in the *San Jose Mercury News*, July 26, 1987.

p. 224 "was never the perfect wife" is from author's interview with Eleanor Coppola.

14 Back to the Future

p. 227 "Zoetrope is an idea" is from author's interview with FC.

p. 228 "Even now, if I'm on a trip": ibid.
"Coming from the theater": ibid.

p. 229 "He's really an advanced director": ibid.
"When I first started": ibid.
"because I know that": ibid.

p. 230 "It's a story of a little girl": ibid.

p. 231 "a pure, kind of god-given talent: ibid.
"You have a million ideas": ibid.

"I'm the kind of person": ibid.
"I figured, well, it doesn't seem": ibid.
"I have a temper": ibid.

p. 232   "Francis had this idea" is from author's interview with Richard Beggs.
"I don't enjoy anything so much" is from author's interview with FC.

p. 233   "I feel it's a good inclination": ibid.

p. 238   "If I were Michael..." is from "Turmoil on the Set of *Godfather III*," by
Peter J. Boyer, in *Vanity Fair*, New York, June 1990.

p. 245   "This bankruptcy filing" is from *Daily Variety*, Hollywood, July 1, 1992.

p. 245   "Originally as a kid" is from "Coppola's Dracula" in *Cinefantastique*,
Forest Park, Illinois, December 1992.

p. 246   "Give me something" comes from *Entertainment Weekly*'s "Holiday
Movie Preview," October 1992.

p. 246   "I don't really like rehearsing" comes from *Bloodlines*, a documentary
produced by Columbia in 1992.

p. 247   "I never had such good screenings" is from *Daily Variety*, Hollywood,
September 16, 1992

p. 249   "Souls reaching out" is from "Journals 1989-1993", by Francis Ford
Coppola, in *Projections* (Faber and Faber, London, 1994).

p. 251   "I think the main difficulty" is from "Coppola's Dracula" in
Cinefantastique, Forest Park, Illinois, December 1992.

p. 251   "You're stepping off a cliff" is from *Bloodlines*.

Index

Other DA CAPO titles of interest